ANTHROPOLOGICAL PAPERS OF
THE UNIVERSITY OF ARIZONA
NUMBER 76

T0340905

Los Primeros Mexicanos

Late Pleistocene and Early Holocene People of Sonora

Guadalupe Sánchez

THE UNIVERSITY OF
ARIZONA PRESS

TUCSON

The University of Arizona Press
www.uapress.arizona.edu

© 2016 The Arizona Board of Regents
All rights reserved. Published 2016

Printed in the United States of America

21 20 19 18 17 16   6 5 4 3 2 1

ISBN-13: 978-0-8165-3063-2 (paper)

Library of Congress Cataloging-in-Publication Data
Sánchez, Guadalupe, author.
    Los primeros Mexicanos : late pleistocene and early
holocene people of Sonora / by Guadalupe Sánchez.
        pages cm. — (Anthropological papers of the University
of Arizona ; number 76)
    Includes bibliographical references and index.
    Abstract also in Spanish.
    ISBN 978-0-8165-3063-2 (pbk. : alk. paper)
    1. Paleoindians—Mexico—Sonora (State) 2. Excavations
(Archaeology)—Mexico—Sonora (State) 3. Sonora (Mexico :
State)—Antiquities. I. Title. II. Series: Anthropological
papers of the University of Arizona ; no. 76.
    F1219.1.S65S26 2016
    972'.1701—dc23
                    2015016362

♾ This paper meets the requirements of ANSI/NISO
Z39.48-1992 (Permanence of Paper).

About the Author

Guadalupe Sánchez was born in Mexico City and received her B.A. in archaeology at the Escuela Nacional de Antropología e Historia, and her M.A. and Ph.D. degrees at the School of Anthropology, University of Arizona. Over the past 20 years, her investigations have concentrated on Northern Mexico, with varied topics encompassing Pleistocene-Holocene hunter-gatherers, the introduction of early maize and agriculture, human adaptations, paleoethnobotany, paleoecology, geoarchaeology, and the organization of lithic technology. At present, she is investigating the Fin del Mundo site in Sonora, the first site known where Clovis people and gomphotheres interacted. Her current research is primarily concerned with long-duration human adaptation and climate change in the Sonoran Desert. She has published numerous articles in English and Spanish on these topics.

Cover

Excavation at Locus 1 at Fin del Mundo, along with a Clovis point recovered at the site. Photographs courtesy of Guadalupe Sánchez.

DEDICATION

To Juancho Carpintero "alma de mi alma."

To Nene (Mom) and Tavo (Dad) for their unconditional love and support in my life.

To Julio Cesar Montané Martí and C. Vance Haynes for showing me the way to the fascinating world of the First Americans.

To Julian Hayden for all the stimulating discussions and tales drinking bacanora on his patio.

Contents

FIGURES

TABLES

Acknowledgments

My eternal gratitude is extended to John Carpenter for listening, debating my ideas, and for fixing my Spanglish. I thank Vance Holliday for believing in me and supporting my research, for sharing his geo-archaeological expertise, for making arrangements to process samples at different University of Arizona laboratories, and for being such a good partner in the field. To Michael Collins, I owe no small debt of gratitude for all that I learned in Austin. I thank Bruce Huckell for all his assistance and encouragement over these many years. The publication of this book is possible thanks to the magnificent editorial work of T. J. Ferguson, David Anderson, and an anonymous reviewer. Linda Gregonis copyedited the manuscript, José Raúl Ortiz drafted two figures, and Richard Flint translated the epigraph that begins Chapter 1. InDesign consultant Doug Goewey formatted the publication.

I am extremely grateful to the various organizations that provided funding for this research: the Arizona Archaeological and Historical Society, the Institute for the Study of Planet Earth, the Argonaut Archaeological Research Fund (University of Arizona Foundation) established by Joe and Ruth Cramer, and the Instituto Nacional de Antropología e Historia. Special thanks are due to Laura Pescador of the Instituto Nacional de Antropología e Historia for granting special project funds. I am grateful to Michael Brack and Bill Doelle from Desert Archaeology, Inc., for making the topographic maps for Fin del Mundo. This monograph is dedicated to all of my professors and colleagues: Elisa Villalpando, Paul Fish, Suzy Fish, Karen Adams, Owen Davis, Alejandro Pastrana, John Olsen, Vance Haynes, Tom Sheridan, Robert Cobean, and Manuel Gándara. I thank the Sonorenses, Leopoldo Velez, Ing. Bustamante, Julian Robles, and Fernando Tapia for sharing information and providing assistance over the years. I am especially grateful to Don Gustavo Placencia for his hospitality and friendship.

Finally, I wish to express my heartfelt thanks to the many people who have collaborated and contributed with the investigations in Sonora over the years, especially Beto Peña, Ismael Sánchez-Morales, and Natalia Martinez. My appreciation and gratitude goes to Edmund Gaines for supervising the field work at Fin del Mundo and for his assistance in taking photographs and drafting some of the drawings that we made during the 2007 and 2008 field seasons.

CHAPTER ONE

Of Paradigms and Parapets

The Peopling of the Americas, Clovis, and the First Peoples of Mexico

… y así no puede escapar de ser tenido por hombre temerario y muy arrojado el que se atreviere a prometer lo cierto de la primera origen de los Indios, y de los primeros hombres que poblaron las Indias.

Thus, one who is so incautiously bold as to claim certainty about the earliest origin of the Indians and about the first people who settled the Indies cannot avoid being taken for one who imprudently takes chances and is a rash man.

—José de Acosta, 1590

The Jesuit priest José de Acosta, in his 1590 chronicle, wrote about his puzzlement over human origin in the New World. It was clear that Native Americans had the same origin as people in the Old World, but how and when people inhabited the Americas and developed complex societies—such as the Incas and the Aztecs—was unknown. To begin answering these questions, Acosta proposed that a land bridge connecting Asia with the New World must have existed, making it possible for humans to cross and inhabit the New World (Acosta 1954 [1590]).

Four hundred years later, questions of when and how people first inhabited the North and South America are still being debated. The more that we know, the more complex the explanation gets. The initial peopling of the continents is difficult to reconstruct. For one thing, sites have been around longer and are thus more prone to disturbance and loss of data; for another, the sites are ephemeral due to the highly mobile lifeways of the early hunter and gatherer groups (Dillehay 2009; Kelly and Todd 1988; Kelly 1996, 1999, 2003; Surovell 2000). Over the last century, interest in the peopling of the Americas has not waned, and the topic continues to be popular in many scientific fields. Archaeologists, anthropologists,

biologists, geneticists, and linguists, as well as paleontologists and other geoscientists, have been involved in exploring and studying artifacts, genes, bones, soils, feces, other kinds of biological remains, languages, footprints, and nanodiamonds. The number of papers published on topics related to the peopling of the Americas each year is astounding. In 2011, Pitblado (2011) noted that in order to synthesize what had been written in the previous decade about the migration of the first Americans, she read over 300 articles published in journals ranging from the *American Journal of Human Genetics* to *Earth and Planetary Sciences*. In spite of this large volume of work, there are many competing propositions. The academic community is still highly divided and has yet to reach consensus on many important issues.

In a recent survey carried out by Amber Wheat (2012), with the participation of 215 researchers specialized on the study of the First Americans, the lack of consensus among scholars is evident. Although 86 percent of those surveyed accepted the existence of a coastal migration route and 67 percent of the participants validated the Pre-Clovis occupation of Monte Verde in Chile, consensus about other Pre-Clovis sites was lacking (Wheat 2012:11). Wheat's survey found no consensus regarding when the respondents thought people first arrived in the Americas—58 percent answered before 15,000 cal year B.P., while 42 percent thought that the peopling of the Americas occurred after 15,000 cal year B.P. (Wheat 2012:13). Although there is little agreement among scholars about the timing of migration into the Americas, the majority of them agreed that the colonization of the continent originated in western Beringia and that there was more than one migration route. Eighty-one percent of the researchers surveyed believed that a coastal migration route existed and that it probably was the route that the

Pre-Clovis people followed to get to the Monte Verde site in southern Chile. Monte Verde has at least two secure radiocarbon dates that place the antiquity of the site at 12,310 and 12,290 ^{14}C years (Dillehay 1989, 1997; Dillehay and others 2008; Pitblado 2011; Kelly 2003; Meltzer 2009).

The diversity of existing paradigms about the first Americans clearly indicate that much needs to be known before we fully understand issues about the timing, geographic extent, and origin of the first peopling of the Americas (Dillehay 2009). Although researchers from various fields have contributed to explanations for how and when the first people arrived in the American continents, ultimately data are needed from archaeological sites in which the relationships between artifacts, stratigraphy, and dating are impeccable (Meltzer 2009).

CLOVIS AND THE PEOPLING OF THE AMERICAS

Clovis is the name given to the earliest well-established human culture on the North American continent (Collins 1999a). Clovis people were the first big game hunters of the Paleoindian tradition—although they were surely not the first people in the Americas. The first people are generally called Pre-Clovis. Clovis projectile points and culture are named after the town of Clovis, New Mexico, where the first Clovis point was found at nearby Blackwater Draw (Haynes 1966; Sellards 1952; Wormington 1957). University of Pennsylvania archaeologist Edgar B. Howard visited the Blackwater Draw locality in 1932 and reported the findings in *The Scientific Monthly*. This marked the beginning of decades of extensive archaeological work in the area (Holliday 2005; Howard 1935a). In the spring of 1933, Howard's excavation crew at Blackwater Draw found fluted lanceolate points in direct association with the remains of mammoth and bison. These points, which came to be known as Clovis points, were distinctive from the more finely made fluted points found several years earlier at Folsom, the nearby locality that became the site type for the Folsom culture (Figgins 1933; Howard 1933:524, 1935a).

Howard (1935b), along with the geologist Ernst Antevs (1931, 1934, 1935), proposed a scenario for the peopling of the North America. In this scenario, between 15,000 and 20,000 years ago, the Bering Strait was dry land and a glacier-free corridor was open along the east side of the Rocky Mountains in what is now Canada (Meltzer 2009:241). According to Howard and Antevs, this frozen passage was used by the people who came to Blackwater Draw, so the site must be 15,000 years old. The precise dates for Clovis and Folsom points could not be established before radiocarbon dating was developed, but Howard and Antevs were certain that people were in North America during Pleistocene times. Once it was established that humans arrived in the Americas during the Pleistocene, sites containing megafauna with associated artifacts were discovered in many places (Holliday 2005; Meltzer 1989:477). During the 70 years following the discovery of Folsom and Clovis, similar sites were found all over North America in areas where ice sheets were not present (Collins 1999a:35; Faught 1996; Anderson and others 2010).

THE CLOVIS PEOPLE: CHRONOLOGY, HEARTLAND, AND HUMAN BEHAVIOR

The Clovis complex became recognized for its characteristic bifacially flaked fluted projectile point. Wormington (1957:263) defined this type of point as lanceolate-shaped, with flutes that originate at the base and extend no more than half way up to the tip. With the discovery of additional Clovis sites throughout the Plains, Sellards (1952) offered a broader definition of the Clovis complex, which he termed the Llano complex. Green (1963) was the first archaeologist to link blade production to Clovis people, and he highlighted the importance of a unique behavior known as caching (Smallwood 2011). The technological details of the Clovis lithic assemblage have only been published in the last two decades, probably because Clovis sites with substantial lithic assemblages are rare, and a substantial amount of fieldwork has been done at Clovis sites in the last 20 years. Today, concepts such as the Llano complex are no longer used, and Clovis complex is applied to label this distinctive Pleistocene-age technological assemblage (Bradley and others 2010; Huckell 2007; Smallwood 2011; Waters and others 2011; and Gingerich 2007)

The Clovis complex represents the oldest widespread cultural complex in North America. Clovis points have been found across much of the unglaciated parts of the continent (including Mexico and Guatemala). For more than 40 years, researchers have looked for the origin of Clovis fluting technology in Siberia and in other places between Alaska and the Northern Plains, but the heartland of the Clovis complex has not been found. The absence of a region outside of North America that can be identified as the origin place for the Clovis complex appears to indicate that Clovis lithic technology, including fluting, was invented in the northern area of North America (Meltzer 2009).

Several sites in North America that are not affiliated with Clovis may predate the Clovis complex by 600 years (Meltzer 2009; Waguespack 2007). The Clovis complex, however, represents the first group of people inhabiting large portions of North America who shared a cultural affiliation. Clovis sites with fluted points have been found all over the interior of North America in diverse settings, landscapes, and environments. Although these sites share the unique Clovis projectile point that identifies them as part of the same complex, the regional interaction of Clovis groups and their integration during the Pleistocene are little understood. The span of time for the Clovis complex is an important variable in understanding the relationships among groups of people who shared a lithic technology.

Many archaeologists think the Clovis complex spanned a period of eight hundred to a thousand years, from 11,700 to 10,700 ^{14}C yr B.P. (Batt and Pollard 1996; Fiedel 1999; Ferring 1994; Haynes 1980, 1993, 2000a; Taylor and others 1996; Waters and Stafford 2007). Waters and Stafford (2007:1123), however, recently challenged the long-established timing of Clovis. Using 43 dates from 11 Clovis sites, they suggested that Clovis spanned a period of 450 years, from 11,250 to 10,800 ^{14}C yr B.P., or 13,250 to 12,800 calendar years B.P. (Waters and Stafford 2007:1123). Waters and Stafford argued that older ^{14}C dates proved the presence of Pre-Clovis populations in the Americas, and that the Pre-Clovis occupation probably extended across a large area, with Clovis technology spreading quickly along an existing cultural corridor (Waters and Stafford 2007:1125). The data Waters and Stafford present, however, are not directly relevant to this proposition (Haynes and others 2007). Waters and Stafford (2007:1123) noted that 22 Clovis sites have been directly dated, but in their analysis they disregard 11 of these sites. One of the sites not included in their analysis is the Aubrey site in Texas, a classic Clovis site with two dates that averaged 11,570 ^{14}C yr B.P. The dates from the Aubrey site may be erratic or not clearly associated with human activity, but in the absence of additional contradictory dates for this component, they should not simply be dismissed (Haynes and others 2007).

During the 2012 field season at the Fin del Mundo site in Sonora, Mexico, we found three pieces of charcoal associated with a Clovis feature found at Locus 1. This archaeological feature, buried in 1.5 m of stratified deposits, was composed of the articulated bones of two juvenile gomphotheres associated with four Clovis points and 21 flakes. A date of 11,560 ^{14}C yr B.P. was obtained from charcoal. This date is equivalent to the dates at the Aubry site that were dismissed by Waters and Stanford (2007). Given the new data obtained from an intact Clovis feature at Fin del Mundo, a span of 800 years for the duration of the Clovis complex should be reconsidered.

The origin of the Clovis complex presents another problem of interest to the academic community. The lack of evidence for a Clovis origin outside the North American heartland drove archaeologists to look at the Great Plains and the Southwest as possible places of origin because the oldest dates for Clovis have been found in these two regions (Meltzer 2009:242). Using distribution maps of Clovis points, another group of researchers has suggested that the eastern United States as the place where Clovis fluting technology was invented because this region has more variety in fluted points than any other place (Meltzer 2009:242). However, fluted point distribution maps alone are inadequate for determining the origin of fluted point technology (Prascuinas 2008). The main problem for archaeologists in the eastern United States is the paucity of stratified sites with datable material (Anderson 2005; Dunnell 1990; Miller and Gingerich 2013; Steponaitis 1986). Without adequate radiocarbon dates to provide chronological control it does not matter where the greatest concentrations of fluted points occur because the densest concentrations do not necessarily represent the oldest points (Prascuinas 2008:52). Furthermore, in the eastern United States, fluting technology continued until late Paleoindian times.

The new, secure date of 11,560 ^{14}C yr B.P. obtained at the Fin del Mundo site, and the fact that at least 114 Clovis points have been reported in Sonora, along with 12 extensive Clovis sites, need to be taken into consideration. I suggest that the Sonoran Desert region (including southern Arizona, northern Sonora, Baja California, and the islands of the Sea of Cortez and the Pacific Ocean) may be the site of origin for the Clovis complex. Although Monte Verde in Chile is widely accepted as a Pre-Clovis site that is 600 years earlier than the oldest Clovis site, it is unlikely that the early settlers of Chile were the ancestors of the Clovis peoples, and Monte Verde does not seem related to Clovis sites in North America (Dillehay 1989, 1997).

Clovis points have been found all over North America. Their widespread distribution is astonishing; Clovis points are the only Precolumbian artifact style that expanded to a continental scale. The widely disseminated Clovis technology probably implies social interaction among people who spoke the same language and shared a geographic and linguistic corridor for the transmission of ideas. Unfortunately, the majority of Clovis materials are limited to small surface scatters and isolated finds of projectile points. Clovis sites with stratified sedimentary deposits are rare (Meltzer 1993), and only 23 sites have yielded radiocarbon dates (Waters and Stafford 2007). We thus know very little about Clovis subsistence, diet, mobility, territoriality, social organization, and interaction (Meltzer 2009).

The high archaeological visibility and spectacular nature of megafauna kill sites shaped early perceptions of Clovis adaptations and established the Clovis people as big-game hunting experts (Haynes 1964; Meltzer 1993:301; Wormington 1957). Sellards (1952:17) described the Clovis people as "the elephant hunters." Martin (1973) characterized Clovis subsistence as focused on hunting, and thought that hunting explained Clovis colonization. To date, there are 15 accepted extinct proboscidean kill sites in all of North America: 12 mammoth kill sites, two mastodon kill sites, and—with the recent discovery of Fin del Mundo in Sonora, Mexico—one gomphothere kill site (Cannon and Meltzer 2008; Meltzer 2009; Haynes 2002; Sánchez and others 2009).

Traditional models of Clovis subsistence and social organization have been constructed based on kill sites, the small size of campsites, the low densities and apparent homogeneity of Clovis lithic assemblages, and the use of exotic fine-grained cherts and other cryptocrystalline raw materials obtained from distant quarries. These models characterize Clovis groups as small bands of hunters whose diet consisted almost entirely of megafauna, with an adaptive strategy that required high logistical, residential and territorial mobility (Haynes 1966, 1969, 1980; Jelinek 1971; Kelly 1995; Kelly and Todd 1988; Martin 1967, 1973; Saunders 1980; Surovell 2000). However, more recent investigations of Clovis sites have produced alternative models that propose that the dispersal of the Clovis complex was a slower-paced, stepwise process influenced by regional resources (Anderson 1990, 2010; Meltzer 2009).

The Clovis lithic tool kit, with the sophisticated point as its centerpiece, has charmed researchers for decades (Haynes 1964). Significant advances in Clovis lithic studies began with the experimental work of Crabtree (1972), Sollberger (1977), and Callahan (1979). Their replicative experiments shifted the focus of study from point typology to a more thorough understanding of reduction techniques. Specifically, Callahan's (1979) description of the process of biface manufacture demonstrated aspects of technology now considered unique to the Clovis complex (Bradley and others 2010). Based on artifact assemblages from the High Plains, Bradley (1993) provided detailed descriptions of Clovis biface production and defined two Clovis thinning techniques: overshot flaking and fluting. Other site-level analyses by Morrow (1997) and Huckell (2007) demonstrated the prevalence of these diagnostic signatures in Clovis biface assemblages throughout North America. Likewise, Collins (1999a) brought blade production to the forefront. His work has shown that blade technology is a Clovis diagnostic, although blades are not present at all Clovis sites.

Recent analyses of lithics from large habitation sites demonstrate that Clovis people used local raw materials of medium quality to make a variety of tools including utilized flakes, a variety of scrapers, core tools, retouched flakes, blades, bifaces, denticulate tools, and points (Bradley and others 2010; Collins 2002; Collins and others 2003; Gingerich 2007; Smallwood 2011; Waters and others 2011). These tools were used to perform diverse activities. The Clovis tool kit was versatile and could be adapted to the available raw lithic material and regional subsistence opportunities.

Recent investigations of Clovis sites in various regions of the United States and Mexico indicate that there is still much to be learned about Clovis people. Big habitation sites with distinct activity areas have been found in some regions (Bradley and others 2010; Collins 2002; Collins and others 2003; Smallwood 2011; Waters and others 2011). In other areas, Clovis sites using local lithic raw materials of medium quality have been found (Anderson 2013; Gingerich 2007; Sánchez 2010). While the strategic emplacement of tool stone caches occurs in the midcontinent (Kilby 2008), these features are not present at the Sonoran Desert or the eastern United States (Ballenger and others 2011). There are several indications that subsistence strategies varied by region (Anderson 2013; Ballenger and others 2011; Gingerich 2007, 2011; Meltzer 2009). In the near future, new paradigms will be required to accommodate the new data being collected about Clovis people in diverse habitats.

THE PLEISTOCENE PEOPLE OF MEXICO AND SONORA

Mexico is a significant region for understanding the colonization of the continent (Aveleyra Arroyo de Anda 1967; Frison 2000; Faught 1996; Hayden 1987; Haynes 1969;

Meltzer 1989, 1995, 2009; Owen 1984; Sellards 1952; Stanford 1991; Waters 1985; Wormington 1957). The country is shaped like a funnel: when the first Americans moved inland from Beringia to South America, they crossed what is now the U.S.-Mexican border, a territory that it is more than 1,600 km long, and walked south to the Isthmus of Tehuantepec, a narrow strip of land 200 km wide that separates the Pacific and Atlantic oceans.

The archaeological record of the first people of Mexico is scarce, and the previously published information is confusing and unsystematic. In the last decade, however, investigations of Paleoindian sites have increased exponentially, even though only a handful of Mexican researchers focus their investigations on Pleistocene sites. Systematic investigations of Paleoindian sites in the state of Sonora, in particular, have added enormously to

what is known about the Pleistocene landscape and the first people who inhabited this region.

The purpose of this book is to present the reader with the current corpus of data about the Pleistocene archaeology of Mexico, with an emphasis on Sonora. Chapter 2 offers an analytical synthesis of the archaeological record related to the first American in Mexico. Chapter 3 presents a synthesis of the Sonoran landscape, paleoenvironment, and physiographic provinces, together with a regional cultural history of Sonora. Chapter 4 presents the corpus of data from Sonoran sites. Chapter 5 presents the lithic Clovis industry of the El Bajío site. Chapter 6 defines the Late Pleistocene Clovis occupation of Sonora, exploring topics such as patterns of land use, subsistence strategies, the organization of labor, the timing of Clovis in Sonora, and Sonoran Clovis interaction and integration.

CHAPTER TWO

The First People of Mexico

*A Critical Review of Archaeological Investigations
and the Future of Research*

Mexico is a significant region for understanding the colonization of North and South America because it constitutes an obligatory land pathway between the continents (Aveleyra Arroyo de Anda 1967; Frison 2000; Faught 1996; Hayden 1987; Haynes 1969; Meltzer 1989, 1995, 2009; Owen 1984; Sellards 1952; Stanford 1991; Waters 1985; Wormington 1957). Human occupation of the Terminal Pleistocene and Early Holocene periods in Mexico remains poorly known. In 1952, the Instituto Nacional de Antropología e Historia (INAH), the governmental federal agency that oversees archaeology in Mexico, created the Departamento de Prehistoria to study the colonization of Mexico and the North American continent. Although many archaeological projects were carried out over the next 35 years, very little evidence of the first peoples that inhabited Mexico was found. In the past 15 years, however, the number of scholars investigating the first inhabitants of Mexico has tripled.

Here I critically review the existing data from Mexico to provide a historical background of Paleoindian investigations. The data from Mexico are diverse, so in order to evaluate the reported archaeological finds of late Pleistocene and early Holocene in Mexico, I use the minimum requirements suggested by Haynes (1969) and Waters (1985:125) for determining early sites: (1) presence of previously documented diagnostic projectile point types or styles; (2) stone tools in clear association with extinct Pleistocene fauna; (3) directly dated human bones; and (4) a demonstrated relationship between the artifacts and a well-documented stratigraphic sequence. The locations of the major sites I discuss in this chapter are depicted in Figure 2.1.

ANTEDILUVIAN MEN AND NINETEENTH-CENTURY FINDS

The first accounts of the existence of Pleistocene humans in Mexico were reported by the *Commission Scientifique du Mexique*, a group of French antiquarians and naturalists commissioned in Mexico from 1864 to 1867, during the years of the French intervention in Mexico. The charge of this commission was to gather information about the "antique" cultures of Mexico. Eugéne Boban, E. Guillermin-Tarayre, and Cornel Doutrelaine were devoted to collecting exotic archaeological and ethnographic artifacts that they later sold to European museums. They became interested in discovering the remains of "antediluvian man" in Mexico, influenced in part by Boucher de Perthes' proclamation that he found fossilized human bones with artifacts in the Pleistocene gravels of Menchecourt in the Somme Valley of France (Aveleyra Arroyo de Anda 1964:384–385; Gullermin-Tarayre 1867; Hamy1884; Lorenzo 1988:30; Riviale 2001).

The commission reported three possible finds of "early man" in Mexico. A crude lanceolate biface was collected from a Quaternary fossil deposit in the locality of Cañada de Marfil in Guanajuato. A uniface chert tool allegedly was found in an unaltered deposit eight meters below the surface at Cerro de las Palmas in Tacubaya, Mexico City, a locality famous for the abundance of fossils. An axe resembling the Acheulean bifaces of the early Paleolithic period in Europe was found in an alluvial deposit on the Juchipila River in Zacatecas (Aveleyra Arroyo de Anda 1964).

Although none of the reports made by the French commission were proven to be valid, they did succeed in

Figure 2.1. Paleoindian sites in Mexico. Cartography by José Raúl Ortiz.

1. Cañada de Marfil, Guanajuato
2. Cerro de las Palmas, Tacubaya
3. Tequixquiac, Mexico
4. Peñon de los Baños, Mexico City
5. Tlapacoya, Mexico
6. Naharon, Quintana Roo
7. Lake Texcoco, Mexico
8. Tepexpan, Mexico
9. Santa María Iztapan, Mexico
10. Santa Isabel Iztapan, Mexico
11. Los Reyes Acozac, Mexico
12. San Bartolo Atepehuacan, Mexico
13. Santa Lucia, Mexico
14. San Miguel Tocuila, Mexico
15. Cerro Tlapacoya, Mexico
16. Valsequillo Reservoir, Puebla

17. Hueyatlaco, Pueblo
18. El Cedral (Rancho La Amapola), San Luis Potosi
19. Babisuri, Isla Espíritu Santo, Baja California Sur (BCS)
20. Ocozocoautla, Chiapas
21. Guilá Naquitz, Oaxaca
22. Rancho El Batequi, BCS
23. Rancho El Mezquital, BCS
24. Cueva Pintada, BCS
25. Isla Cedros, Baja California Norte
26. Timmy Site, Chihuahua
27. Lago Bustillos, Chihuahua
28. Palo Blanco, Chihuahua
29. Alamo de Villa, Chihuahua
30. Atotonilco, Jalisco

31. Lake Zacoalco, Jalisco
32. Cerro del Tecolote, Jalisco
33. El Platanillo Cave, Guerrero
34. Oyapa, Hidalgo
35. La Calzada, Hildago
36. San Juan Guelavia, Oaxaca
37. El Pocito, Oaxaca
38. Istmo de Tehuantepec, Oaxaca
39. San Isidro, Nuevo León
40. Puntita Negra, Nuevo León
41. La Morita, Nuevo León
42. Salmalayuca Basin, Chihuahua
43. C75-01 site, Chihuahua
44. Mesa de Las Tapias, Durango
45. Cueva de los Grifos, Chiapas

opening a new door for the study of the first Mexicans. By the end of the nineteenth century, Mexican geologists, paleontologists, naturalists, and archaeologists began to investigate archaeological materials that appeared to be of great antiquity, including the discovery of human bones claimed to be associated with Pleistocene deposits in the vicinity of Mexico City. Mariano Bárcena and Manuel del Castillo—known as the fathers of Quaternary geology and paleontology in Mexico—were the first scientists to study early sites and finds (Aveleyra Arroyo de Anda 1964:387; Gio-Argaez and Rodríguez Arevalo 2003).

In 1870, a laborer digging a well at Tequixquiac found the "modified" sacrum of a fossilized camel in a Pleistocene deposit 12 meters beneath the surface. This deposit had a high concentration of fossil material in a stratum known as the El Tajo Formation. The engineer in charge of the drainage operation first gave the camelid bone to Alfredo Chavero in 1880, then to Manuel Orozco y Berra in 1881, and finally to Mariano Bárcena in 1882. After studying the bone and its provenience, the three researchers concluded that the fossilized sacrum was an ornament carved into an animal face before the bone was fossilized, which made it extremely old (Chavero 1881; Orozco y Berra 1880; Bárcena 1882; Aveleyra Arroyo de Anda 1965). When Mariano Bárcena, a geologist, reported the important find at the International Congress of Americanists in Mexico City in 1897, he was met with much skepticism. Bárcena's unexpected death shortly after the meeting, and the misplacement of this putative artifact for nearly 60 years, added drama to the story.

In 1951, Luis Aveleyra Arroyo de Anda reanalyzed the sacrum and agreed with Bárcena´s initial determination that it was indeed a modified bone that had been carved before it was fossilized (Bárcena 1882). Using the drainage system map, he determined the exact location of the find and conducted surveys in the arroyos of Tequixquiac. There he collected approximately 20 artifacts at a gravel deposit that appeared to be the Becerra Formation, which is associated with the Pleistocene fossils (Aveleyra Arroyo de Anda 1965, 1967). The famous camel sacrum is now curated at the Laboratorio de Arqueozoologia at the Subdirección de Laboratorios y Apoyo Académico, Instituto Nacionál de Antropología e Historia (INAH), in Mexico City. This sacrum was studied recently by Lorena Mirambell and Oscar Polaco, and after finding no evidence of use wear, they concluded that the bone was not modified by human agency (Lorena Mirambell, personal communication 2007).

Peñon de los Baños is a rocky hill close to the Mexico City International Airport. This locale was named "de los Baños" due to the hot springs that emerge there. When the Spaniards arrived at Tenochtitlan in 1521, the Peñon de los Baños was an island in Lake Texcoco. Today, it is an isolated rocky hill in more or less flat terrain, forming a unique landscape feature. At least three sets of human remains have been recovered at Peñon de los Baños, all of which appear to be from late Pleistocene deposits at the site.

The first set of remains was found in 1884, embedded in a well-developed travertine deposit that was exposed during an excavation using dynamite. After finding a skull, Mariano Bárcena and Manuel Del Castillo conducted a detailed geological study, and they located the rest of the skeleton in situ. Bárcena and Del Castillo (1885) reported on the geological data and concluded that the human remains were embedded in a calcareous travertine deposit of great antiquity. The naturalist John Newberry (1885) was skeptical about the Peñon de los Baños discoveries, however, and argued that the travertine that sealed the deposits could have been formed in more recent times.

In 1958, more human bones were found at Peñon de los Baños during construction of a road. When Luis Aveleyra Arroyo de Anda (1967:14) examined the site, he found that the deposits had been completely destroyed by road construction. Later that year, human remains were discovered during the excavation of a well. This find, designated Peñon III, was reported to the Departamento de Prehistoria of INAH, and Arturo Romano and Francisco González Rull recovered a mostly complete human skeleton at the site. Romano and González Rull, along with Aveleyra Arroyo de Anda, carried out a detailed study of the area, including the geomorphology, stratigraphic relationships, and paleo-vegetation (Gonzalez and others 2003:381; Gonzalez, Jimenez, and others 2006). The skeleton was located 3 m from the surface in a dark stratum sealed by a travertine deposit. Aveleyra Arroyo de Anda (1964, 1967) proposed that the skeleton was of late Pleistocene age (Bopp 1961).

DIRECTLY DATED HUMAN BONES

With a grant from the Natural Environment Research Council of the United Kingdom, Silvia Gonzalez, a geologist from John Moors Liverpool University, and José Concepción Jiménez, a physical anthropologist from INAH, directly radiocarbon dated 11 human skeletons presumed to be from old contexts, all of them curated at the Museo Nacional de Antropología in Mexico City. After the bone was purified to obtained collagen, only four samples contained enough carbon for dating, and only two of these yield dates of Paleoindian age. From the Peñon III locality, a skeleton found in 1957 was dated with a radiocarbon age of 10,755 ± 75 (OxA-10112) (Gonzalez and others 2003:381; Gonzales, Jiménez, and others 2006:69). A cranium found by workmen making a road near the Tlapacoya site in the early 1960s produced a radiocarbon age of 10,200 ± 65 (Gonzalez and others 2003:381; Gonzales, Jiménez, and others 2006:69).

The Tlapacoya site is located along the margins of ancient Lake Chalco, in the southeastern corner of the Basin of Mexico. There, José Luis Lorenzo excavated at least 18 localities between 1965 and 1975. He argued for an early human occupation of Tlapacoya in two loci dated at approximately 23,000 years ago. C. Vance Haynes visited the site twice during the excavation and collected several radiocarbon samples. While the archaeological record of a 23,000 year-old human occupation at Tlapacoya is controversial, better evidence exists to support an occupation from 7,000 to 10,000 years ago. A feature near the slope of the Tlapacoya Hill, designated Tlapacoya XVIII, consisted of a dense concentration of lithic artifacts and an extended human burial that yielded a radiocarbon date of 9920 ± 250 (I-6897) (Lorenzo and Mirambell 1986a:84; Nárez 1990:30). Recently, Gonzalez and colleagues (2003; Gonzales, Jiménez and others 2006:69) directly dated a human cranium from Tlapacoya that is curated in the INAH Physical Anthropology Department. This skull, discovered at Tlapacoya by workmen during road construction during the late 1960s, yielded a radiocarbon age of 10,200 ± 65 (OxA-10225).

On the Yucatán Peninsula, several caves were recorded during the Proyecto Atlas de Sitios Arqueológicos de Quintana Roo. Although the caves are underwater today, they were unquestionably dry at the end of the Pleistocene, when the water of the Caribbean Sea was much lower than today. The cave deposits have suffered some mixing due to sea currents, but some archaeological contexts and paleontological specimens have been found (González-González and others 2006). In three caves, charcoal flakes, presumably from human occupation, and at least three human burials yielded radiocarbon dates between 9,000 and 8000 years B.P. (Table 2.1; González-González and others 2006:87). One burial designated Naharon I, Quintana Roo, was directly dated, and an 11,670 ± 60 radiocarbon age was

Table 2.1. Radiocarbon Dates from Caves in Quintana Roo

Sample No.	^{14}C Age (B.P.)	Material	Cave
INAH-2123	6941 ± 39	Charcoal	Las Palmas
B-1666199	9180 ± 60	Charcoal	Aktun Ha
INAH-2009	9318 ± 37	Charcoal	Aktun Ha
INAH-2011	9139 ± 23	Charcoal	Aktun Ha
UGA-6637	9524 ± 84	Charcoal	Aktun Ha
UCR-4000/ CAMS-87301	11,670 ± 60	Human bone	Naharon I
UGA-6828	8050 ± 130	Human bone	Las Palmas

Source: Gonzalez and others 2006.

obtained. According to Taylor (2009:184), who processed the sample, the Naharon I bone contained less than 0.1 percent of the residual organic carbon found in bones and did not exhibit a collagen-like profile. Therefore, the sample should be regarded as problematic. Several attempts to date more bones from the Naharon I burial have failed due to the lack of collagen (Alejandro Terrazas, personal communication 2011). More studies need to be performed at the Yucatán caves in order to evaluate the stratigraphic contexts and to understand the nature of the archaeological elements and their relationship with the paleontological finds.

MAMMOTHS AND HUMANS IN THE BASIN OF MEXICO

The first written report of giant bones observed in central Mexico date to the sixteenth-century chronicles of Bernal Diaz del Castillo (1939:268–269). This report states that the Tlaxcaltecas showed Hernán Cortés a giant femur that appeared to have been buried in the ground, demonstrating that giant people and animals existed in this land. Cortés was so impressed with the giant bone that he sent the sample to Spain with the first lot of goods offered to King Carlos I.

Presently, 150 mammoth finds have been reported from within the Basin of Mexico; at least 40 of them have been completely excavated (Arroyo-Cabrales and others 2003, 2006, 2007; Carballal, editor 1997; García Bárcena 1989; Johnson and others 2006; Lorenzo and Mirambell 1999). Only a few of these finds provide evidence of association with humans.

When the Departamento de Prehistoria was established in the Instituto Nacional de Antropología e Historia in 1952, the staff included Pablo Martinez del Río (director), Manuel Maldonado-Koerdell (paleontologist), A. R. V. Arellano (consultant stratigrapher), Luis Aveleyra Arroyo de Anda (archaeologist), José Luis Lorenzo (archaeologist), and Arturo Romano (physical anthropologist). This department was the first scientific organization to specialize in the study of Paleoindians in North America (Kreiger 1950b). The first investigation carried out by the staff of the Departamento de Prehistoria, under the direction of Aveleyra Arroyo de Anda, was the excavation of mammoths at Santa Isabel Iztapan (Aveleyra Arroyo de Anda 1955, 1961, 1962, 1964, 1967; Aveleyra Arroyo de Anda and Maldonado-Koerdell 1953).

Aveleyra Arroyo de Anda, who served as the director of the Departamento de Prehistoria from 1954 to 1956, was instrumental in promoting archaeological investigations of the first Mexicans during the 1950s and 1960s. Aveleyra Arroyo de Anda received his bachelor's degree in anthropology, with an expertise in archaeology, at the Escuela Nacional de Antropología e Historia. He earned a graduate degree in anthropological sciences in Europe, where he received additional paleontological training. Aveleyra Arroyo de Anda began his education with Helmut de Terra, Kirk Bryan, and Alberto Arellano, the scholars responsible for the first coordinated scientific study of the early inhabitants of Mexico. This group used volcanology and glaciology to reconstruct the stratigraphic sequence of the Late Pleistocene and Early Holocene periods in the Basin of Mexico (Arellano 1946a, 1951; Bryan 1946, 1948; De Terra 1947a, 1947b, 1957).

In the 1960s, José Luis Lorenzo became a significant figure in the investigation of early humans in Mexico. He was named director of the Departamento de Prehistoria in 1961, shortly after returning from a two-year long stay at the University of London, where he studied under Frederick Zeuner and V. Gordon Childe, pioneers of environmental archaeology and interdisciplinary methods. With this perspective, Lorenzo began forming laboratories of paleozoology, paleobotany, geology, pedology, and sedimentology. He directed several long-term interdisciplinary studies and systematic investigations at the Departamento de Prehistoria, including the development of a glacial chronology for the volcanoes in central Mexico (Lorenzo 1958, 1969).

By 1950, the population of Mexico City began its meteoric growth, with the population doubling every 20 years. The urban center of Mexico City was greatly expanded, and substantial construction was carried out in the suburbs of the city. This led to an increase in the discovery of megafauna, mostly in lacustrine deposits. Central Mexico is characterized by highly dynamic landscapes that underwent complex transformations throughout the Late Quaternary period. The Basin of Mexico was formed by tectonic activities and fractures; the basin filled with material derived from the mountains that was redeposited by rivers. By the end of the Pleistocene, the Valley of Mexico had become a closed basin supporting a system of marshy lakes. Unquestionably, the lakes provided an oasis-like setting for many animals, including herds of mammoths, as well as for the first human groups who arrived in the Basin of Mexico (Carballal 1997; Lorenzo and Mirambell 1986a:20; Sedov and others 2010).

The northeastern and eastern sectors of the Lake Texcoco shoreline provide the setting for numerous finds of late Pleistocene fauna, especially mammoth, both with and without associated human artifacts. The greatest concentration of bones are in the north, where proboscidean remains, particularly mammoths, have been found across the basin. The Departamento de Prehistoria was instrumental in the excavation of mammoths found in the vicinity of Lake Texcoco between 1952 and 1980.

According to Lorenzo and Mirambell (1986a), the remains of 15 mammoths were excavated in the Basin of Mexico between 1952 and 1980. Seven of these paleontological finds show possible associations with artifacts; however, after a careful analysis of the archaeological data, only three have indications of human-mammoth interactions. Margarita Carballal Staedtler (1997) published a detailed compilation of mammoths and other Pleistocene fauna found by the Department of Salvage Archaeology of INAH from 1980 to 1997. None of the 20 mammoths reported by Carballal were associated with evidence of human activity; many of the finds were recovered in deep excavations (10 m beneath the present surface) when subway lines and underpasses were constructed in the city. A few mammoth finds in the Basin of Mexico are more than 35,000 years old, but most of them are between 10,000 and 12,000 years in age.

Mammoth and Man in Tepexpan

In December 1945, workers digging a trench at the Tepexpan Hospital in the Basin of Mexico found the remains of a mammoth (Arellano 1946b:2). The skeleton of the mammoth was almost complete and showed evidence of butchering. The skull was overturned and the base was damaged, probably in order to extract the brain (Arellano 1946b). One of the iliac bones was missing and the remaining one was overturned with the femoral cavity facing up. The right foreleg was completely articulated and in an upright position, suggesting that the animal was trapped in a swamp and died before it was butchered (Arellano 1946a; Lorenzo and Mirambell 1986a:116). A small flake (3-cm long) made of a white chert was found between the skull and the head of the humerus. The stratigraphic unit where the mammoth was deposited is a gray-green lacustrine lime deposit sealed by caliche, which apparently corresponded to a desiccation period of Lake Texcoco (Arellano 1946b). A short time later, another, less complete mammoth was found in this same ditch.

During the same year, at least five mammoths were found over a 2-km area (De Terra and others 1949). According to Helmut De Terra, all the fossils were found in the Becerra Formation, defined by Bryan and Arellano as an alluvial deposit with numerous fossils from the late Pleistocene. This formation was thought to have a regional distribution (Arellano 1946a; Aveleyra Arroyo de Anda 1967; De Terra and others 1949).

De Terra arrived in Mexico City in 1945 and began to coordinate the geological investigations at Tepexpan. Two years later, after a detailed survey of the Tepexpan area, he found a human burial eroding out of a wall profile that appeared to be "in situ" within a stratigraphic unit that he called the "formación Risco," representing the younger, sandy face of the Late Pleistocene Becerra Formation (De Terra and others 1949:26). De Terra also defined a lithic industry in Tepexpan that he called the San Juan Industry, represented by coarse, unifacially flaked choppers and other simple unifacial tools. Several researchers were critical of De Terra's conclusions about Tepexpan. These critics did not agree that the lithic complex was human-made, and they questioned the provenience of the burial, criticized the excavation techniques, and disparaged the methods used for dating the archaeological context (Avelyra Arroyo de Anda 1950; Black 1949; Krieger 1950a, 1950b; Lorenzo 1967). Alex Krieger (1950b) visited the site and concluded that the skull originated from an Archaic period occupation that was well represented at Tepexpan.

The controversy surrounding the antiquity of the human remains recovered at Tepexpan continued until 1989, when Tom Stafford directly dated some fragments of long bones. The bone was pretreated by Stafford and dated at the University of Arizona, yielding a ^{14}C date of 1980 ± 330 B.P. (AA-2667). At the same time, the skeleton was examined by a physical anthropologist and identified as a female (Lorenzo 1991). Silvia Gonzalez and colleagues (2003:385; Gonzalez Jiménez and others 2006; Gonzalez, Morett, and others 2006) attempted to independently date the Tepexpan skeleton, but the considerable chemical contamination of the remains with preservatives made it impossible. Recently, Sergey Sedov and colleagues (2010) carried out a series of investigations at Tepexpan with the purpose of reconstructing the past climate in relation to the human occupation of the valley. Sedov recorded a stratigraphic deposition of sediments at least 30,000 years old (Sedov and others 2010). Although controversial, the Tepexpan site is one of the few localities that has not been destroyed by urban development because the area is a protected INAH zone. The archaeological record of Tepexpan should be reevaluated in the future.

The Articulated Mammoths of Santa Isabel Iztapan I and II

Santa Isabel Iztapan was the site of the first archaeological investigation carried out by the Departamento de Prehistoria. In July 1950, while digging an irrigation ditch in the town of Santa Isabel Iztapan at the northeast edge of Lake Texcoco, workers found fragments of mammoth bones and tusks (Iztapan 1). In July 1952, José Luís Aveleyra Arroyo de Anda, Manuel Maldonado-Koerdell, and Arturo Romano began excavations at the locality. After four days of work, a projectile point was found lodged between two mammoth ribs. Further work revealed the presence of five more artifacts associated with the remains. Eighty percent of the skeleton was recovered. One femur lay more than 1.8 m away from the rest of the skeleton, suggesting that it had been moved during the butchering process (Aveleyra Arroyo de Anda and Maldonado-Koerdell 1953; Wormington 1957:92–93). The projectile point associated with the mammoth bears a general resemblance to the Scottsbluff type; the maximum chronological range for this type is 9900 to 8300 B.P.

In June 1954, Arturo Romano, under the direction of Aveleyra Arroyo de Anda, excavated a second mammoth, designated Iztapan 2. Iztapan 2 was located approximately one kilometer from the first mammoth, apparently within the same stratigraphic horizon. The second skeleton was complete and showed clear evidence of butchering with cut-marks on bone made by stone tools. Like the Tepexpan mammoth, the skull was overturned and the base of the cranium was smashed. Three artifacts were found in direct association with the bones. One of these is a lanceolate projectile point with a straight base. It has broad overall flaking on both faces and an extremely fine marginal retouch. This point somewhat resembles an Angostura point, as well as some of the Great Basin lanceolate Paleoindian points, but it cannot be directly correlated with those types. A second projectile point is laurel-leaf-shaped, pointed at both proximal and distal ends (Aveleyra Arroyo de Anda 1955; Aveleyra Arroyo de Anda and Maldonado-Koerdell 1953). This second point is similar to the Lerma type defined by MacNeish (1950), a type that remains poorly dated.

The Iztapan mammoths were found within the same gray-green lacustrine lime deposit that was associated with the Tepexpan mammoth (Aveleyra Arroyo de Anda 1955; Aveleyra Arroyo de Anda and Maldonado-Koerdell 1953). A radiocarbon age obtained from the organic fraction of the sediments associated with mammoth kill at Locus 1 yielded a date of about 9000 B.P. Lawrence Kulp, who processed this sample at Columbia University, does not believe this date is reliable because only a single organic remnant was obtained during the pretreatment. In a letter to Aveleyra Arroyo de Anda, Kulp suggested that this date may represent the minimal reliable age (Aveleyra Arroyo de Anda 1964:402). García Bárcena (1975:30) obtained relative dating using the obsidian-hydration technique on three obsidian artifacts associated with the first Tepexpan mammoth. García Bárcena's results are not very precise and are somewhat confusing, with three different hydration rim widths equivalent to 8100, 6200, and 7000 years old. García Bárcena (1975:30–31) noted that the soil alkalinity of the area may have affected the readings.

There is no doubt that the mammoths of Iztapan I and II are the best examples of mammoths associated with humans in the Basin of Mexico. When Maldonado-Koerdell realized the importance of the first find, he sent telegrams to Marie Wormington at the Denver Museum of Natural History, Alex D. Krieger at the University of Texas, and E. H. Sellards at the Texas Memorial Museum. On March 20, 1952, these archaeologists, along with many Mexican researchers, witnessed the removal of the artifacts from the bone bed.

There are rumors that the artifacts found associated with the mammoths of Iztapan were a hoax orchestrated for political reasons, to obtain funding for future investigations and to demonstrate the importance of the Departamento de Prehistoria (Gianfranco Cassiano, personal communication 2008; Fernando Lopez Aguilar, personal communication 2001). Beatriz Braniff, a professor

emeritus at INAH, was a student in 1952 and part of the excavation crew at the Iztapan site. She was present when the first stone tool was found at and she denies that the find was a hoax. However, Braniff remembers that plastic bags and other modern materials were found under and above the bones during the excavation, indicating that it was not a sealed context (Beatriz Braniff, personal communication 2002). Dr. Jane Kelley, then a student, accompanied H. M. Wormington to Mexico City to see the site, and she also agrees that it was not a hoax (Jane Kelley, personal communication 2008). Roberto García Moll, former director of INAH and president of the Consejo de Arqueología from 2006 to 2009, worked with Luís Avelyra and Maldonado Koerdell on several investigations. García Moll describes them as professional and superior researchers, and he also denies the hoax theory (Roberto García Moll, personal communication 2007).

Los Reyes Acozac Mammoth

In 1956, Arturo Romano and José Luis Lorenzo carried out a meticulous and systematic excavation of a mammoth located in the northern section of the Basin of Mexico at Los Reyes Acozac. An excavation area of at least 12 m by 12 m was opened and three mostly disarticulated mammoths were exposed. Two flakes, one of basalt and the other of obsidian, were found in the excavation area but not in direct association with the bones. The stratum of the bone bed was defined as a silty, lacustrine deposit located approximately 2 m below the surface. The bones were sparse throughout the 1.2-m thick stratigraphic unit, a possible indication that the bones are not in a primary sealed context. An obsidian flake from the excavation was dated at 10,000 years B.P. by obsidian hydration (Lorenzo and Mirambell 1986a:51; García Bárcena 1975).

Mammoth of San Bartolo Atepehuacan

In 1957, when digging a drainage ditch at San Bartolo Atepehuacan, Colonia Vallejo, in the northern Basin of Mexico, workers found the remains of a semi-complete mammoth. Arturo Romano was placed in charge of excavating the mammoth. The mammoth was found between 3.2 m and 3.7 m beneath the ground surface in a sandy stratum with charcoal flecks that was below a caliche-like horizon. The mammoth was semi-articulated with several articulated vertebrae, many ribs preserved in anatomical position, articulated long bones, and a pelvis. The cranium had been destroyed by the workers who found the mammoth.

A concentration of 59 flakes and chips of obsidian and fine-grained basalt was found in association with the articulated vertebrae in the south section of the excavation area. At least one of the flakes was utilized. Pleistocene hunters at this site apparently resharpened their tools while butchering the mammoth (Aveleyra Arroyo de Anda 1962:42–43, 1964, 1967:45–46; Lorenzo and Mirambell 1986a:57). Numerous dispersed charcoal flecks were found among the bones. A radiocarbon age obtained from the combined sample of several charcoal flecks gave a date of 9670 ± 400 B.P. (M-776). An obsidian flake found in the concentration of tools was dated by the obsidian-hydration method and produced a result of approximately 9400 B.P. (García Bárcena 1975; Lorenzo and Mirambell 1986a).

Lake Texcoco Mammoth

In 1972, a mammoth was discovered eroding out of mud deposits in a remnant of the southeastern portion of Lake Texcoco; this find was excavated by Lorena Mirambell and a team of archaeologists from the Departamento de Prehistoria. The skeleton had been recently exposed and it was semi-articulated and semi-complete; only the skull and the lower extremities were missing. Thirty-one square meters were excavated; the skeleton was located less than 40 cm deep in a pyroclastic deposit created by multiple volcanic events. Two obsidian flakes and one basalt flake were associated with the bones (Lorenzo and Mirambell 1986a:91; Mirambell 1972). Because the mammoth was found on the surface, however, it is impossible to know if the spatial association between the bones and the artifacts represents the same behavioral event.

In order to determine if there was a late Pleistocene hunter's encampment surrounding the mammoth, Mirambell (1972) tested an area of about 400 square meters for phosphates. She found an area with a high concentration of phosphates, which could be interpreted as an area of high human activity; however, no artifact cluster suggesting a camp area was found. It is important to point out that Lake Texcoco has been heavily populated since 4,000 B.P. García Bárcena (1975:37) obtained an obsidian-hydration date about 12,600 years B.P. from one of the obsidian flakes. He noted, however, that this flake was very close to the surface so the margin of error is unknown and the date is not reliable.

Santa Lucia I: Mammoths and Pleistocene Fauna

In 1976, Pleistocene fauna were found during construction of a platform at Air Force Base No. 1 in Santa Lucia, Estado de México, at the northern end of Lake Texcoco. Jesús Mora and Oscar Rodriguez were in charge of the excavation of this site. Two semi-articulated mammoths, a semi-articulated camelid, and isolated bones of a saber tooth cat were found about 2 m below the surface in lacustrine-alluvial deposits. One obsidian flake and two andesite flakes were found in the same stratum as one of the mammoths (Mora and Rodriguez 1979, cited in Lorenzo and Mirambell 1986a:99). Two dates from the fossil-bearing strata were obtained. A soil sample from the upper part of the stratum dated to 23,900 ± 600 B.P. (I-10.427), and a soil sample from the lower part dated to 26,300 ± 880 B.P. (GX-6,628). A pollen column obtained from the excavation profile revealed that the plant community associated with the mammoths of Santa Lucia I was represented by pine, oaks, cypress, and elms, corresponding to a period of cool but dry weather (González Quintero and Sánchez 1980:200).

Tocuila Locality

In July 1996, a mammoth skull was found about 3 m below the surface during the excavation of a water cistern at San Miguel Tocuila, in Texcoco, Estado de Mexico. Luis Morett and Joaquin Arroyo Cabrales investigated the paleontological find for three months, excavating five disarticulated mammoths. Horses, camels, bison, and rabbits were also found in the same bone-bearing stratum. The Pleistocene fauna were found in a 1.5-m deep mudflow channel. The bones had been transported into the channel from their primary context (Arroyo Cabrales and others 2001; Morett and others 1998; Gonzalez and others 2001). Although some bones at the site were articulated, most of the mammoth bones were not. The articulated bones are indicators that the mammoth bones were not transported far. Although the mammoth skeletons were recovered within a 10-m by 10-m area, the Tocuila channel does not represent a primary archaeological context. Several ^{14}C dates were obtained from combined wood charcoal, seeds, soil samples, and mammoth bone. The set of dates provided an average age of 11,100 years B.P. for the deposit (Table 2.2) (Gonzalez and others 2001; Morett and others 1998, 2003). According to Siebe and Urrutia-Fucugauchi (1999:1550), the mammoth remains were situated in a stratum created by a 14,000 year-old volcanic eruption. This appears to indicate that the bones were redeposited in an older stratigraphic unit.

Arroyo-Cabrales and colleagues (2001) argue for a human presence at the Tocuila paleontological locality,

Table 2.2. Radiocarbon Dates from Tocuila

Sample No.	Depth	Material	¹⁴C Age (B.P.)
INAH-1658	170–173 cm	Wood charcoal	11,277 ± 139
INAH-1659	170–205 cm	Wood charcoal	11,274 ± 116
INAH-1660	205–230 cm	Seeds and charcoal	11,541 ± 196
INAH-1661	230–270 cm	Seeds	11,296 ± 270
INAH-1662	270–300 cm	Seeds	10,553 ± 188
AA23161 (AMS)	204 cm	Soil	10,220 ± 75
AA23162 (AMS)	305–306 cm	Soil	12,615 ± 95
OXA-7746 (AMS)		Mammoth skull bone	11,100 ± 80

Source: Modified from Table 1 in Morett and others 2003.

based on the presence of a mammoth tusk flake from which two secondary flakes were detached. The two detached flakes can be refitted to the core because they were left in place. The "core" was found together with semi-articulated bones. However, the secondary nature of the bone-bearing stratum, and the fact that the bones are embedded in a Pleistocene lahar, appear to indicate that the mammoth bones might have been fractured by non-human agents (Haynes 2002:135). Nonetheless, the Tocuila locality represents an important region for future investigations. According to Luis Morett and Joaquin Arroyo Cabrales (personal communication 2009), there are at least three unexcavated mammoths in the more intact lake deposits near the Tocuila site, so the prospect for finding a human association in a more pristine deposit is feasible.

MISCELLANEOUS ARCHAEOLOGICAL RECORDS

In addition to mammoth finds, an eclectic array of sites with evidence of first Mexicans has been reported. The sites occur in different regions of Mexico, and some are thought to be more than 20,000 years old. Here I critically review the archaeology of six sites that have been identified as full glacial, Late Pleistocene sites.

The Tlapacoya Site

In 1965, José Luis Lorenzo documented a recently exposed large profile in the lower bajada of the andesitic Cerro Tlapacoya that contained stratified deposits showing several lake shorelines, lahars, peats, and paleosols, together with burned red deposits that appear to represent fire features associated with Pleistocene bones (Lorenzo and Mirambell 1986b:3). Tlapacoya Hill is located along the margins of ancient Lake Chalco in the southeastern corner of the Basin of Mexico.

Eight field seasons were carried out at the site between 1965 and 1973. The research strategy consisted of excavating a series of trenches from the Tlapacoya Hill to the old lakeshore (Tlapacoya I–XVIII). Tlapacoya represents one of the few localities in the Basin of Mexico that has a complete stratigraphic record for the last 40,000 years. In other areas, the high volcanic activity characteristic of the Late Pleistocene has destroyed much of the stratigraphic record (Huddart and Gonzalez 2006; Lozano and others 1993). The reconstruction of the stratigraphic sequence, geochronology, geomorphology, and the environment at Tlapacoya provide the most important information available for understanding the Late Pleistocene and Early Holocene environment of the Basin of Mexico.

Lorenzo (Lorenzo and Mirambell 1986b:10, 31; Mirambell 1994:194) argued for an early human occupation of Tlapacoya in two loci. At Tlapacoya I (Trenches Alfa and Beta) the early evidence consists of three cleared circles, each measuring 1.15 m in diameter, with burned soil, charcoal flakes, and very rough artifacts made of the andesitic rocks of Cerro Tlapacoya. A radiocarbon age of 24,000 ± 4000 B.P. (A-794b) was obtained from a sample composed of very fine charcoal flecks inside the feature.

The other archaeological context reported by Lorenzo to have great antiquity was found at Tlapacoya II. A burned log of *Taxodium mucronatum* (Montezuma cypress or ahuehuete) was found in the trench at this location, with a prismatic blade lying underneath it. The log was radiocarbon dated to 23,950 ± 950 B.P. Lorenzo proposed that the minimal age for the blade, therefore, must be 23,000 years. However, Lorenzo found no evidence of an encampment, kill site, or other archaeological feature (Lorenzo and Mirambell 1986b).

C. Vance Haynes, Jr., visited the site twice during the excavations. He collected and processed several charcoal samples for obtaining radiocarbon dates, and also examined the stratigraphic profiles at Tlapacoya I and II (Haynes 1967). According to Haynes, both loci are problematic; the cleared circular feature associated with the first locus may represent bear "beds" (C. Vance Haynes Jr. personal communication 1997), or may be the result of tree rooting in the sediment (Waters 1985). Huddart and Gonzalez (2006:98) reopened the Alfa Trench at Tlapacoya I, and they concluded that there is no evidence of human occupation between 24,000 and 10,000 years B.P. With regard to the second locus at Tlapacoya II, the prismatic obsidian blade is clearly an intrusive artifact associated with overlying Archaic and ceramic period occupations at the site. The position of the blade in the trench may be the result of a large fissure that was clearly visible in the profile (C. Vance Haynes, Jr., personal communication 1997). It is possible that volcanic activity between 24,000 and 9000 years B.P. could have altered the formation processes of the archaeological record at the site, and that some of the artifacts from later occupations slipped down into earlier deposits.

The archaeological evidence for a 23,000 year old human occupation at Tlapacoya is controversial, but the Early Holocene occupation (10,000 to 7,000 years old) is much more substantial and well represented. The best archaeological component of Early Holocene age was found during the excavations conducted in 1970 and 1971 at Tlapacoya XVIII, located 25 m south of Trench Beta, where a dense concentration of lithic artifacts was found near the slope of Tlapacoya Hill. This feature yielded at least one ^{14}C date of 7000 B.P. An extended human burial with the face down was excavated from the underlying unit (IV). The horizon associated with this burial was radiocarbon dated at 9920 ± 250 B.P. (I-6897) (Lorenzo and Mirambell 1986b:84; Nárez 1990:30). Aside from the burial, unit IV had few lithic artifacts. These artifacts included two cores, 12 flakes from the local quarry, and one obsidian flake (Nárez 1990:142). The lithic collection from Tlapacoya XVII is abundant, and is curated at the Museo Nacional de Antropología in Mexico City. Future analysis of the lithic material is necessary to assess if a Pleistocene industry is represented at the site

Recently, Gonzalez and colleagues (2003; Gonzalez, Jiménez and others 2006:69) directly dated a human cranium housed in the INAH Physical Anthropology Department. This skull was found at Tlapacoya in the late 1960s by workmen while constructing a road. The radiocarbon age obtained from this cranium is 10,200 ± 65 B.P. (OxA-10225).

The Valsequillo Reservoir, Puebla

Juan Armenta Camacho, an enthusiast antiquarian, spent many weekends during the 1950s looking for sites with Pleistocene fauna at Valsequillo Reservoir in the state of Puebla, southeast of the Basin of Mexico. Over 20 years, he documented more than 100 localities, some of which were associated with bones and artifacts. Most of the sites were located in the eroded walls of the arroyos that emptied into the reservoir (Armenta 1957, 1959). The Hueyatlaco locality, the most important site documented by Armenta, apparently contained various deposits associated with Pleistocene fauna and artifacts. In 1962 and 1964, Cynthia Irwin-Williams conducted excavations in two outcrops at this locality, documenting exposed profiles that contained a series of fine alluvial deposits with Pleistocene fauna and artifacts (Irwin-Williams 1967:338).

According to Irwin-Williams (1967), evidence for early human occupation at the Hueyatlaco locality is represented in several strata. Unit C contained large quantities of horse and camel remains and five stone tools, none of which is considered diagnostic. Unit E_1 contained abundant fossil remains of horse and camel, along with a few horned antelope and mammoths. Unit E_1 also contained a Lerma-like point and a tip of a bifacially flaked artifact that were found between the ribs and vertebrae of a semi-articulated horse skeleton. Unit E_2 contained a concentration of mastodon bones representing a single individual. The mandible of this mastodon was split, and a chopping tool was discovered inside the fragmented mandible near the tooth row. A burin-like tool was also recovered from inside the tooth cavity of the mastodon mandible. Unit G had abundant fossil remains with inclusions of a distinctive volcanic ash. A unifacial pointed tool was recovered from under a large ungulate rib in unit G (Irwin-Williams 1967). Although the Hueyatlaco locality appears to be an extraordinary site with Pleistocene fauna in direct association with artifacts, the dates of the deposits are controversial. These dates, obtained using the uranium-series method, yielded ages of more than 200,000 years B.P. (Steen-McIntyre and others 1981; Irwin-Williams 1981).

Recent investigations carried out at the locality of Hueyatlaco provide new data. In 2001, a group of investigators (Ochoa Castillo and others 2003; Hardaker 2007; Malde and others 2007) reopened and cleaned some of the Irwin-Williams' excavations of the 1960s. In 2004, Waters and colleagues (Renne and others 2005; Waters and others 2008) opened several test pits and relocated the walls of the old excavations made by Irwin-Williams in order to study the stratigraphic sequence, reconstruct the geochronology of the site, and assess the relationship among artifacts, fossils, and deposits. Silvia Gonzalez and colleagues did geological work in 2003 near the Hueyatlaco locality to reconstruct the Quaternary geological sequence in the valley. They claim to have found human footprints in a volcanic ash deposit that dates more than 40,000 years B.P. (Gonzalez and Huddart 2007, Gonzalez, Jiménez, and others 2006; Gonzalez, Morett and others 2006).

Michael Waters and his colleagues' (2008) are seeking to understand the formation process of the archaeological record at Hueyatlaco. Their investigations are still in process, but they have reviewed the established stratigraphic sequence and proposed a new geochronological sequence. They found that the Hueyatlaco ash is 450,000 years old. This dating was obtained using different methods, all of which produced similar dates. The investigations of Waters and his colleagues demonstrate that the artifacts recovered from Irwin-Williams' excavations are not a hoax, as was claimed by Lorenzo (1978). These artifacts are located at an unconformity in the stratigraphic sequence. A uranium-series determination in bone from the so-called "bifacial level" gave a date of 245,000 ± 40,000 B.P. However, due to the unconformity, this bone bed date does not reflect the age of the artifacts, which are likely of Holocene age (Waters and others 2008). In order to understand the geochronology of the Valsequillo Valley, Waters and colleagues also dated volcanic episodes present in different profiles using diverse dating techniques, including fisson track, tephra-hydration, U/TH(he), Ar-Ar- normal, and reverse polarity.

The Ar-Ar and reverse polarity dating of the Xalnene Tuff deposit where Gonzalez and colleagues (Gonzalez, Huddart, Bennett and Gonzalez-Huesca 2006; Gonzalez, Huddart, and Bennet 2006) claim to have found a site composed of human and other animal footprints yielded a date of 1,300,000 years B.P. (Renne and others 2005; Waters and others 2008). After almost 50 years of speculation; Waters and colleagues are beginning to resolve the many questions that have been raised concerning the archaeology of the Valsequillo Reservoir.

El Cedral (Rancho La Amapola), San Luis Potosí

Rancho La Amapola is located in the town of El Cedral in the state of San Luis Potosí, near the road between Matehuala and Saltillo. It is located in an area with abundant springs, where a high water table formed extensive but superficial lakes in the past.

El Cedral (Rancho La Amapola) was investigated by Mirambell (2012) over eight field seasons from 1977 to 1991. The site consisted of Pleistocene bone beds that contained semi-articulated mammoth, camel, horse, bear, and tapir skeletons (Mirambell 1994, 2012; Lorenzo and Mirambell 1985, 1999). Seven concentrations of preserved wood and wood charcoal at the site were interpreted as hearths. Artifacts included one circular chert scraper and some modified bones (Mirambell 1994, 2012; Lorenzo and Mirambell 1999). Thirty samples for radiocarbon dates were obtained from soil, charcoal, and preserved wood; the hearths dated between 37,694 ± 1963 B.P. (INAH-305) and 25,682 ± 1418 B.P. (INAH-303).

The relationships between the in situ artifacts, possible hearths, and the Pleistocene bones at the site are not well understood. Mirambell's (2012) recent publication analyzing the environmental, geomorphological, geochronological, and sedimentological contexts of El Cedral provides a baseline for future research at the site. El Cedral is an important site that should be investigated further.

Babisuri Shelter, Isla del Espíritu Santo, Baja California Sur

In 1996, Harumi Fujita, an archaeologist from the Centro INAH Baja California Sur, discovered the Babisuri Shelter site on the island of Espíritu Santo, located 30 km from the mainland in the Sea of Cortez. She argued for a 40,000 year old human occupation at the cave. In stratum III, the lowest stratigraphic unit above the bedrock of the cave, the occupation is represented by basalt and rhyolite flakes and scrapers, ground stone, and many shells that had been transformed into artifacts (Fujita 2002, 2007, 2008). The age of the occupation was determined by radiocarbon dating the shell artifacts, which yielded dates of 40,000 years old. Stratum II, above Stratum III, is described as having an occupation very similar to that in stratum III but it has been dated to 10,000 years B.P. According to Fujita, the transition between Strata II and

Table 2.3. Selected Radiocarbon from Babisuri Shelter, Espíritu Santo Island

Sample No.	Stratum	Material	¹⁴C Age
B159190	B3 V a inferior	Charcoal	1860 ± 40 B.P.
B159188	B2IV a inferior	Charcoal	1550 ± 40 B.P.
B211114	E3 III g inferior	Charcoal	1400 ± 40 B.P.
INAH-2266	G4 II c superior	Charcoal	1356 ± 22 B.P.
B159194	B4	Human bones	800 ± 40 B.P.
B211120	H2 IIIj inferior	Charcoal	1270 ± 40 B.P.
B159189	B2 V a inferior	Charcoal	450 ± 40 B.P.
B159191	B4-V	Small charcoal	480 ± 60 B.P.
B159193	B3	Fish bone	8280 ± 40 B.P.

Sources: Fujita 2007, 2008.

III is continuous, and there are very few distinctions between the two layers—both contain loose silty sand sediments (Fujita 2007, 2008).

At least 88 radiocarbon dates have been obtained from Babisuri shelter. Twenty-two of the radiocarbon dates on bulk shells (*Glycymeris* sp., *Dosinia* sp., and *Laevicardium* sp.) are at least 35,000 years old (Fujita 2008). Seven charcoal samples have been radiocarbon dated, all of which date to the late Archaic age (1800 to 1300 cal B.P.; see Table 2.3). Two of the dated charcoal samples were recovered in Stratum III (the unit dated at 40,000 years old). One radiocarbon date of 8280 ± 40 B.P. on a fish bone came from Stratum V (Fujita 2007 and 2008).

In summary, the Babisuri site appears to represent a late Archaic occupation of the island. The similarities of the three occupations of the cave described by Fujita are comparable to Archaic sites in Sonora, with the presence of ground stone and fire-cracked rock. The early dates obtained from the shell artifacts surely represent the use of fossil shells, which the inhabitants of La Covacha Babisuri obtained from a natural relict shell deposit of Pleistocene age, and the shell dates do not represent the age of the occupation of the shelter.

Ocozocoautla, Chiapas (Cueva de los Grifos and Cueva Santa Marta)

Joaquin García Bárcena excavated two caves at Ozococoautla, Chiapas, between 1974 and 1977. Cueva de los Grifos, a moderately sized cave measuring 24 m wide and 8 m deep, is one of three continuous caves located at Ocozocoautla. This cave contained stratigraphic deposits less than 1.5 m in depth. (Santamaría and García Bárcena 1984:7). An unfluted, lanceolate chert projectile point was found in the earliest level, along with denticulate tools, scrapers, bifacial thinning flakes, and bone fragments (Santamaría and García Bárcena1984, 1989). Although identified as a Clovis point (García Bárcena 1979; Santamaría and García Bárcena 1989:76), the point is not fluted and the fine collateral pressure flaking and basal thinning present in this specimen is unlike Clovis-type points. The artifact appears to be more similar to a Plainview or Milnesand point (Sellards 1955; Holliday 1997:141). Unfortunately the location of the point is unknown at present time. Two radiocarbon dates were obtained from combined charcoal flecks. A radiocarbon date of 8930 ± 150 B.P. (I-10760) was obtained for the lower stratum containing the point, and a date of 9460 ± 150 B.P. (I-10761) was obtained for the unit lying immediately above the point (Santamaría and García Bárcena 1984:13, 1989:99–100).

Cueva Santa Marta is located at the northeast margin of the valley. The cave is 24 m wide and 8 m deep, and contains 2.5 m of sediment. MacNeish and Peterson (1962) conducted test excavations at Santa Marta Cave between 1958 and 1959. García Bárcena and Santamaría of INAH opened an area of 58 square meters in three different units (García Bárcena and Santamaría 1982). García Bárcena and Santamaría found a stratigraphic sequence with at least 15 different well-defined units. The lowest units yielded two radiocarbon dates about 9000 B.P. (Table 2.4).

In 2005, Guillermo Acosta Ochoa from the Instituto de Investigaciones Antropológicas at the UNAM carried

Table 2.4. Radiocarbon Dates from Santa Marta and Los Grifos Caves

Laboratory No.	Provenience	¹⁴C Age (B.P.)	Cave	Source
I-9260	Stratum XVI	9330 ± 290	Santa Marta	Garcia Bárcena and Santamaria (1982)
I-9259	Stratum XVI	9280 ± 290	Santa Marta	Garcia Bárcena and Santamaria (1982)
I-10760	Unit 15, above Plainview point	8930 ± 150	Los Grifos	Santamaria and Garcia Bárcena (1974)
I-10761	Unit 16, below Plainview point	9460 ± 150	Los Grifos	Santamaria and Garcia Bárcena (1974)
UNAM 07-22	Stratum XVI, Level 7	10,055 ± 90	Santa Marta	Acosta (2008)

out new investigations at Cueva Santa Marta for his doctoral dissertation. Acosta reported the presence of corn pollen, proto-metates, and some flakes at unit XVI that he dated at about 10,000 B.P. (see Table 2.4) (Acosta Ochoa 2008a; 2008b). Acosta Ochoa (2008b) claims that two tomato seeds (*Solanum* sp.) and pollen of *Zea mays* were recovered at Cueva Santa Marta. Wild tropical seeds such as *nanche* (*Byrsonima crassifolia*) and *zapote* (*Lucuma mammosa*) were recovered from the 10,000 year-old horizon. No diagnostic lithic tools were found in unit XVI, although expedient flakes and tools are present along with ground-stone artifacts. More laboratory and field investigations need to be carried out to understand the relationships between the archaeological record and the stratigraphic units before a 10,000 year-old tropical environment with domesticated plants can be accepted.

Guilá Naquitz, Oaxaca

Guilá Naquitz is a small shelter at the base of a large ignimbrite canyon wall located high above the Tlacolula branch of the Valley of Oaxaca. During 1966 and 1967, excavations were conducted by Kent V. Flannery (1986) in two caves: Guilá Naquitz and Peña Blanca. The earliest Naquitz phase (6900–4700 year B.P.) was attributed to the early Archaic period (Flannery 1986:32). However, recent direct AMS dating of a seed and peduncles of *Cucurbita pepo* with morphological indications of domestication from the lower levels of Guilá Naquitz, provided dates of 8990 ± 60 B.P. (β-100766) and 8910 ± 50 B.P. (β-100764) (Smith 1997:933). One projectile point found in zone E of Guilá Naquitz could be assigned to the Paleoindian complex (Hole 1986:116). The point is laurel leaf in outline and diamond shaped in cross section, with

a pointed end. Although this artifact was identified as a Lerma point, it appears to be similar to the specimens found in association with extinct Pleistocene fauna at Iztapan and Hueyatlaco. Marcus Winter (personal communication 2008) affirmed that two Clovis point bases were recovered from an open site about 500 m from Guilá Naquitz Cave.

CLOVIS, FOLSOM, AND PLAINVIEW-LIKE POINTS AND SITES

Temporally diagnostic artifacts of Late Pleistocene and Early Holocene age provide useful clues to the identification of Mexico's early settlers. Clovis, Folsom, and Plainview projectile points have been found in several Mexican states. Clovis points are well represented in the state of Sonora but they diminish in the area south of Sonora. Northern Chihuahua, northern Hidalgo, and Oaxaca also have a relatively high occurrence of Clovis points, and probably Clovis sites. Folsom, Plainview-like, and later Paleoindian points are more common east of the Sierra Madre Occidental than west of that mountain range. Chihuahua and Nuevo León have Folsom sites, and at least one Plainview site in northern Hidalgo has been dated (Table 2.5).

Sonora

The Clovis complex is well represented in Sonora and it is the central theme of this book. A variety of sites, isolated Clovis points, and artifacts have been found in the northern half of the state, mainly in the Sonoran Desert. To date, more than 114 Clovis points have been found in Sonora. While there are no reports of Folsom

Table 2.5. Distribution of Paleoindian Points in México

State	Clovis	Folsom	Plainview
Sonora	114	0	18 unfluted bifaces
Baja California	5	0	0
Chihuahua	9	16	14
Jalisco and Guanajuato	5	0	0
Northern Hidalgo and Veracruz	8	0	8
Oaxaca	3	0	0
Nuevo León	2	14	3
Sinaloa	2	0	0
Durango	1	0	1
Tlaxcala	1	0	0
Chiapas	0	0	1
Zacatecas	0	0	6
TOTAL	150	30	51

and Plainview points in the state, at least 18 lanceolate-shaped, unfluted bifaces resembling unfluted Golondrina and Plainview projectile point types have been recorded from private collections (Gaines and others 2009b). Unfortunately, the surface damage, breakage, and reworked processes present in these lanceolate-shaped points makes it impossible to attribute them to a specific type.

Baja California

At least five Clovis points have been reported from the Baja California peninsula; two of these come from the midsection of the peninsula. In 1949, Homer Aschmann (1952) found a complete Clovis point made of fine basalt at the Rancho San Joaquin locality. In 1993, the Proyecto Arte Rupestre found a basal fragment of a Clovis point made of obsidian in the vicinity of Rancho El Batequi (Gutierrez and Hyland 1994). X-ray fluorescence source analysis of this point fragment indicates that the obsidian came from the Valle de Azufre quarry, located 43 km northeast of where the point was found (Gutierrez and Hyland 1994, 1998). Lucero Gutierrez found a Clovis point during archaeological survey in the middle of Baja California (Lucero Gutierrez, personal communication 2007).

In addition to Clovis finds, Pleistocene fauna have been reported from Baja California. Mammoth remains have been reported at Rancho El Mezquital, 1 km southwest of San Joaquin (Gutierrez and Hyland 1994). Gutierrez and Hyland (2002:329) reported a radiocarbon date of 10,860 ± 90 from charcoal collected from an archaeological stratum that was 30 cm to 40 cm below the surface at Cueva Pintada in Baja California Sur. In 2005, Mathew Des Lauriers and his team found the base of a Clovis point on the surface of Isla Cedros, off the west coast of Baja California. This Clovis fragment is heavily patinated and made from a dark brown cryptocrystalline raw material. Although the Clovis point base found at Isla Cedros is a surface find, Des Lauriers reported agave charcoal from a hearth feature at the same site dated to 10,095 ± 30 B.P. (UCIAMS-12859) (Des Lauriers 2008, 2011:168).

Chihuahua

Paleoindian points are well represented in the northwestern portion of the state of Chihuahua, where at least 44 Paleoindian points have been reported. These include 9 Clovis points, 16 Folsom points, and 14 Plainview-like points (Martinez and others 2011). Charles Di Peso (1965) documented the first Clovis point reported in Chihuahua when he described a fluted point collected by a hunter at the Timmy Site. The Timmy Site is situated at the crest of a volcanic hill about 8 km north of Boca Grande, Chihuahua, near the border between Mexico and New Mexico. The majority of the Paleoindian points and sites in Chihuahua are associated with lake systems located in the northern section of the state. However, two Clovis points were found in the middle part of the state in the vicinity of Lago Bustillos (Martinez and others 2011).

Based on their investigation of Palo Blanco and Alamo de Villa, Rafael Cruz of INAH and Vance Holliday and Natalia Martinez of the University of Arizona, concluded that these two sites have the potential to contain in situ artifacts associated with Pleistocene fauna (Cruz 2012; Martinez and others 2011). Further investigation of Palo Blanco and Alamo de Villa is needed for understanding the first human occupation of Chihuahua.

Jalisco and Guanajuato

Four Clovis points were collected from the surface of the Zacoalco-Sayula Basin near Guadalajara in Jalisco, an area known as the Great Central Lakes of the Mexican Plateau. The lake deposits of this basin are rich in fossils of extinct Rancholabrean fauna that have been recovered from Pleistocene gravels (Aliphat 1988:147). Stone tools associated with extinct fauna have been reported near Atotonilco, in the vicinity of the Lake Zacoalco. In 1957, Federico Solorzano documented an obsidian flake with extensive retouch associated with the remains of a semi-articulated mammoth found on the surface (Aveleyra Arroyo de Anda 1962, 1964:405). In 1983, during the survey phase of the Proyecto Zacoalco-Sayula, some highly deteriorated large animal bones, together with a fragment of a "lermoid" or "laurel-leaf" point, were found on the surface in the same locality as that described by Solorzano (Aliphat 1988:161).

In 1963, Howard Smith, George Mitchell, and José Toscano located two fluted projectile points made of obsidian on the surface of Cerro del Tecolote, a volcanic hill that separates Zacoalo Lake from San Marcos Lake. Both of these projectile points are 5 cm long, with a flute on one side and basal thinning on the other. Basal and lateral grinding indicates that the points are finished tools. The two points were described and illustrated by Lorenzo in 1964, and they are currently exhibited at the Museo Regional de Guadalajara. Otto Schondube found a brown chert fluted biface fragment during a visit to Cerro del Tecolote in 1983 (Aliphat 1988:161, 2008; Otto Schondube, personal communication 2008). Bruce Benz (2002, 2005) described a complete Clovis point made of brown chert, discovered during his reconnaissance of the Zacualco-Sayula Basin while searching for evidence of early agriculture. Although we do not know much about the nature of the early Paleoindian occupation of

the Zacualco-Sayula, it is clear that an archaeological investigation of this area should be carried out.

Brigitte Faugere (1996, 2006) found two Paleoindian points in a Classic period archaeological context at El Platanillo Cave, located on the alluvial plain of the Lerma River in northern Guanajuato. These include a Clovis point that is 7 cm long and an Eden or Yuma point that is 10 cm long (Faugere 1996:126). Faugure excavated several caves in the immediate area looking for early occupations but did not find any archaeological occupations younger than 6000 B.P. (Brigitte Faugere, personal communication 2007).

Hidalgo

The region of Meztitlan and Metzquititlan in the state of Hidalgo in central Mexico comprises the southernmost end of the Sierra Madre Occidental. A total of 12 sites associated with Paleoindian occupations, including both open and cave sites, have been documented in this area (Cassiano 1998). Four basal fragments of Clovis points fabricated using a white chert from a nearby source were recovered from a low terrace at the Oyapa site, along with Clovis end scrapers and blades (Cassiano and Vasquez 1990:26; Cassiano 2008). Several points and bifaces from other locales may be Paleoindian artifacts (Cassiano 1998, 2008). Some of the points resemble styles of the Cody complex and Plainview series, as well as the Golondrina, Angostura, and Lerma projectile point types. These points are poorly known with respect to chronology and affiliation (Faught and Freeman 1998:48; Hester 1977; Hesse and others 2000; Holliday 1997:154; MacNeish 1950). Gianfranco Cassiano and Ana Maria Alvarez recently excavated some of these localities. At the La Calzada site, they obtained a radiocarbon date of 9,200 B.P. from a piece of charcoal found in a feature consisting of a lithic workshop containing a fragment of a Plainview-like point, (Ana María Alvarez, personal communication 2012).

Oaxaca

Three Clovis points have been collected from the surface of archaeological sites in the state of Oaxaca. In the municipality of San Juan Guelavia in the Tlacolula Valley, a Clovis point base made from brown chert was found by Richard Orlandini (Winter and others 2008). This artifact is currently exhibited at the Museo de Santo Domingo (Marcus Winter, personal communication 2008). Two Clovis point bases have been found west of Mitla, in an open site on the lower bajada about 100 m from the Río Mitla and 500 m from the site of Guilá Naquitz. One of these Clovis bases was found by Richard Orlandini in 2006 and the other by Marcus Winter and colleagues in 2007. One point was manufactured using a brown chert; the other displays a heavy white patina (Winter and others 2008). The site where these Clovis bases were found, which has not been excavated, appears to be a late Pleistocene or Early Holocene knapping station that also contains several bifaces and bifacial thinning flakes. It is possible that additional early sites are present on the lower bajada in this area (Winter and others 2008). A Clovis point base was also found at the Guhdz Bedkol site east of Mitla (Marcus Winter, personal communication 2008).

Extinct fauna that are possibly associated with humans have been also found in Oaxaca. In 2006, during the Salvamento Arqueológico Carretera Oaxaca-Istmo, a poorly articulated *Gomphotherium* sp. skeleton was excavated at the El Pocito Site, located about 6 km east of Mitla. Although this find was close to the surface, a denticulate scraper and a multiplatform core made from a reddish chert were found near the Pleistocene bones (Winter and others 2008). In August of 2012 a 10-cm long fluted Clovis biface was found during an archaeological survey of the Isthmus of Tehuantepec. This Clovis biface had been broken by cattle trampling (Patricia Abarca, personal communication 2012).

Isolated Clovis Finds and Late Paleoindian Points

Isolated surface finds of Clovis points diminish considerably south of Sonora. A total of four isolated Clovis points have been reported from the states of Sinaloa (Guevara 1989), Durango (Lorenzo 1953), and Tlaxcala (García Cook 1973). All of these isolated Clovis points are either surface finds or from private collections with unknown proveniences. In the state of Nuevo León only two Clovis points have been found on the surface, although Folsom points are more common. The fact that at least 14 Folsom points, one Folsom site, and other styles of late Paleoindian points have been found in Nuevo León means that a late Paleoindian occupation is well represented there.

Jeremiah Epstein (1961) carried out a reconnaissance survey at San Isidro and Puntita Negra sites in Nuevo León. The San Isidro Site is situated on a lower bajada, where several thermal features are exposed on the surface. Crudely flaked bifacial choppers are the most abundant tool type, although a small polyhedral core and nine chert projectile points were also found at the site. The nine projectile points include three Plainview-like points,

two Tortuga points, one Langtry-like point, one point of lanceolate form, and one nondescript type. A heavy patina covers each of the artifacts. The Plainview points are similar to the classic Plainview type but the basal concavity is slightly deeper (Epstein 1961). At the Puntita Negra Site, Epstein recovered a fluted point tip. The fluting on this artifact carries through to the tip of the point, prompting Epstein (1961) to classify it as a Folsom point.

During the 2002 field season of the Catalogo de Sitios de Nuevo León project, Moises Valadez from the Centro INAH Nuevo León, found La Morita rock shelter, located at Villadama about 100 km west of Monterrey. The cave has two chambers; the irregularly shaped main chamber measures 18 m by 7 m. During 2003 and 2004, 50 square meters were excavated during exploration of the principal chamber, revealing a stratified deposit. The lowest stratum is about 3 to 4 m from the actual cave floor (Strata IV–V). This stratum is composed of compacted silts that contained retouched flakes, polished bones, and burned molars of a horse (*Equus* sp.). Four Folsom point fragments were recovered from this unit. Two ^{14}C ages were obtained from charcoal: 9230 ± 45 B.P. (OxA-17377) and 8935 ± 66 B.P. (Valadez Moreno 2006, 2008; Moises Valadez, personal communication 2008). There is no doubt that the ongoing investigations at La Morita will provide essential information of the Folsom occupation in Nuevo León.

Aveleyra Arroyo de Anda (1961) reported the surface find of a classic Folsom point base from the Salmalayuca Basin, near Ciudad Juarez, Chihuahua. Several bones of extinct animals have been found in this vicinity but not in association with artifacts.

During the project La Ocupación de Agricultura Temprana en el Sur de Chihuahua, Art MacWilliams and colleagues found a Plainview point fragment at a cave designated as the C75-01 site. This site, located on the highway between Cuauhtemoc and Chihuahua, apparently was associated with an occupational surface that contained dispersed charcoal. The charcoal was dated by radiocarbon at 9120 ± 50 B.P. (B185635) (MacWilliams and others 2006:10). Unfortunately, the contexts at the cave are disturbed and no primary contexts remained of the Plainview occupation (Art MacWilliams, personal communication 2007). At least 16 Folsom points and 14 Plainview-like points have been found in the northernmost part of Chihuahua in the lake system region (Martinez and others 2011).

In 2004, José Luis Punzo and Bridget Zavala (2007:190) reported that a Plainview base of chert was collected from a later prehistoric context at the Mesa de Las Tapias Site in the Guadiana Valley, Durango. In 1953, J. Charles Kelley found a Clovis point at the Weicker Site, also in the Guadiana Valley (Lorenzo 1953; Punzo and Zavala 2007:190). Ciprian Ardelean recently carried out fieldwork in the northern section of Zacatecas state with the objective of identifying its earliest inhabitants. So far, Ardelean has found several late Paleoindian styles of bifaces on the surface, as well as some paleontological locations with Pleistocene fauna (Ciprian Ardelean, personal communication 2012).

As described previously, a burned, complete Plainview point made of chert was found among the earliest stratigraphic deposits at Cueva de los Grifos, Chiapas (Santamaría and García Bárcena 1984, 1989). Two radiocarbon ages were obtained from combined charcoal flecks. The stratum containing the Plainview point yielded a radiocarbon age of 8930 ± 150 B.P. (I-10760), whereas the unit immediately above the point yielded an age of 9460 ± 150 B.P. (I-10761) (Santamaría and García Bárcena 1984:13; 1989:99–100).

ARCHAEOLOGICAL DATA AND PROPOSITIONS ABOUT THE EARLY OCCUPATION OF MEXICO

After extensively reviewing the existing archaeological data about the first humans in Mexico, I can say with confidence that to the present day there is no site with convincing evidence of a human occupation older than 13,000 to 13,500 years ago. The four Mexican sites that researchers claim to have great antiquity—Tlapacoya, Mexico City; Hueyatlaco (Valsequillo), Puebla; El Cedral, San Luis Potosí; and Babisuri, Baja California—do not pass scientific scrutiny and cannot be considered early sites associated with the glacial maximum. There is no doubt that the archaeological record of mammoths and humans in the Basin of Mexico is somewhat enigmatic. Artifacts have been found with at least five mammoths, however, a secure association of those artifacts with mammoth bones has been demonstrated for only three proboscideans—Iztapan I and II and San Bartolo Atepehuacan, all of which were excavated before 1960. It is indisputable that before 9,000 years ago, the Columbian mammoths (*Mammuthus columbi*) were present in the Basin of Mexico, where 150 of the animals have been reported (Arroyo and others 2003, 2006; García Bárcena 1975; Carballal 1997; Gonzalez, Morett and others 2006; Lorenzo and Mirambell 1986a). The human bones from El Peñon and Tlapacoya that were directly radiocarbon

dated offer proof that humans were present in the Basin of Mexico at least 10,500 B.P. I think there is little chance of finding earlier sites in the Basin of Mexico that will modify what we know about the first colonists of the basin. The center of Mexico is one of the most studied regions on the American continent. Three-quarters of the 400 archaeologists of the Instituto Nacional de Antropología e Historia work in central Mexico, and most of the salvage and research projects that take place in Mexico are developed in that region. In contrast, adjacent areas such as the state of Tlaxcala have been little studied. Several mammoth finds have been reported from that state, but they have not been thoroughly investigated (Linda Manzanilla, personal communication 2009). A research program focusing on paleontological finds should be implemented with the purpose of understanding the Late Pleistocene and Early Holocene of central Mexico.

The cultural affiliation of the first people in the Basin of Mexico is unknown. The projectile points found in association with the mammoths at Iztapan are diagnostically confusing. One of the points from Iztapan resembles an Angostura point and some of the Great Basin lanceolate Paleoindian points, but it cannot be directly correlated with those point types. A second projectile point has a laurel-leaf shape, pointed at each end (Aveleyra Arroyo de Anda 1955; Aveleyra Arroyo de Anda and Maldonado-Koerdell 1953). The point is similar to the Lerma type defined by MacNeish (1950), which remains poorly dated.

Unquestionably, the Paleoindian sequence established for North America can be traced southward into Mexico. The available information from Mexico clearly shows that that the Clovis occupation is well represented in Sonora and diminishes greatly to the south, although isolated points have been reported as far south as Costa Rica and Guatemala in Central America (Brown 1980). Baja California, Sonora, Chihuahua, Jalisco, and Hidalgo are states where four or more Clovis points have been found. The relatively high number of Clovis points and artifacts at Meztitlan, in the state of Hidalgo in central Mexico, is striking. The investigations carried out during the last 10 years by Alvarez and Cassiano (2013) suggest that the principal reason for the abundance of remains in Meztitlan has to do with the presence of high-quality obsidian and chert sources that probably attracted Clovis and later Paleoindian groups. The lack of Clovis points in the Basin of Mexico is puzzling, especially given the fact that more than 159 mammoths have been found in Central Mexico.

Clovis points and bifaces with a possible Clovis affiliation, found on the Isthmus of Tehuantepec, Oaxaca, in southern Mexico are notable. The narrow isthmus, only 200 km wide, would have been the major land route for people moving into Central and South America. The Clovis points and sites that have been found in Guatemala (Brown 1980; Pearson 2004:100) and Venezuela indicate that Clovis people probably traversed the isthmus. In conclusion, the Clovis complex is well represented in Sonora, making this state one of the most important places for studying the First Americans and the Clovis complex. Archaeologists did not know anything about Paleoindian archaeology in Sonora 15 years ago, but a systematic and interdisciplinary project under the direction of Vance Holliday and me has been successful in locating Clovis points and finding good archaeological contexts. Outside of Sonora, the scarce and confusing records of the late Pleistocene and Early Holocene human occupation indicate that few people inhabited Mexico at that time. The domesticated *Cucurbita* at Guilá Naquitz, Oaxaca, during Early Holocene times, directly dated at 8990 ± 60 B.P. (β-100766) and 8910 ± 50 B.P. (β-100764) (Smith 1997:933), together with possible early corn pollen, suggests that the mobility of hunter and gather groups decreased early in the cultural history of human occupation in Mexico.

I recommend that archaeologists in Mexico follow the research strategy undertaken by C. Vance Haynes in evaluating Paleoindian contexts in the United States in the 1970s. This strategy employs an active program of radiocarbon dating and stratigraphic trench exploration in the significant sites excavated before 1980, as well as in those localities that are only known through their surface material. In addition, a geoarchaeological research program investigating the peopling of Mexico should be developed following the methodology of the well-established research on early humans within the United States. Only after this research program is implemented will we be able to truly discuss the chronological and cultural sequences for the first Mexicans.

CHAPTER THREE

Frameworks for Sonoran Early Prehistory

The state of Sonora is located in northwest Mexico. Encompassing 184,934 square kilometers, Sonora is the second largest state in Mexico, constituting slightly more than 9 percent of the country. According to its biogeographical location, Sonora is a transitional region between the Neotropic and Nearctic ecozones.

Within Mexico, Sonora extends to the state of Baja California and the Gulf of California to the west, to the state of Sinaloa to the south, and to the state of Chihuahua to the east. The northern border of Sonora forms an international boundary with the states of Arizona and New Mexico in the United States. Sonora is considered an arid region with diverse ecosystems. Large portions of Sonora are covered with desert scrub, but the southern part of the state supports tropical deciduous forest, while the Sierra Madre Occidental in the eastern half of the state is characterized by pine-oak forest (Molina-Freaner and others 2010).

Sonora has a great history of human occupation with resilient populations that were able to adapt to the rapid environmental changes of the late Pleistocene age, the severe dry conditions of Middle Holocene ages, and the carnage of the Spanish conquistadors and Mexican authorities in the historic period. Here, I present an overview of the past and present landscapes and environments of Sonora, a history of archaeological investigations, and a regional cultural-historical chronology.

THE SONORAN LANDSCAPE

Sonora is part of the Basin and Range physiographic province. Virtually the entire state is situated in this physiographic province, which continues to the south to central Mexico (McDowell and others 1997:1349).

This terrain resulted from fracturing of the earth's crust and the formation of block-faulted basins and mountain ranges with volcanic intrusions. In eastern Sonora, near the foothills of the Sierra Madre Occidental, the fault-block ranges have been subjected to extensive erosion, which has formed deep, rugged canyons. The debris from this erosion filled the intervening basins. A few of these basins have major drainages such as the Río Sonora and the Río Mátape (Fig. 3.1).

The same geologic structures are found in the northwest section of Sonora, where they are deeply buried beneath debris from their own erosion. The broad alluvial plains of Sonora are formed by sediment eroded from the foothills (McDowell and others 1997), giving rise to the description "Buried Ranges" for this part of the state (Cserna 1975). This block-faulted area dropped down as the Gulf of California opened more than 5 million years ago (Bailey 2002; McDowell and others 1997).

The mountain ranges west and southwest of Santa Ana are only partially buried. To the northwest, west, and southwest of Hermosillo, however, the ranges are more deeply buried, underlying a flat open alluvial plain that I refer to as the "Llanos de Hermosillo" (Gaines and others 2009b). This plain begins in the foothills of the Sierra Madre Occidental to the east and northeast of Hermosillo, and slopes gently down to the west and southwest into the Gulf of California. It is likely composed of deltaic deposits of the Río Sonora and alluvial fan sediments derived from the partially buried ranges to the north. The Llanos de Hermosillo is dotted with low hills that rise abruptly above the level terrain. These hills include Tertiary volcanic intrusions and isolated, unburied remnants of the "buried ranges." The Llanos de Hermosillo has poorly developed drainage, probably

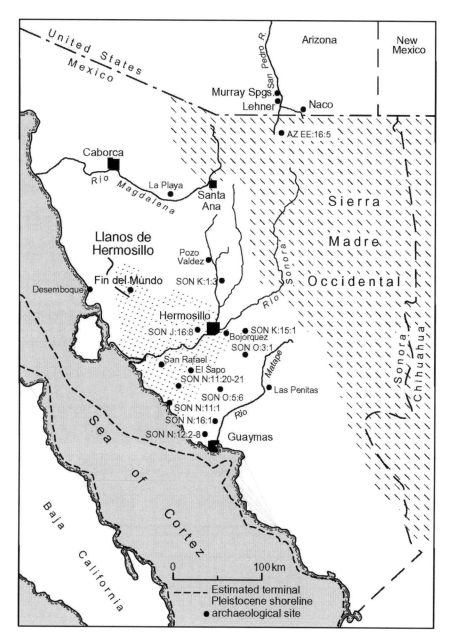

Figure 3.1. Sonora and surrounding areas showing key towns, physiographic features, and archaeological sites. From Gaines and others (2009:307).

because of its relative youthfulness and low gradient. As a result, topographic lows locally form lakes, or playas in dry years. Sand dunes are also locally common across the surface of the plain, some derived from the coast of the Gulf and others derived from sand in the alluvium. Some dunes are associated with the playas, but it is unclear whether these dunes formed as a result of wind erosion of the playa basin (lunettes) or if they are

dune ridges that helped contain the playas (Gaines and others 2009b).

The hydrology of the northern section of Sonora is composed of perennial surface arroyos with underground aquifers that are the principal sources of water. At present, these aquifers are over-exploited and have been contaminated with salt water from the sea. The study area for this monograph is located in three hydrological basins: the Río Sonora, the Río Bacoachi, and the Río Mátape (Vega Granillo 1992).

The Río Sonora is the largest of the three basins; it begins in the vicinity of Cananea. The Río Sonora basin is composed of three rivers: the Río Sonora, the Río San Miguel, and the Río Zanjon. The three rivers merge near Hermosillo and form a delta that empties into the sea. Dry washes or *zanjones* drain off of the foothills into the river or out across the alluvial plain. The basin of the Río Bacoachi has a perennial flow with many underwater aquifers that reach the surface in small springs in the central segment of the area. The basin of the Río Mátape begins near the town of Mazatán and extends in a north-south direction before turning to the southwest and emptying into the Sea of Cortez near Guaymas. Today, the underground fresh water aquifers of the Río Mátape are contaminated in the middle of the basin by an older highly mineralized aquifer that contains calcium and magnesium chloride. Aquifers at the southwestern end of the basin are contaminated with salt water (Vega Granillo 1992).

It has been known for 40 years that the sea level fluctuated enormously between glacial and interglacial cycles, and during the glacial maximum about 20,000 years ago. The greatest documented fluctuation is a sea level 120 m below the present shore line (Flemming and others 2003; Muhs and others 2004). During the terminal Wisconsin, the Sea of Cortez would have been at least 40 m lower than it is today, with vast expanses of dry land exposed in the upper gulf from the midriff islands to the present Colorado River delta. Based on bathymetric data (Lohman 1969; Lavín and Marinone 2003), and assuming no subsequent tectonic activity, it is possible to estimate northern gulf late-glacial shore levels (Fig. 3.1). Differences in the horizontal shoreline location would have been greater on the gently sloping Sonoran side of the gulf than on the steep Baja coastline, and the northern Sonoran coast would have been on average about 60 to 70 km west of its current location. Most of the upper gulf would have been dry land, with a 20- to 40-km wide channel extending from Isla de la Guardia to the mouth of the Colorado River. Isla Tiburón would have been connected with the Sonoran mainland, and the associated landmass would have been separated from the Baja peninsula by less than 20 km of water (Fig. 3.1).

PALEOENVIRONMENTAL RECORDS

The focus of this monograph is the Sonoran Desert biome that began to develop about 11,000 years ago. For Sonora, the information needed to reconstruct the Late Pleistocene environment is sparse, and the interpretation of paleoenvironments remains general. The best proxy data for studying climate and vegetation are plant remains recovered from packrat (*Neotoma* spp.) middens investigated in Sonora and the surrounding areas (Van Devender and others 1987, 1990).

A preliminary interpretation of changing climate and plant succession over the last 16,000 years is possible using data from packrat middens, pollen profiles from the region (Davis and Anderson 1987), and a recent study of bulk carbon ($\delta^{13}C$) and oxygen ($\delta^{18}O$) isotopes from nine mammalian fossils recovered from Sonora (Nuñez and others 2010). Paeloenvironmental reconstructions are provided in Antevs (1955), Ballenger and others (2011), Haynes (1968), Irwin-Williams and Haynes (1970), Long (1966), Martin (1963), Sánchez and Carpenter (2012), and Van Devender and Spaulding (1979).

Environmental changes in the Sonoran Desert in general have been unidirectional, with a tendency toward desertification that commenced at the end of the Pleistocene and continues today (Nabhan 1985; Van Devender 1990). The macrobotanical record obtained from packrat (*Neotoma* spp.) middens and pollen records suggests that by the end of the Pleistocene a stable pinyon-juniper-oak woodland was present under a winter-dominated precipitation regime (Davis and Shafer 1992; Van Devender and Spaulding 1979). The upslope retreat of pinyon (*Pinus monophylla*) that occurred about 9,000 years ago in the Sonoran Desert left juniper-oak woodlands, chaparral shrub, and some modern desert plants including saguaro, prickly pear, agave, and nolina (Van Devender 1990; Van Devender and others 1994).

In the southernwestern United States, summer grasses are rare in late Pleistocene packrat middens (Betancourt 1990), indicating that the northern reach of summer monsoon moisture was truncated at that time (Ballenger and others 2011; Holmgren and others 2007). A winter precipitation regime persisted until about 8,000 years ago, when the rain pattern became bimodal with summer and winter rains and the Sonoran Desert Province and Subprovince developed its modern characteristics (Van Devender and Spaulding 1979:702). Humans entered Sonora during the Pleistocene and encountered megafauna just before the big animals went extinct. There are 54 localities of Late Pleistocene age with megafauna known in Sonora, where the remains of 38 proboscideans, 28 horses, 21 bison, and 13 camels have been found (White and others 2010:53).

THE ENVIRONMENTAL SETTING OF THE SONORAN LANDSCAPE

The Sonoran Desert Biome

The Sonoran Desert is a unique sub-tropical desert with a relatively high biodiversity that developed after the Pleistocene (Nabhan 1985). Within Sonora, this province extends along the Arizona border from the Colorado River eastward to Nogales, and southward to a point approximately halfway between Guaymas and the Río Yaqui.

Although northwestern Sonora lies entirely within the Sonoran Desert, this region presents a mosaic of several biotic communities (Brown and others 1994). The Lower Colorado River Valley subdivision predominates in the northwest and extends south along the coast approximately to Puerto Lobos, where it is replaced by the Central Gulf Coast subdivision. The Arizona Uplands subdivision is predominant to the north of Highway 2 between Sonoyta and Santa Ana. The Plains of Sonora subdivision extends along the interior approximately from Santa Ana south to Guaymas (Fig. 3.2). The Southern Coastal Belt Province and the Sierra Madre Occidental are adjacent to the Sonoran Desert Province.

Lower Colorado River Valley Subprovince

The Gran Desierto de Altar is an area in the northwestern corner of Sonora that extends from the Colorado River eastward to the Río Sonoyta. This area is marked by extreme aridity—median annual precipitation is a mere 89.8 mm, and temperatures often reach 45°C (113°F) or higher (Pérez Redolla 1996:142). The Colorado River and the ephemeral Río Sonoyta are the only significant drainages in the region. Large expanses of sand dunes and desert pavement are common. Vegetation is generally limited to creosote bush (*Larrea tridentata*) and white bursage (*Ambrosia dumosa*). Sonoran pronghorn (*Antilocapra americana sonoriensis*), desert cottontail (*Sylvilagus audubonii*), and antelope jackrabbit (*Lepus alleni*) are the principal mammalian species.

The volcanic disconformity represented by the Sierra Pinacate is an isolated subprovince surrounded entirely by the Gran Desierto de Altar. The Sierra Pinacate, encompassing approximately 1,500 km², is characterized by dozens of volcanic cones and craters of varying sizes, along with extensive basalt lava flows resulting from two million years of volcanic activity that ended in the lower Pleistocene (Hayden 1998:14). Natural bedrock basins, or tinajas, provide the only source of water in this region.

Historically, desert bighorn sheep (*Ovis canadensis nelsoni*) and Mexican wolf (*Canis lupus baileyi*) inhabited the Pinacate region.

The Arizona Uplands Subprovince

The Arizona Uplands subprovince lies to the east of the Río Sonoyta. In this region, elevations are generally above 500 m, and temperatures are extreme, occasionally dropping below 0°C (32°F) during the winter months and soaring to 47°C (117°F) in the summer. The annual precipitation ranges between 200 and 300 mm, and has the bimodal distribution characteristic of the Sonoran Desert region. Slightly more rain falls during the summer *chubascos* (cloudbursts) than in the winter *equipatas* (light showers). Compared with that of the Lower Colorado River Valley subdivision, the vegetation is more dense and more varied. The vegetation includes creosote bush, ocotillo (*Fouquieria splendens*), ironwood (*Olneya tesota*), velvet mesquite (*Prosopis velutina*), littleleaf palo verde (*Parkinsonia* [*Cercidium*] *microphylla*), organ pipe cactus (*Stenocereus thurberi*), senita (*Pachycereus* [*Lophocereus*] *schottii*), saguaro (*Carnegiea gigantea*), numerous species of prickly pear and cholla (*Opuntia* spp.), and barrel cactus (*Ferocactus* spp.). The fauna is more abundant and varied here than in other parts of Sonora. Animals include desert bighorn (found within the isolated mountain ranges), mule deer (*Odocoileus hemionus*), javelina or collared peccary (*Pecari tajacu*), coyote (*Canis latrans*), American badger (*Taxidea taxus*), the ubiquitous complement of lagomorphs, and a host of rodent, reptilian, and avian species. The Río Magdalena and Río Concepción form the principal drainage basin in this region, with several major tributaries, including the Río Boquillas and the Río Altar, rising among the uplands along the international border between Sasabe and Nogales.

To the south of the Baboquivari Mountains, where elevations generally exceed 900 m (2,970 feet), semidesert and plains grasslands predominate. True Madrean evergreen woodland is restricted to the Sierra de Humo and the Sierra del Mezquital, two small mountain ranges between Altar and Sasabe, and to the Sierra Cibuta to the southwest of Nogales (Brown and others 1994). White-tailed deer (*Odocoileus virginianus*) are generally restricted to these upland areas.

Plains of Sonora Subprovince

The Plains of Sonora subprovince extends along the interior from a few kilometers south of Santa Ana to just

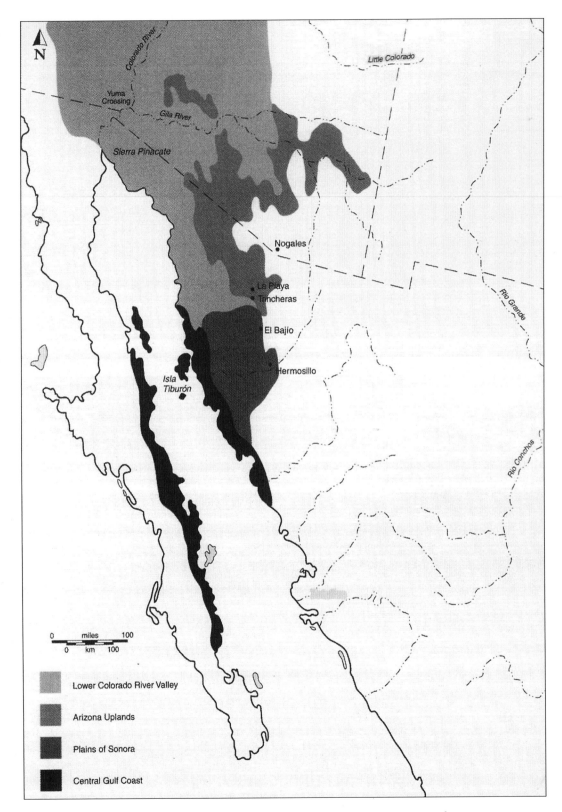

Figure 3.2. Biotic communities in Sonora. From Carpenter and others (2008:Figure 102), courtesy of Statistical Research, Inc.

north of Guaymas, with elevations generally less than 500 m. Here, desert grasslands intermixed with creosote (*Larrea tridentada*) predominate, along with several short tree species, including ironwood *(Olneya tesota)*, mesquite (*Prosopis* sp.), palo verde (*Parkinsonia* [*Cercideum*] *microphylla*), and tree morning glory (*Ipomoea arborescens*). Organ pipe (*Stenocereus thurberi*), senita (*Lophocereus schotti*), several species of prickly pear and cholla (*Opuntia* spp.), and barrel cactus (*Ferocactus* spp.) are interspersed throughout this subprovince (Perez Redolla 1985:124–125; Turner and Brown 1994: 218–220).

Within this region of the Sonoran Desert, elevations generally exceed 500 m. Temperatures may occasionally dip below 0° C (32° F) during the winter months and typically reach 47° C (117° F) in the summer. Annual precipitation ranges between 200 and 300 mm. The Río Sonora and its tributary Río San Miguel provide the most significant drainage systems within the Plains of Sonora subprovince.

The Central Gulf Coast Subprovince

The Central Gulf Coast subprovince incorporates the Sonoran coast between Puerto Lobos and Guaymas. Here, red mangroves (*Rhizophora mangle*), along with black mangrove (*Avicennia germinans*), white mangrove (*Laguncunaria racemosa*), and sweet mangrove (*Maytenus phyllanthoides*) are found in brackish estuary environments. Species often associated with the Baja peninsula are found here, including the boojum tree (*Fouquieria columnaris*) and elephant or torchwood tree (*Bursera microphylla* and *B. hindsiana*) (Perez Redolla 1985:146; Rzedowski 1981:342; Turner and Brown 1994:212–214). Columnar cardón cactus (*Pachycereus pringlei*), a variety of prickly pear, cholla, and barrel cactus species, along with ocotillo (*Fouqueria splendens*), are also common. Precipitation along the central coast averages less than 200 mm a year, and there is a general absence of the shrub cover that is common elsewhere in the Sonoran Desert (Turner and Brown 1994:212).

In addition to the usual complement of desert mammals, the coastal waters are home to California sea lions (*Zalophus californianus*), dolphins (*Delphinis delphis*), and whales (*Balaenoptera* spp., various species, but especially *B. physallus*), along with the green sea turtle (*Chelonia mydas*), various species of mollusks and crustaceans, and a host of fish species, including totoaba (*Cynoscion macdonaldi*), mojarra (*Diapterus peruvianus*), mullet (*Mugil cephalus* and *M. curema*), spotted sand bass (*Paralabrax maculatofasciatus*), grouper (*Mycteroperca jordani*), snapper (*Lutjanus* sp.), mackerel (*Scomberomorus* sp.), and several species of sharks.

In terms of protein per square meter, the Sea of Cortez ranks among the richest marine environments anywhere in the world. However, there are no significant stream systems between the Río Concepción and the Río Sonora, and the availability of fresh water is limited to only a few widely dispersed springs and tinajas, or bedrock catchment basins.

The Southern Coastal Belt Province

The Southern Coastal Belt encompasses the southern limits of the coastal plain, which becomes a narrow band extending southward into Sinaloa. This province is dominated by the broad alluvial deposits of the Yaqui and Mayo rivers. In this region, the Sonoran Desert vegetation blends with Sinaloan Thornscrub. From just north of the Río Mayo, the mesophyllic Sinaloan Thornscrub becomes predominant (Rzedowski 1981:209). Acacia (*A. cymbispina*) is the primary plant on the coastal plain (Shreve 1937), forming both open and dense woodlands. Other plants associated with the acacia woodland include tree morning glory, pitahaya or organpipe cactus (*Stenocereus thurberi*), senita (*Lophocereus schotti*), hecho (*Pachycereus pecten-aborignum*), agaves (*Agave schotti* and *A. ocahui*), ironwood (*Olneya tesota*), torote (*Bursera* sp.), cassias (*Cassia atomaria* and *C. emarginata*), greythorn (*Ziziphus sonorensis*), Sonoran ebony (*Pithecellobium sonorae*), palo colorado (*Caesalpinia platyloba*), *Lonchocarpus megalanthus*, copalillo (*Jatropha cordata*), palo verde (*Cercidium torreyanum*), mesquite (*Prosopis* sp.), mauto (*Lysiloma divaricata*), and palo blanco (*Piscidia mollis*) (Brown 1994:101–104; Rzedowski 1981:210).

Sierra Madre Occidental Province

Lastly, the eastern margins of Sonora are defined by the massive blocks of rhyolite that form the Sierra Madre Occidental. Oak woodlands are prevalent on the lower mountain ranges that form foothills above 1000 m. The uppermost reaches of the Sierra Madre Occidental, at elevations of between 2000 and 3000 m, are populated by conifers including Douglas fir (*Pseudotsuga menziesii*) and various species of pines, *Pinus ponderosa, P. arizonica, P. engelmannii,* and *P. leiophylla* var. *chihuahuana* among them (Rzedowski 1981:297).

HISTORY OF PALEOINDIAN AND ARCHAIC RESEARCH IN SONORA

The first discovery suggesting the possible existence of early humans in Sonora was made in January 1937 at the Chinobampo Ranch, 32 km southeast of Navajoa. There, Howard Scott Gentry and John C. Blick discovered a human skull embedded in a caliche-like deposit of probable Pleistocene age. This stratum also contained the remains of camel, horse, and wolf. The skull, along with a 50-pound stratigraphic block, was removed during a second visit to the locality in March of the same year, and transported back to New York (Blick 1938).

Gordon Ekholm and Carl Sauer visited the Chinobampo locale the following year, affirming that it was indeed plausible that this find was a genuinely ancient deposit. Ekholm and Sauer concluded that if the skull exhibited evidence of having been within a lime deposit it is probably legitimate (Ekholm 1938:46). Ekholm (1937, 1940) also reported seeing slab metates, cobble manos, and projectile points at several locations near the Rio Mayo and at a large shell midden at Topolobampo in northernmost Sinaloa, suggesting that these assemblages were comparable to the (as yet unpublished) Cochise tradition that had only just recently been defined by Sayles and Antevs (1941).

Malcolm Rogers, recognized today as the "father of desert archaeology," believed that coastal Sonora had served as a corridor for "early man" (Hayden 1956:19). In the early 1940s, Rogers urged Julian Hayden to explore this region further. Hayden (1956, 1965, 1967, 1969, 1976; personal communication 1997) subsequently recorded a large Archaic shell midden located on an ancient, relic estuary at Estero Tastiota, along with several Archaic period sites in the Sierra Pinacate, the region to which he would devote his attention over most of the ensuing five decades.

With the principal objective of defining the southern extent of the Cochise Archaic tradition, Donald Lehmer (1949a:4) and Bryant Bannister undertook an extensive jeep survey of Sonora in 1949. Several sites that they compared to "later Cochise horizons" were recorded in the Río Sonora, Zanjón, Estero Tastiota, and Arroyo Cuchujaqui areas (Lehmer 1949a:5). They also reexamined the Arroyo Chinobampo locale, but were unable to locate any bones or artifacts (Lehmer 1949b).

During the 1950s, George Fay (1955, 1967) defined the "Peralta Complex" on the basis of 17 Archaic sites he recorded to the west of Hermosillo. Paul Ezell (1954)

collected several Archaic projectile points, including Pinto points, in his survey of the Papaguería Borderlands, which incorporated extreme northwestern Sonora. Thomas Hinton (1955) reported three San Pedro points as the only Archaic artifacts observed during his survey of the Altar Valley. Frank Holzkamper (1956) collected several projectile points at Estero Tastiota that were subsequently identified by Rogers as San Dieguito II through Amargosa I types (Hayden 1956:22). Eduardo Noguera (1958) carried out a brief, but extensive, reconnaissance in the vicinity of Guaymas and Bahía Kino, and described several sites as being affiliated with the Archaic Cochise culture.

In the following decade, Ronald Ives (1963) recorded cultural materials and shell middens associated with a fossil *Chione* shell shoreline in the region between Estero Tastiota and Bahía Adair. Ives noted that another, earlier *Turitella* shoreline that was presumably associated with the late Pleistocene lacked cultural materials. In 1965, Charles Di Peso (1965) reported on two fluted Clovis points that were found by a collector in an old estuary 30 miles north of Guaymas. In 1968, Walter W. Taylor and José Luis Lorenzo carried out excavations at the Tetabejo Cave (SON O:5:6) located south of Hermosillo in the Sierra Libre (Julio Montané, personal communication 2007; Richard Pailes, personal communication 2007).

In the years prior to the establishment of the office of the Instituto Nacional de Antropología e Historia (INAH) in Hermosillo in 1973, the late Manuel Robles, Director of the Museo de la Universidad de Sonora in Hermosillo, and an amateur archaeologist, undertook the responsibility of documenting the cultural resources reported in Sonora. Robles spent countless weekends working with a group of local amateur archaeologists to prospect for archaeological sites, particularly Clovis sites. Robles also invited Vance Haynes from the University of Arizona and James Ayres from the Arizona State Museum to visit the some of the sites he documented. In 1972, Robles and Manzo Taylor (1972; Robles 1974) reported on 11 localities associated with 25 Clovis points located in the northern half of Sonora. Six of these localities are near the Gulf of California, with the others distributed in the basin and range province and on the Llanos de Hermosillo. Although we have not yet relocated all the sites reported by Robles and Manzo Taylor, our knowledge of the sites that we have visited, and the evaluation of the collections deposited at the Centro INAH Sonora and the Museo Regional de la Universidad de Sonora, are beginning to provide an indication of the

Paleoindian occupation of Sonora. Julian Hayden, who visited and studied the Estero Tastiota site with Manuel Robles, assured us that the Clovis occupation was associated with the shell middens on the coast (Julian Hayden, personal communication 1994). Unfortunately, the area around Estero Tastiota has been impacted by the development of shrimp ranches that modified the land and destroyed archaeological sites.

Among the sites reported by Robles, El Bajío (SON K:1:3) is clearly the most remarkable and may represent the largest Clovis period site in western North America. In the summer of 1975, Kenneth and Marian McIntyre, schoolteachers from Vancouver, Canada, conducted an archaeological survey, made surface collections, and conducted limited test excavations at the site. They identified 600 roasting pits or hearths on the surface (McIntyre and McIntyre 1976). The next researcher to work at the site was Julio Montané, from the Centro INAH Sonora. Montané was the archaeologist who excavated the well-known early Chilean site associated with gomphothere remains and artifacts at Laguna Taguatagua (Montané 1968:1137). Between 1977 and 1981, he excavated a series of trenches in 10 localities within El Bajío and collected many artifacts from the surface of the site (Montané 1985, 1988). Unfortunately, neither of these studies was completed, and no field notes or reports from the research are known to exist. However, 10 boxes containing an estimated 300,000 artifacts (tools and debitage) recovered by the McIntyre and Montané projects at El Bajío are currently curated in the Centro INAH Sonora. The collection of artifacts housed at the Centro INAH Sonora show a clear association with the early Paleoindian period and indicates there was a dense occupation at El Bajío.

The Centro de Estudios Mexicanos y Centroamericanos (CEMCA) carried out several field seasons in Sonora during the 1980s with the goal of defining a cultural sequence from Pleistocene groups to the Hia-Ced O'odham, the Piman hunter-gatherers who persisted in this region until the late nineteenth century. The archaeological evidence from Quitovac, a sacred site of the Tohono O'odham situated near the international border, has been the source of considerable controversy regarding the association of Pleistocene fauna and Paleoindian hunters. In report on excavations at Quitovac, Rodríguez and Silva (1987) noted the association of stone tools with the remains of a mammoth in what they described as a paleo-lake. However, the description of these materials is vague and no clear evidence is presented to substantiate

their claim of association between the tools and the faunal remains. In a subsequent publication, Rodríguez-Loubet reports that the faunal remains were almost completely deteriorated, thus prohibiting them from establishing a positive association with the lithic artifacts, and that the poor state of bone preservation prevented the identification of cut-marks, butchering scars, or "fractures that could be attributed to human origin" (Rodríguez-Loubet and others 1993:212, my translation). In arguing that there was a human presence at Quitovac during the Pleistocene, Rodriguez-Loubet and others (1993:262) indicate only that stone tools and faunal remains were recovered from the same stratigraphic association.

In 2004 and 2005, Edmund P. Gaines (2006) carried out geoarchaeological investigations in the Upper San Pedro Valley for his master´s degree at the University of Arizona. The principal goal of this study was to look for Clovis sites and to try to correlate the late Pleistocene stratigraphy on the Upper San Pedro in Sonora with that found along the river in Arizona, where the sites of Naco, Navarrete, Lehner, Murray Spring and Escapule are located. Gaines spent several months investigating geoarchaeological, alluvial, and paleontological contexts, locating one Clovis site. Although no buried archaeological deposits of late Pleistocene age were observed, Gaines (2006) documented three localities with fine raw material sources (chert, petrified wood, and quartz crystal) suitable for manufacturing stone tools.

CULTURAL-HISTORICAL CHRONOLOGY OF SONORA

Investigations during the last 15 years in the Sonoran Desert have greatly improved our understanding of the ancient people of Late Pleistocene and Early Holocene age, including chronology and human adaptations. In constructing a provisional cultural sequence for the earliest periods of human occupation in northwestern Mexico, we rely on diagnostic projectile point types that can be correlated with established North American Paleoindian and Archaic sequences. The radiocarbon dates that recently have been obtained allow us to place these projectile points in chronological order.

Early Paleoindian Occupation of Sonora

The early Paleoindian occupation of Sonora is the principal focus of this monograph and will be discussed over the next chapters; here I will only point out that this period is well represented in Sonora. The large number of early Paleoindian sites provide us with a new corpus of data that is changing and improving the explanations of the early Paleoindian occupation of western North America.

Late Paleoindian Occupation

One striking aspect of the Sonoran Desert Paleoindian record is the absence of Folsom points. Of the various post-Clovis Paleoindian traditions in the United States, Folsom is by far the best known and best documented. Folsom is classically a Great Plains tradition (Hofman and Graham 1998), although significant Folsom occupations and collections are also documented in the central Rio Grande valley and adjacent basins (Judge 1973; Amick 1996; Holliday 2005). The frequency of Folsom finds drops significantly farther west, especially to the southwest in southern Arizona (Ballenger and others 2011; Holliday 2005; Mabry and Faught 1998). The absence of Folsom materials west of the Sierra Madre Occidental in Mexico, therefore, is in keeping with the larger pattern of Folsom distribution (Gaines and others 2009b). In contrast, Folsom artifacts are reported from northern Mexico east of the Sierra Madre Occidental, but Clovis materials are extremely rare in that region (Sánchez 2001).

At the sites of El Bajío, Fin del Mundo, and SON N:11: 20-21, a variety of unfluted lanceolate bifaces have been found. These bifaces do not appear to be related to Late Paleoindian varieties, such as Golondrina or Plainview, as was previously thought (Gaines and others 2009b). At El Bajío a dozen triangular bifaces with square bases and overshot flaking, some in the process of manufacture and others finished, were found in a workshop feature. Their chronology is unknown, and the use wear and breakage pattern they exhibit appear to indicate that they were used primarily as knives.

Certainly, the late Paleoindian occupation of Sonora is not well represented. This could be interpreted as a decrease in human population in Sonora. In the adjacent area of southeastern Arizona, Ballenger and others (2011) describe a noticeable 1,400-year hiatus in the archaeological record following the Clovis occupation and late Pleistocene extinctions. But the available evidence also could be interpreted to mean that after Clovis a regionalization of hunter-gatherer groups took place in Sonora. An early Archaic subsistence pattern appears to have evolved soon after the Clovis occupation of the Sonoran Desert, as has been previously proposed by Cordell (1997) and Mabry (Mabry and Faught 1998).

Early Holocene Archaic Period Occupations

Unfortunately, stratified deposits with artifacts of possible early Holocene contexts have yet to be reported. The following discussion draws upon artifacts from surface collections at the La Playa site and from four sites with a documented Clovis component (SON K:15:1, SON K:1:3, SON N:11:20, and SON O:3:1).

The Malpais Phase of the San Dieguito Complex

The San Dieguito complex was defined by Malcolm Rogers (1939), based on his research in Southern California. The complex orginally was divided into an earlier Malpais industry and a later San Dieguito industry. Rogers (1958) later proposed a new subdivision using San Dieguito I, II, and III phases. Julian Hayden (1967, 1976, 1987) revived the term Malpais to describe an industry that he considered to be an early and distinct basal stage of the San Dieguito complex. As used by Hayden, the Malpais phase is represented by heavily patinated chopping and scraping tools from the Sierra Pinacate. Hayden thought these tools were part of a pre-projectile point lithic industry associated with small bands of foragers.

A Malpais phase lithic component was recognized at La Playa (Martinez and others 2002). The local stratigraphy in this area of the site is comprised of a late Pleistocene basin fill with a well-expressed red soil ("Big Red" with Bt-Bk horizonation) locally buried by a gravel stratum that probably represents an inverted Pleistocene stream channel (Fig. 3.3). The Malpais phase lithic assemblage is located on top of the inverted channel. The location of the Malpais phase tools indicates that the archaeological component was deposited sometime after the channel was abandoned. Thus, the archaeological feature cannot be older than the early Holocene.

García Moreno (2008:194–195) carried out a technological and morphological analysis of more than 1,000 artifacts at La Playa, based upon the degree of patination present on the artifacts. She concluded that at least 50 percent of the assemblage is representative of the San Dieguito Phases I or II (with a wide range of probable chronology from 9,000 to 5,000 B.P.). At least 29 percent of the artifacts are representative of San Dieguito Phase III or later (Garcia Moreno 2008:195). However, a heavily patinated grooved-axe fragment, dating to no earlier that A.D. 1000, was also identified within the La Playa Malpais assemblage, contributing to doubts regarding the presumed correlation between the formation processes of desert varnish and the purported antiquity of artifacts.

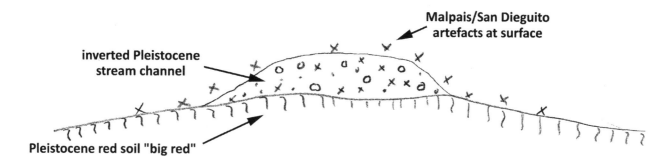

Malpais/San Dieguito
artefacts at surface

inverted Pleistocene
stream channel

Pleistocene red soil "big red"

Figure 3.3. Schematic cross-section of stratigraphy at the Malpais locality at La Playa.

Tapering Stem Point Styles

Within the southwestern United States, tapering stemmed projectiles have been variously named Jay, Lake Mojave, Silver Lake, and Ventana Amargosa (Lorentzen 1998:142); however, all of these points share morphological, technological, geographical, and chronological attributes, and they can be described in the same group. These points have a long, contracted stem that is frequently edge ground, a trait that is likely correlated with shaft technology (Lorentzen 1998:142). Jay points have gentle shoulders and a lightly contracting stems; Lake Mojave points have pointed contracting stems, with the longitude of the stem greater than that of the body and weak shouldering (Sliva 1997:49); Silver Lake points are smaller than other points in this group, with wide contracting stems and light shoulders (Justice 2002a, 2002b).

Lake Mojave and Silver Lake projectile points are generally dated to about 6000 B.C. in the Great Basin, and may represent types associated with the San Dieguito complex. The Jay points are thought to date between 6000 and 4800 B.C. (Sliva 1997:49). In regions west and south of the Colorado Plateau, the Lake Mojave and Silver Lake point types have been found within the southern Basin and Range Province and the lower valley of the Colorado River (Lorentzen 1998:142; Mabry 1998a:57), and they are also reported from sites in southern California (Justice 2002a:108). In contrast, the Jay point type is restricted to the Colorado Plateau, Rio Grande Valley, and Chihuahua Desert regions (Huckell 1996:360).

In Sonora, tapering stem points have been documented from six sites, including La Playa near Trincheras, Apasco, and SON O:3:1 in the Río Matape basin (Fig. 3.4), El Bajío, SON N:11:20 on the Central Coast, and at a site near Carbó. The variety of landscapes where this point style have been recorded suggest that during

CM

Figure 3.4. Tapering stem
point from SON O:3:1.

the early Archaic and middle Archaic periods, hunter and gatherer groups were familiar with and explored a wide range of territories, playas and estuaries near the coast, the Plains of Sonora, and the upland of the Basin and Range Province. Unfortunately, all the points are surface finds and none of the archaeological contexts are dated.

Middle Holocene or Altithermal Archaic Traditions

The Middle Holocene, or Altithermal period, was initially defined by Antevs (1955) as a shift to higher temperatures and decreased precipitation, the severity of which is still contested. Although Middle Archaic points account for 15 percent of the total assemblage, only seven of the 254 projectile points (2.7 percent) are identified as Pinto or San Jose types at La Playa. At Fin del Mundo, 50 Pinto points have been found (Sánchez Morales 2012).

We suspect that La Playa, along with much of the lowland desert borderlands, was likely abandoned during at least a portion of the Altithermal, consistent with models previously proposed by Berry and Berry (1986), Hayden (1976), Mabry (1998a), and others. Altithermal period projectile points, such as the Pinto and San Jose types, probably reflect brief incursions by northern groups from the Great Basin or Colorado Plateau, or both, into the Sonoran Desert during sporadic periods of ameliorative climatic conditions (Carpenter and others 2001).

Increased use of the Boquillas Valley apparently coincides with a return to wetter climatic conditions when the Altithermal ended around 4500 B.P. Several soil formations showing evidence of wetter conditions at about 5000 to 4500 years B.P. have been seen at some sites in addition to La Playa.

At La Playa, 13 percent of the Middle Archaic projectile points are best associated with the early portion of the late Holocene—immediately prior to the Early Agriculture period. These Middle Archaic points include four Chiricahua points (4800 to 2500 B.P.), 27 Cortaro points (4300 to 2300 B.P.), and two Gypsum points (4500 to 1500 B.P.) (Lorenzten 1998:144–147). Several archaeologists have noted the apparent discontinuity in the Middle Archaic sequence associated with the beginning of the Late Holocene (Berry and Berry 1986; Huckell 1996; Mabry 1998a, 1998b). The appearance of contracting-stem points, including a number of regional variants considered under the general rubric of "Gypsum Cave" points, coincides with the beginning of the Late Holocene. This point style co-occurs with maize in the Coxcatlan phase in the Tehuacan Valley, and represents a new technology using adhesives to attach the dart point to the foreshaft, suggesting that independent technologies diffused together (Carpenter and others 1997, 2002; Mabry and others 2008).

Late Archaic and Early Agriculture Periods

Initial cultivation of maize began in the Sonoran Desert around 2000 B.C. The La Playa site represents the single largest Early Agriculture period site yet known within Northwest Mexico and the U.S. Southwest. La Playa comprises at least 10 square kilometers along either side of the Río Boquillas, approximately 37 km to the southwest of Santa Ana, Sonora, and 10 km north of Cerro de Trincheras, the extensively terraced basalt hill considered to be the type site for the Trincheras culture of northwestern Sonora (Carpenter and others 2005).

The Río Boquillas rises on the western flanks of the Sierra Cibuta, southwest of Nogales, and flows in a southwesterly direction to its confluence with the Río Magdalena and Río Concepción some 15 km to the west of Estación Trincheras. The Río Boquillas flows along the northern side of the alluvium-filled basin, close to the pediment of the Boquillas Mountains. Although the Río Boquillas is presently dry for most of the year, as recently as the early 1960s it was considered to be a perennial river (Johnson 1963). Today, the Río Boquillas is deeply entrenched, in some areas as much as 5 m below the surrounding ground surface; however, during the occupation of La Playa, the river flowed on a higher terrace that was an active alluvial fan and floodplain (Carpenter and others 2005; Sánchez 1998).

La Playa (SON F:10:3) is a predominantly Early Agriculture period site with significant Archaic components, along with a Clovis point, bifaces, and partially fossilized antler billets of probable Paleoindian affiliation. In addition, the remains of numerous species of Pleistocene fauna (*Equus, Camelops, Mammuthus, Bison antiquus, Sigmodon*, Cervids, and *Antilocapra*, along with an exceptional number of tortoises—*Gopherus* or Hesperatudae) were identified within a Pleistocene paleosol and the alluvial deposits lying directly above it (Carpenter and others 2005:20; Jim Mead, personal communication 2003; Sánchez and Carpenter 2012).

La Playa has been investigated for more than 18 years (Carpenter and others 1996, 1997, 1999, 2003, 2005, 2009; Carpenter 2009; Villalpando and others 2009, 2010, 2012). The artifacts and features of La Playa are similar to those found at San Pedro (1200 to 800 B.C.) and Cienega phase (800 B.C. to A.D. 50) sites in southeastern Arizona. The 267 human burials recovered at La Playa, dated to the Early Agriculture period, provide the largest burial sample for this period. More than 550 prehistoric archaeological features have been investigated at La Playa. In addition to the burials, they include human and animal cremations, dog burials, a variety of pits, flaked stone scatters, ground stone caches, two structures located on the slopes of the Cerro Boquillas, a probable pit house, geoglyph figures, petroglyphs, about 35 ha of probable linear-bordered agricultural fields, and irrigation canals (Carpenter and others 2009; Villalpando and others 2012). Archaeological data indicate that humans intermittently used the Río Boquillas valley since Late

Pleistocene times. The earliest archaeological feature dated at La Playa is a female burial with a radiocarbon date of 3720 ± 320 B.P. During recent geomorphological investigations carried out by Copeland and others (2012:2937), an occupational surface was identified in two different profiles. Charcoal at these occupational surfaces was radiocarbon dated to 4330 ± 90 and 4160 ± 80, suggesting that the Boquillas Valley was inhabited without interruption once the Altithermal period ended and environmental conditions improved (Carpenter and Sánchez 2013).

The arrival of maize in the Sonoran Desert changed the lives of the people living there. Permanent agricultural villages began to appear in alluvial plains with well-drained soils and adequate water for agriculture. The Archaic way of life that prevailed for thousands of years was replaced by a less mobile life in river valleys, where sophisticated water control systems were built. Communities with an economic base dependent on farmed goods and supplemented with products obtained from the surrounding lands became the most common way of life in the Sonoran Desert. Distinctive cultural regions with the varied languages, traits, and traditions emerged all over Sonora.

The notable Clovis presence on the coastal plain and in the central river valley systems suggests that these regions of Sonora supported long-term residential settlement for both Paleoindian and Archaic hunter-gatherer groups. Binford (1980) and Kelly (1992, 1995) posit that the most important condition determining mobility strategies of hunter-gatherer groups is the natural environment, which defines the distribution of food and water. The fundamental resources for hunter-gatherer groups are permanent water and lithic raw material for tool making; these are indispensable within a given territory. The Llanos de Hermosillo and surrounding areas offered Paleoindian and Archaic groups all the resources they needed.

The nascent Sonoran Desert flora and fauna provide a relatively high biomass for human exploitation, with many of the desert plants producing seeds and fruits high in nutrients throughout various seasons of the year (Nabhan 1985, 1989). Accessibility of edible resources is a key variable in determining mobility and the number of residential campsites occupied during the yearly rounds of hunter-gatherers. The archaeological data available for Sonora has permitted us to reconstruct a preliminary cultural history, although this reconstruction will need to be updated as additional research is conducted.

ARCHAEOLOGICAL PRACTICE AND SITE VISIBILITY

The state of Sonora is allocated less than 1 percent of the Mexican federal budget for archaeological investigations; most of the funding goes to the investigation and restoration of monumental pre-Columbian urban centers with attractive pyramids for tourists, such as Teotihuacan, Tajín, and the Templo Mayor. Foreign scholars carried out the first archaeological explorations in Sonora at the end of the nineteenth century. The Instituto Nacional de Antropología e Historia (INAH) established a branch at Hermosillo in 1973, and Mexican archaeologists began to develop archaeological projects in Sonora. Data collected by Cesar Villalobos Acosta (2007) shows that by 2003 a total of 57 archaeological research projects were carried out in Sonora, with 69 percent of these supported with foreign funding. In the last 10 years, 22 projects have been carried out in Sonora, and at least half of these projects were sponsored by foreign institutions. A total of 12 regional survey projects have been conducted in Sonora, with five of these developed in the last eight years. In contrast, during the same period in Arizona, 60 projects were carried out annually.

At any given time, there are 25 archaeologists employed full-time in Sonora. In contrast, the Arizona State Museum estimates there are about 1,200 archaeologists employed full-time in Arizona (Paul Fish, personal communication 2012). Sonora encompasses an area of 184,933 square kilometers, Arizona is about 40 percent larger than Sonora, encompassing 295,253 square kilometers. There is therefore one archaeologist for every 1,233 square kilometers in Sonora, while in Arizona there is one archaeologist for every 246 square kilometers. In the Tucson Basin, Stephanie Whittlesey, Suzanne Fish, and Paul Fish (personal communication 2012) estimate that there is one archaeologist for every 4 square kilometers. Some regions in Arizona are, therefore, more intensively investigated than comparable regions in Sonora.

Sonora, unquestionably, has the highest density of Clovis sites in the region. A total of 114 Clovis points are known in Sonora; in the neighboring state of Arizona 109 Clovis points are known (Ballenger and others 2011; Prasciunas 2011). The contrast between the two states is even more notable when the low number of full-time archaeologists in Sonora, and the relatively few projects that are conducted every year in the state, are taken into account. Although the total number of Clovis points is similar between Arizona and Sonora, Arizona is much larger than Sonora and there are many more archaeologists working there. If we compare all Clovis artifacts found in Sonora and Arizona, including points, bifaces, endscrapers, blades, blade cores, and tablets, the visibility of Clovis in Sonora is even greater than that in Arizona. Arizona archaeologists have documented 152 Clovis artifacts (Huckell 1978, 1982:3, 2007), while archaeologists have found 618 Clovis artifacts in Sonora. In comparing the number of archaeologists, projects, Clovis points, and Clovis artifacts, it is easy to speculate that Clovis groups used Sonora more intensively than Arizona.

The late Pleistocene and early Holocene archaeological record in Sonora is robust and highly visible, even though the level of investigations is limited. A possible explanation for the high visibility of Paleoindian archaeology in Sonora is that late Pleistocene deposits are still preserved in many places, and that rapidly deflating surfaces contribute to exposing archaeological remains. The eroded surfaces are due to a combination of recent overgrazing, aridity, and groundwater pumping that has dropped the water table. Modern population growth and cultivation are two factors in Sonora that have little effect on the visibility of Clovis points and sites because little cultivation is done in the desert, and only three Clovis points have been found in the city of Hermosillo. About 50 percent of the Clovis points in Sonora have been found by collectors. A group of about dozen collectors were active from 1967 to 1985, and many of the collections were made during that period. There are still several Clovis collectors active in Sonora, and their impact is apparent on sites located within two hours travel from Hermosillo.

It is unlikely that the number of archaeologists working full time in Sonora is going to increase significantly over the next 10 years. However, large infrastructure projects such as pipelines, mines, artificial lakes, and aqueducts planned by the Mexican government are beginning to be developed. These projects will affect large areas that have never been studied, so archaeological assessments that take place as part of these projects will increase our knowledge of zones that will never be studied in any other way.

CHAPTER FOUR

Archaeological Investigations of the Late Pleistocene Occupation of Sonora

Dated at 11,500 radiocarbon years ago, the Clovis industry represents the oldest cultural horizon in the Americas. Several well-known Clovis sites, including Naco, Lehner, and Murray Springs, are located along the San Pedro River Valley in southeastern Arizona (Haury and others 1953, 1959; Haynes 1966, 1969, 1976, 1982, 1987, 2007; Hemmings 1970). These sites, which include mammoth and bison kill sites and camp sites, have an unusually complete record of late Quaternary depositional and erosional events, as well as a robust series of radiocarbon dates (Haynes 1991, 1993, 2000a, 2000b; Huckell 2007; Taylor and others 1996). These San Pedro River sites are located only a few kilometers north of the international border between Arizona and Sonora.

Relatively few systematic archaeological investigations have been conducted within the state of Sonora, a region where even the ceramic period traditions remain vaguely defined. My interests in the Paleoindian and Archaic occupations of Sonora were kindled over a decade ago, when the research I did at the predominantly Early Agriculture period site of La Playa (SON F:10:3) revealed a Paleoindian component at the site. In addition, the remains of numerous species of Pleistocene fauna (*Equus, Camelops, Mammuthus, Bison antiquus, Sigmodon,* Cervidae, and *Antilocapra*, along with an exceptional number of tortoises—*Gopherus* or Hesperatudae) were collected (Jim Mead, personal communication 2003). The bones were deposited in red soil of Pleistocene age (Carpenter and others 2005:20).

In 1997, I began a research project to identify and document Clovis and other Paleoindian artifacts housed in museum collections and private collections. All of the collectors in Sonora were contacted, and photographs of artifacts were taken with the help of Julio Montané, Elisa Villalpando, and John Carpenter. I attempted to relocate and document the localities that had probable Paleoindian contexts. In 2003, the project Geoarqueología y Tecnología Lítica de los sitios Paleoindios de Sonora was funded by the Argonaut Archaeological Research Fund of the University of Arizona, and since then a coordinated effort between geologists and archaeologists from the University of Arizona and INAH has developed to study of the archaeology and the depositional context of Paleoindian sites in Sonora. Our ongoing efforts to document artifact collections and known localities of Paleoindian sites, and our quest to find new Paleoindian sites, indicate that the northern half of Sonora contains a relatively high distribution of Clovis Paleonidian sites and a wide spread distribution of isolated Clovis points.

Our research has identified several sites with the potential of having late Pleistocene buried deposits with intact archaeological features. To date, geoarchaeological investigations have been carried out at seven sites: El Bajío (SON K:1:3), El Gramal (SON N:11:20), SON O:3:1, SON J:16:8; and Fin del Mundo (SON J:6:2). This fieldwork has yielded abundant Paleoindian artifacts and features, and our research team has visited many other Paleoindian localities that are under investigation (Fig. 4.1).

EL BAJÍO (SON K:1:3)

El Bajío, investigated in 2003, has numerous Clovis diagnostic artifacts. This site presents the most evidence for Paleoindian occupation of any place known in Sonora. In many localities within El Bajío, the artifacts appear to have been recently exposed through erosion, and the site thus has the potential to yield buried archaeological contexts.

El Bajío is located approximately 15 km southeast of the town of Opodepe and 40 km northeast of Carbo, on

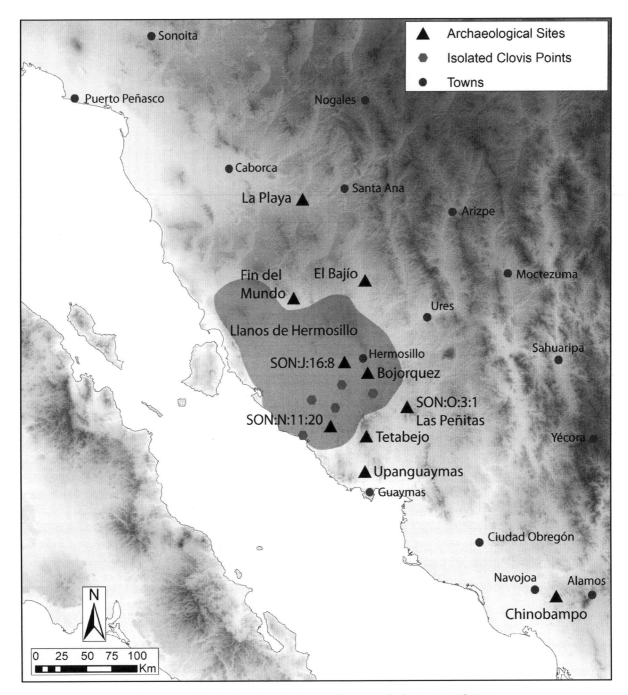

Figure 4.1. Paleoindian sites in Sonora. Cartography by José Raúl Ortiz.

the southwestern piedmont of the Sierra San Jeronimo. The Sierra San Jeronimo is the range that separates the parallel valleys of the Río San Miguel and the wide valley of the Río Zanjon. The Río Zanjon Valley is situated in the parallel valleys and mountain ranges of the Sonoran physiographic province. The broad valley, more than 30 km wide, is filled with sediment. The valley runs in a north-south direction, immediately to the west of the more heavily eroded valley of the Río San Miguel (Fig. 4.2). These two valleys form part of the Río Sonora drainage basin. They both empty into the Río Sonora in the vicinity of Hermosillo. The Río Sonora, in turn, debouches into the Sea of Cortez at Estero Tastiota on the Central Coast.

Figure 4.2. El Bajío site area. Map data © 2010 Google, INEGI, Digital Globe, CNES/SPOT Image.

At a median elevation of 800 m above mean sea level, El Bajío is situated on a pediment that forms a small, slightly inclined, irregularly shaped bajío, or low-lying area. This landform, which trends in a northwesterly-southeasterly direction at the southern edge of El Bajío, was created by the piedmont of the granitic Sierra San Jeronimo to the northwest and a series of volcanic peaks of basalt that comprise the Cerro La Vuelta. The basalt hills near El Bajío represent a recent geological phenomenon that interrupted the more ancient granitic slope of the Sierra San Jerónimo, forming the irregularly shaped, low-lying area for which the site is named. This geomorphological setting promotes the formation of small alluvial fans, possibly creating conditions where water accumulated for short periods of time at the end of the Pleistocene. Presently, springs do not exist within this arid zone.

Annual precipitation in this region is 309.3 mm, of which approximately 190 mm falls during the cyclonic summer storms, or chubascos (Turner and Brown 1994:218). The site is associated with a transitional biotic community. A finger of the Sinaloan thornscrub (*matorral espinoso sinaloense*) extends northward through the adjacent valley of the Río San Miguel, intermixing with the Sonoran Desert vegetation. The local flora consists of thorny shrubs, with riparian plants along the margins of the drainages. The vegetation includes stands of ironwood (*Olneya tesota*), mesquite (*Prosopis velutina*), various species of palo verde (*Cercidium* sp.), ocotillo (*Fouquieria macdougalii*), palo blanco (*Ipomoea arborescens*), and pochote (*Ceiba acuminata*), as well as cacti, including pitahaya or organ pipe (*Stenocereus thurberi*), chollas (*Opuntia* sp.) and various species of agave (*Agave* spp.). Dispersed low shrubs are scarce but include *hierba del vaso* or brittlebush (*Encelia farinosa*) and *sangregado* or limberbush (*Jatropha cardiophilla*). The characteristic fauna include white-tailed deer (*Odocoileus virginianus*), mule deer (*O. hemionus crooki*), coyote (*Canis latrans*), collared peccary (*Dicotyles tajacu*), cottontail rabbit (*Sylvilagus audubon*), black-tailed jackrabbit

(*Lepus californicus*), desert tortoise (*Gopherus agassizi*), numerous rodents (*Neotoma* spp., *Peromyscus* spp., *Perognathus* spp.), and a wide variety of birds (Turner and Brown 1994).

In 1996, Julio Montané took John Carpenter, Elisa Villalpando, and me to El Bajío. Immediately upon our arrival, we found four distal fragments of Clovis points and preforms. Two years later, accompanied by C. Vance Haynes and Paul Fish, we found a nearly complete Clovis point in two fragments separated by a distance of four meters. The fracture of this point was not recent, and the two pieces appeared to have eroded from buried contexts. Considering the large quantity of tools that Manuel Robles, Julio Montané, and the McIntyres collected at this site, El Bajío is one of the largest Clovis sites in western North America.

Initiating research at El Bajío was difficult because Señor Molina, the landowner, prohibited entry to his ranch. After three months of intense negotiations, at every level, Señor Molina at last relented, giving us permission to conduct the fieldwork that we carried out between April 28 and June 7, 2003. In order to better understand the site and its setting, we implemented a research strategy entailing total survey coverage of the area, employing the method proposed by Fish and Kowaleski (1990). The explicit objectives of the systematic survey were to identify the site boundaries, identify the various localities within the site, and identify those loci with the greatest probability of containing buried contexts. We carried out extensive surveys to locate stratigraphic horizons and paleontological elements that were exposed in arroyo cuts. We then made systematic collections of all diagnostic artifacts (Paleoindian and Archaic), conducted test excavations in selected locations, and undertook extensive excavations of several surface features to identify buried Paleoindian contexts and reconstruct the depositional history of the site.

The site extends over an area of 4 square kilometers, with a low-to-moderate distribution of artifacts observed throughout 22 distinct loci that were defined on the basis of surface artifacts (Fig. 4.3). These loci are distributed along the pediment, in the low-lying terrain of the bajío, and on the hilltops. The most important locus is the vitrified basalt that outcrops on Cerro de la Vuelta in the southwestern portion of the site, designated Locus 20 (Fig. 4.4).

Surface artifacts were systematically collected using a standardized dog-leash method with a radius of 1 m. All diagnostic artifacts were also collected. In addition, each locality was evaluated with regard to its probability of containing late Pleistocene or early Holocene deposits. All loci were documented independently of their chronological and cultural affiliation (Table 4.1). Diagnostic artifact types and the degree of patination on artifacts were used to determine the loci with a Clovis or early Paleoindian affiliation.

Eight loci were selected for additional excavation. The selection process was based upon the character of the surface artifacts collected, the immediate geomorphology present, and the observable stratigraphy of each locus. A total of 10 hand-dug test trenches and three 1-m by 1-m test units were excavated. Extensive excavations were conducted at visible surface features, including two knapping stations and 10 fire-cracked thermal features in dispersed locales. Disarticulated roasting pits (hornos) are common features at El Bajío. In 2003, we documented 110 hornos, and the McIntyres had previously registered some 600 of the features. It should be noted that most of the horno features lack contextual integrity, and it appears that the site surface has been subjected to a high degree of alteration. We therefore invested a great amount of time in identifying the 10 intact and semi-intact hornos that were subsequently excavated. Several samples for radiocarbon dates were obtained from different trenches and features (Table 4.2), but no Paleoindian buried features or surface features were found, even though the lithic assemblages at the surface clearly suggest a Paleoindian occupation.

At present, it is impossible to create an accurate cross-section of the site's depositional history. It is evident, however, that a Pleistocene basin fill with a well-expressed red soil underlies the site. We think this Pleistocene soil began to form about 13,000 to 15,000 years ago. This red paleosol was probably the Pleistocene surface where the Clovis people lived. In some of the units on top of the Pleistocene red paleosol, sediments and soils of Middle and Late Holocene age developed; in other localities, the Pleistocene red soils are heavily weathered and exposed at the surface. A silty-clay dark gray stratum that we interpreted as a cienega-like deposit was radiocarbon-dated to between 4500 and 5500 B.P. This deposit, observed in three profiles, likely represents a wetter climatic episode in the region following the Altithermal period.

Locus 20 (Vitrified Basalt Quarry)

Cerro de la Vuelta is the highest landform at El Bajío, and the vitrified basalt raw material source on the southern

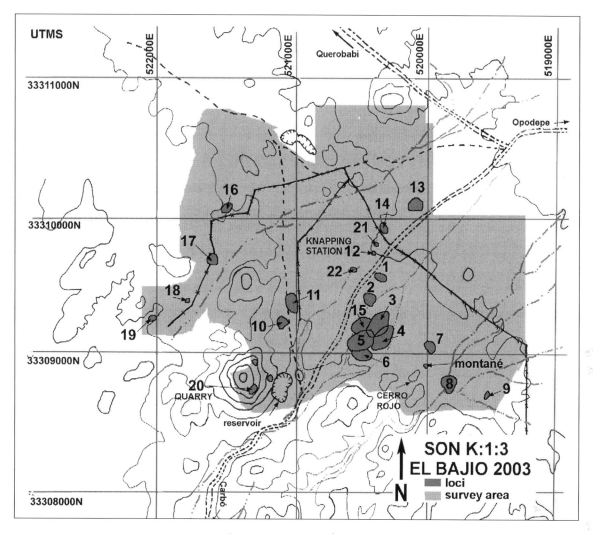

Figure 4.3. Loci at El Bajío.

Figure 4.4. Cerro de la Vuelta and Locus 20
as viewed from Locus 5 at El Bajío.

Table 4.1. Cultural Affiliations of the El Bajío Loci

Cultural Affiliation	Locus Number	Total Number of Loci
Paleoindian	1, 4, 5, 6, 7, 10, 12, 18, 11, 22	10
Paleoindian/ Archaic	20, 2, 3, 15, 8, 16, 21	7
Archaic	9, 14, 19	3
Ceramic	13	1
	TOTAL	21

Table 4.2. Radiocarbon Dates from El Bajío

Sample Number	Locus	Excavation Unit	¹⁴C Date (B.P.)	Material Dated	Stratigraphic Unit
A-13267	11	Trench 2	5390 ± 120	Soil residue	A2 black mat?
A-13268	11	Trench 4	4135 ± 95	Soil residue	A2 black mat?
B-188544	6	Trench 8	3560 ± 40	Charcoal	Occupational surface on a red soil
A-59681-13270	15	Trench 6	2225 ± 35	Soil residue (upper)	Unit 1 clay deposit
A-59681-13270.1	15	Trench 6	1665 ± 50	Soil residue (upper)	Unit 1 clay deposit
A-59680-13269	15	Trench 6	5180 ± 45	Soil residue (lower)	Unit 1 clay deposit
B-188544	12	Hearth	1980 ± 40	Charcoal	
A-15396	5	Horno 50	1260 ± 35	Charcoal	

slope of this hill was undoubtedly the principal reason why Paleoindian groups visited or inhabited this location. Ninety-eight percent of the lithic material documented at the site was derived from this source (Fig. 4.5), along with lithic waste material dumps that extend for a distance of more than 20 m (Fig. 4.6). These dumps contain fragments of biface preforms, hammerstones, and abraders. The principal quarry area extends over a hectare (Fig. 4.7). The vitrified basalt occurs naturally in prismatic and sub-prismatic blocks, and the quality of the raw material with regard to the production of flaked stone tools is unpredictable.

Some blocks are fine-grained, and are thus quite knappable, while others reveal abundant internal fractures or

Figure 4.6. Lithic waste dump at Locus 20 at El Bajío.

Figure 4.5. Vitrified basalt raw material at El Bajío.

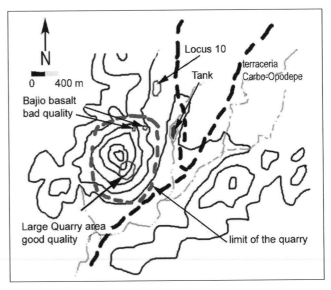

Figure 4.7. Sketch map of Locus 20 at El Bajío.

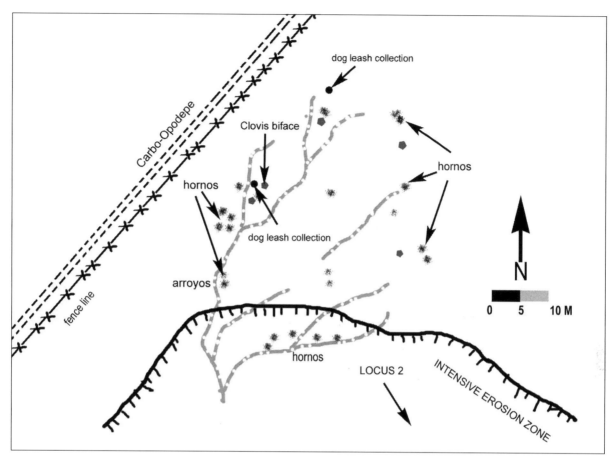

Figure 4.8. Sketch map of Locus 1 at El Bajío.

inclusions of olivine crystals of varying sizes, or both. The raw material color is also extremely variable, ranging from a cream color to jet-black. This material has the characteristic of developing a surface patina; the artifacts at the site can display a thick yellow glaze patina, a thinner greenish patina, and a grey patina. In addition to the principal quarry, there exist at least three other outcrops of raw material within the northeast sector of the Cerro de la Vuelta and the hills adjacent to Locus 20. This quarry appears to have been exploited mainly during Paleoindian and Archaic times. At the only locality where ceramics were documented, we observed that the lithic artifacts were manufactured from water-worn cobbles of basalt, rhyolite, and diorite, with a notable absence of vitrified basalt. Locus 20 needs to be explored in much more detail because it was discovered on the penultimate day of the field season, and our preliminary reconnaissance suggests there may be artificial terraces with deposits that could be excavated at this locus.

Locus 1

Situated in the north-central sector of the site, Locus 1 encompasses an area of 2,750 square meters. This locus is characterized by a moderate distribution of four to five artifacts per m², interspersed with areas of much higher artifact concentrations. There are also 19 probable horno features (Fig. 4.8). A lanceolate biface fragment with a square base of probable Paleoindian affiliation was collected as a diagnostic artifact, along with many biface thinning flakes and biface fragments with a thick patina.

The archaeological materials in Locus 1 appear to be eroding out of the well-expressed red palesol of probable late Pleistocene age. The Holocene deposits in the locus are eroded. The fire-cracked rocks observed on the surface appear to be greatly altered and scattered. An unsuccessful attempt was made to locate a sufficiently intact feature that could be excavated in order to obtain flotation samples and charcoal. No stratigraphic test trenches were implemented.

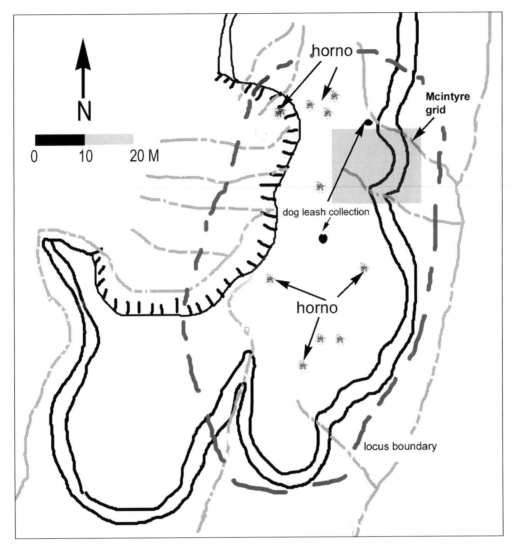

Figure 4.9. Sketch map of Locus 2 at El Bajío.

Locus 2

This locus, about 6,400 square meters in size, is situated 100 m to the southeast of Locus 1. Here the terrain is heavily eroded by gullies up to 2 m deep that delimit the artifact distribution (Fig. 4.9). The artifact density varies from moderate to dense (from 5 to 10 artifacts per m²). The sole diagnostic artifact collected is a large biface that could represent a Clovis preform. In addition, there were a large number of biface thinning flakes, both with patina and without.

Although the surface is heavily eroded, it is possible that buried archaeological features may exist in some places of the locus; however, we did not excavate any test trenches. We located old wooden stakes placed in

a 20-m grid using 5-m by 5-m squares that are unquestionably remnants of the controlled surface collections carried out by Marian and Kenneth McIntyre in 1976. A total of 10 disarticulated hornos were documented at this locus. The excavation of Horno No. 22 revealed a dark matrix lacking charcoal or ash, evidence of a highly disturbed area.

Loci 3, 4, 5, 6, and 15

Five loci are located on a ridge west of Cerro Rojo, where they occupy a 400-m by 300-m area (Fig. 4.10). Here the pediment extends from the northeast to the southwest on a highly dissected alluvial remnant that forms a narrow ridge with the same orientation, with erosional head cuts

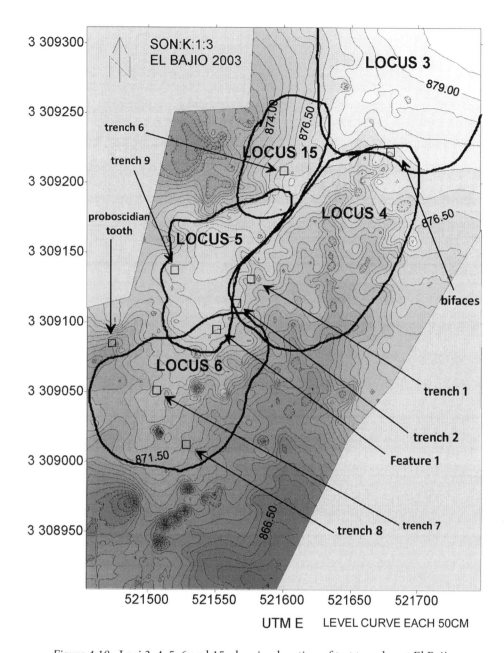

Figure 4.10. Loci 3, 4, 5, 6 and 15, showing location of test trenches at El Bajío.

emanating in every direction but the north (Fig. 4.11). The crest of this ridge has an average elevation of 877 m above sea level. These loci represent the sector of the site with the greatest quantities of Clovis artifacts. The area was divided in five loci, where distinctive surface concentrations of artifacts were observed on the surface.

Locus 3 is the northernmost and the highest locus of the group. A moderate artifact distribution encompassing 15,000 square meters were observed. There are

also eight disarticulated hornos in Locus 3. During the systematic survey in 2003, no diagnostic Clovis artifacts were documented at this locus. However, two San Pedro projectile points dating to the Early Agriculture period were collected, and much of the lithic debitage at the locus lacked patina. Nevertheless, in May 1999, a fluted Clovis preform was found. This Clovis preform was broken into two fragments separated by 6 m, and apparently had been recently exposed by erosion. During a site visit

Figure 4.11. View looking northeast at Loci 3, 4, 5, 6, 7, and 12 at El Bajío.

in 2002, a group of three large bifaces, probably of Clovis age, was documented eroding out of the surface near the southern limit of Locus 3 (Fig. 4.12). Both of these discoveries suggest that there are buried stratified contexts of late Pleistocene or early Holocene age.

Locus 15, to the southwest of Locus 3, encompasses about 2,800 square meters. This locus includes the northwestern portion of the relatively flat alluvial remnant, as well as a segment of the erosional gullies that are oriented to the west (Fig. 4.13). A concentration of bifaces was observed eroding from a small arroyo at this locus; the bifaces appear to have originated in a buried soil. A hand trench, designated Trench No. 6, was excavated in the area where the bifaces were found. Four strata were recognized in Trench No. 6. Stratum 0 was the oldest, and probably represents the Pleistocene surface, which has been eroded away and is missing from most of the trench profile. Stratum 1 represents a clay-sand deposit about 70 cm wide that was dated to 5180 ± 45 B.P. (AA59689-13269). Stratum 1 appears to represent a cienega or wet period. At the 2–3 contact about 60 cm below the surface, a linear group of rocks was observed. Various artifacts were lying on this apparently artificial arrangement of rocks, and this prompted a decision to extend

Figure 4.12. Bifaces from Locus 3 at El Bajío.

the excavation in order to follow the possible occupation surface. An area measuring 4 m x 3 m, designated Extension 2, was opened to the north of the trench (Fig. 4.14). Unfortunately, the rock cap proved to be irregular (Fig. 4.15), although it is unquestionably an Archaic occupation surface with artifacts that included a San Pedro type projectile point and a hearth with charcoal that was dated at 2225 ± 35 B.P. (AA59681-13270).

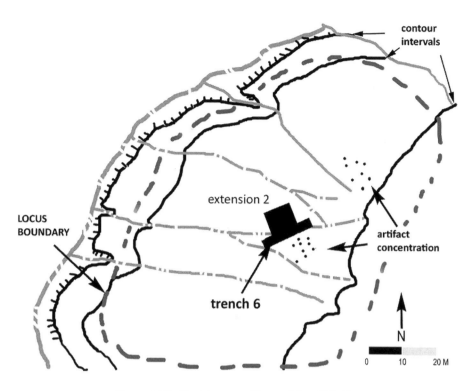

Figure 4.13. Sketch map of Locus 15 at El Bajío.

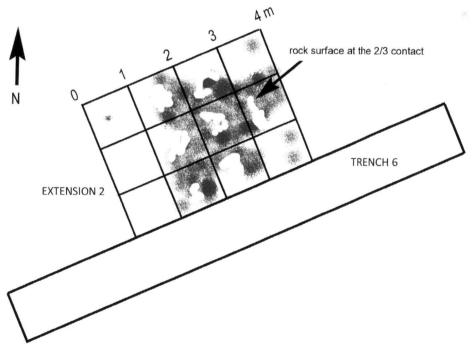

Figure 4.14. Trench 6 and Extension 2, Locus 15, at El Bajío.

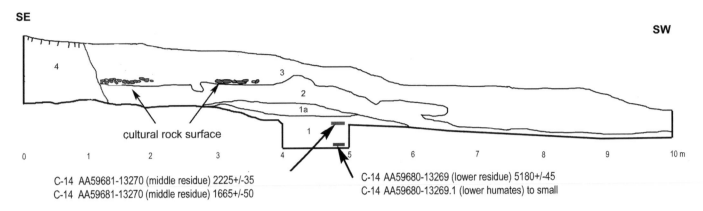

SE

SW

4

3

2

1a

1

cultural rock surface

0   1   2   3   4   5   6   7   8   9   10 m

C-14 AA59681-13270 (middle residue) 2225+/-35
C-14 AA59681-13270 (middle residue) 1665+/-50

C-14 AA59680-13269 (lower residue) 5180+/-45
C-14 AA59680-13269.1 (lower humates) to small

Figure 4.15. Profile of Trench 6, Locus 15, at El Bajío.

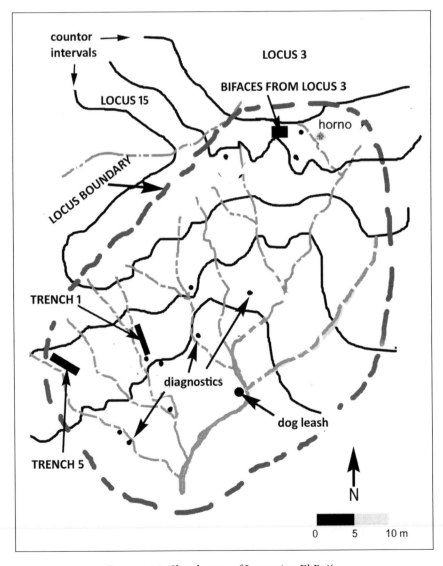

countor intervals

LOCUS 3

BIFACES FROM LOCUS 3

LOCUS 15

horno

LOCUS BOUNDARY

TRENCH 1

diagnostics

dog leash

TRENCH 5

N

0   5   10 m

Figure 4.16. Sketch map of Locus 4 at El Bajío.

Locus 4 is comprised by gullies located south of Loci 3 and 15 (Fig. 4.16). These gully channels are variously oriented north-south and east-west. This locus comprises 12,000 square meters at elevations ranging from 872 to 875 m above sea level. There are many more diagnostic Clovis artifacts around the bajadas than in the less eroded terrain above, prompting us to think that it was likely that the Clovis artifacts originate in the old, well-developed, red soil that appears to represent the buried stratigraphic unit observed beneath the surface deposits at Locus 3. Twenty diagnostic Clovis artifacts were collected at Locus 4, including a basal fragment of a Clovis point, fluted on both sides; a distal fragment of a point of a size and raw material type indicating it is probably a Clovis point; eight bifaces, one of which displays a flute; three prismatic blades; an end scraper on a blade; and a conical Clovis core. Two trenches were excavated to

search for archaeological contexts and samples for dating. Trench No. 1 was 10 meters long (Fig. 4.17), and Trench No. 5 was 7 meters long (Fig. 4.18). We also excavated two shallow horno features but these did not yield samples suitable for dating.

Locus 5 is situated to the south of Locus 15 at an elevation of 876 meters on semi-flat terrain at the crest of the remnant deposits. Locus 15 encompasses an area of 7,500 m² (Fig. 4.19). There is a well-developed red soil at this location, thought to be of Pleistocene age. This red soil is closer to the present surface than it is at Locus 3. The artifacts at Locus 5 appear to be eroding from the upper contact surface of the possible Pleistocene age surface.

Locus 5 contains the highest density of archaeological materials found at El Bajío. The diagnostic Clovis artifacts recovered at this locus include three blades, two bifaces, two unifacial tools, and a flake with a prepared

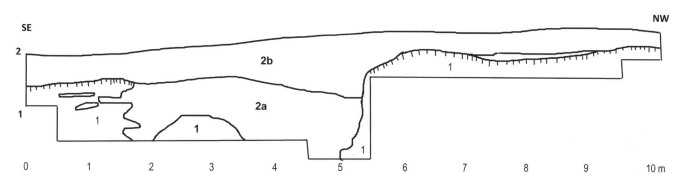

Figure 4.17. East profile of Trench 1, Locus 4, at El Bajío.

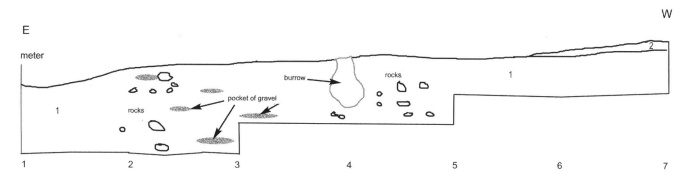

Figure 4.18. South profile of Trench 5, Locus 4, at El Bajío.

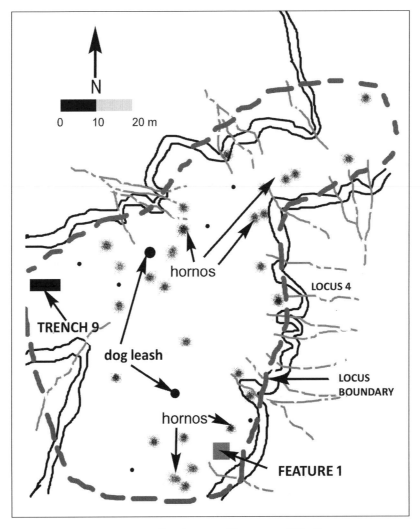

Figure 4.19. Sketch map of Locus 5 at El Bajío.

platform. Twenty-four fire-cracked-rock features were documented, along with an apparent knapping station consisting of blades, debitage, and other artifacts. A single fire-cracked rock feature, designated Horno No. 50 (Fig. 4.20) was excavated; charcoal from the feature was dated at 1260 ± 35 B.P. (A-15396).

In the southeast section of Locus 5, there was a concentration of archaeological materials within a 4-m by 3-m area. There were approximately 250 to 300 artifacts here, including blades, scrapers, large bifaces, and large cores that were brought from the source at Cerro de la Vuelta. A 3-m by 4-m grid composed of 1-m by 1-m square units was established, and the artifacts collected by quadrant (Fig. 4.21). Each unit was subsequently excavated in 10-cm levels to a depth of 30 cm but no

Figure 4.20. Horno 50, Locus 5, at El Bajío.

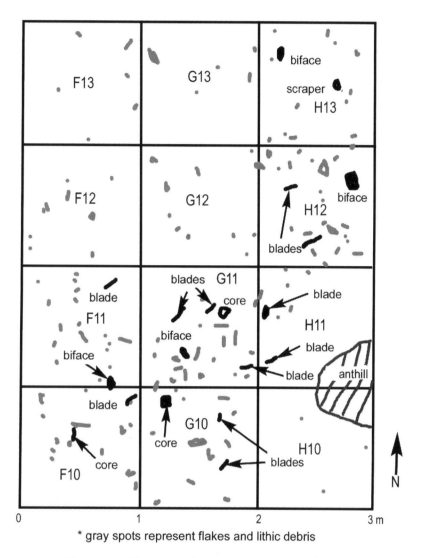

Figure 4.21. Plan view of Feature 1, Locus 5, at El Bajío.

subsurface artifacts were recovered. It appears that this locus had recently eroded to the surface, and it is likely that it had been previously exposed during one or more erosional events and thus lacked contextual integrity. The enamel of a proboscidean tooth was found between Locus 5 and Locus 6 (Fig. 4.22). A 1-m by 1-m unit was excavated to investigate whether there were additional remains of the mastodon but we determined that this element had been redeposited. However, these fossils indicate that there might be more Pleistocene animals buried at the site.

Locus 6 is situated to the west of the Cerro Rojo, encompassing 6,600 square meters (Fig. 4.23). Here the red soil is exposed and forms most of the surface. Due to

Figure 4.22. Highly eroded proboscidean molar between Locus 5 and Locus 6 at El Bajío.

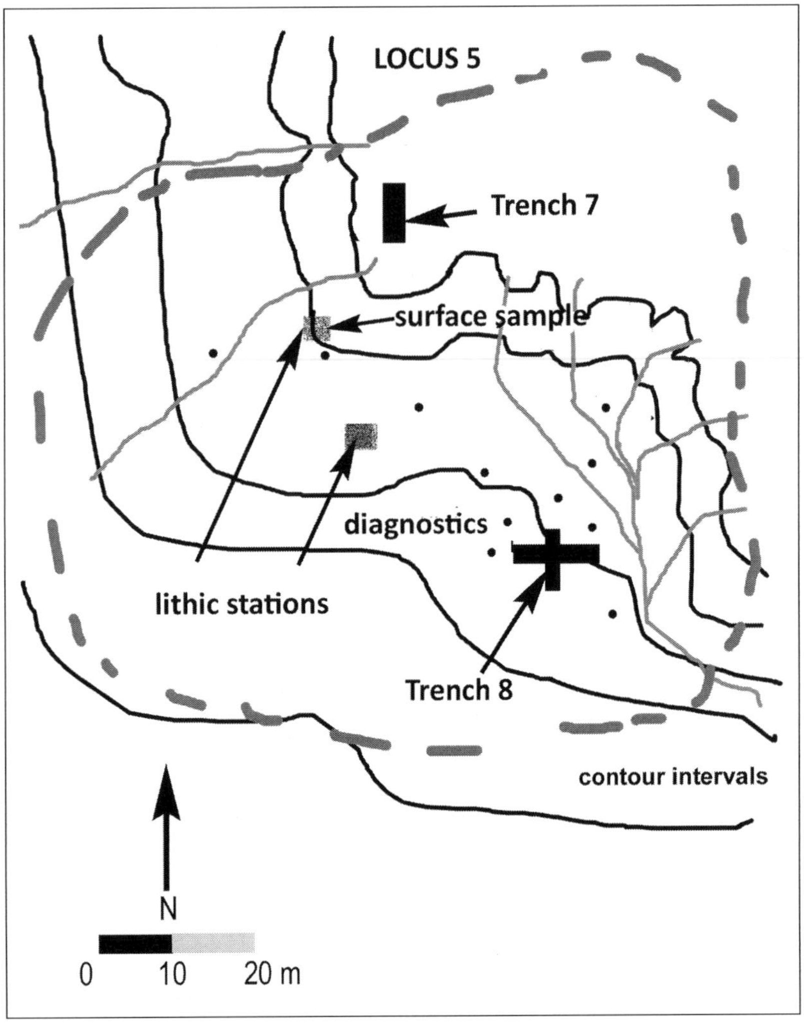

LOCUS 5

Trench 7

surface sample

diagnostics

lithic stations

Trench 8

contour intervals

N

0   10   20 m

Figure 4.23. Sketch map of Locus 6 at El Bajío.

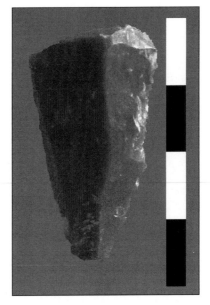

Figure 4.24. Red chert end scraper from El Bajío.

weathering, the red soil is more intense than in other parts of the site, and pebbles of calcium carbonate are present. Locus 6 contains a dense concentration of diagnostic Clovis artifacts and flakes, as well as a large quantity of other lithic artifacts made with nonlocal, high quality raw materials. There are two areas containing cores and debitage where the qualities of raw material were likely tested by the occupants of the site. We collected various flakes of nonlocal cherts and obsidian at this location. Diagnostic Clovis artifacts recovered from this locale include five blades, a conical core, a side scraper, an end scraper, and a large biface. The end scraper was made on a red chert blade (Fig. 4.24). It is similar to one recovered from the Murray Springs site in Arizona (C. Vance Haynes, Jr., personal communication 2003).

Trenches No. 7 and No. 8 were excavated within Locus 6. Trench No. 8 was excavated to investigate a concentration of bifaces and blades that appeared to have recently eroded to the surface from a buried deposit. The trench was placed in a low-lying portion of Locus 6. Three strata were observed (Fig. 4.25). Flakes were found down to the contact with Stratum B1, which is the base of the channel that cut through unit A1. A radiocarbon age of 3560 ± 40 B.P. was obtained from an ash stain with associated flakes within the gravelly sand well-consolidated channel.

In sum, the fieldwork carried out among Loci 3, 4, 6, and 15 demonstrated these areas of El Bajío have the highest quantity of artifacts affiliated with Clovis. Preliminary geoarchaeological investigations indicate that the Clovis

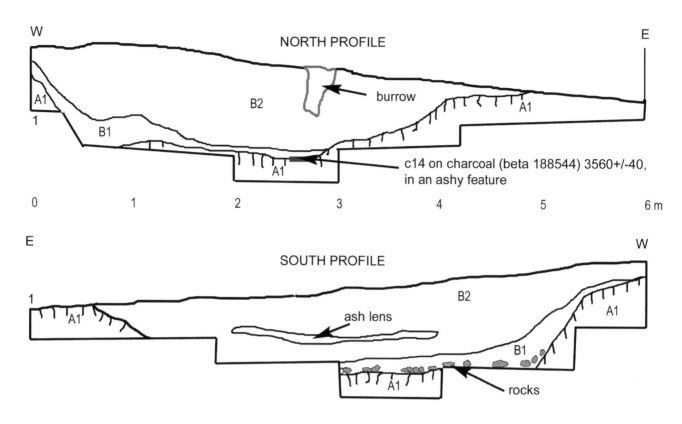

Figure 4.25. Profiles of Trench 8, Locus 6, at El Bajío.

artifacts are eroding from a red paleosol believed to be of Pleistocene age, and perhaps associated with the glacial maximum. It is possible that the red soil was the Clovis surface that was buried in few zones, and now completely eroded in most of El Bajío, including Trenches Nos. 1, 5, and 6 and in Loci 4 and 5.

Cerro Rojo, a small red hill, lies to the east of this group of loci. A great quantity of quartz nodules used in tool production can be found on Cerro Rojo. The hill is also a source of red ochre, an important pigment for Paleoindian people. Julio Montané collected a large quantity of end scrapers and side scrapers with remnants of red ochre pigment during his investigations in the vicinity of Cerro Rojo. Apparently, the hill was an important place for Pleistocene people (Julio Montané, personal communication 2003).

Locus 7

Locus 7 is situated on the pediment, approximately 600 m east of Locus 4. This locus comprises approximately 31,200 square meters within a zone that is heavily dissected by small arroyos (Fig. 4.26). Although the

artifact density at Locus 7 is much lower than previously reported, the majority of the artifacts observed on the surface have a Paleoindian affiliation, and the generally excellent state of preservation suggests a recent exposure. Among the artifacts collected are 12 blades, a conical core, core tablets, and two finely-made end scrapers produced using blades. Trench 10 was excavated here in order to find buried archaeological features.

Trench No. 10 was placed in a dense scatter of Paleoindian surface artifacts consisting predominantly of blades. The artifacts appear to have been exposed to the surface recently, with no evidence of redeposition, and they are in a generally excellent state of preservation. A handful of flakes was recovered within the first 20 cm of subsurface sediments. The trench presents at least six different strata created by alluvial and low-energy depositional processes (Fig. 4.27). Stratum 1, the basal unit, is a silty-sand with calcium carbonate. Stratum 2 is a gray silty-clay matrix that directly overlies Unit 1, and which represents low-energy fluvial deposits, perhaps a pond deposit. Locus 7 is an ideal location to seek buried Paleoindian deposits in the future.

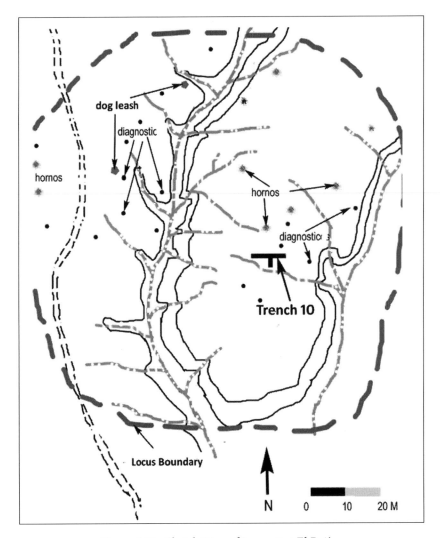

Figure 4.26. Sketch Map of Locus 7 at El Bajío.

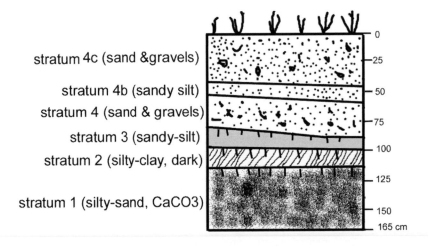

Figure 4.27. Profile of Trench 10, Locus 7, at El Bajío.

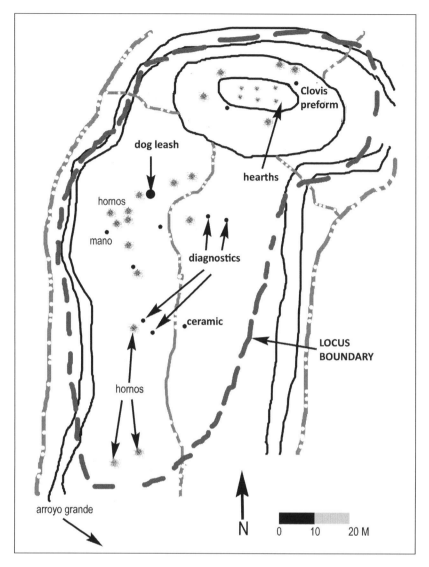

Figure 4.28. Sketch map of Locus 8 at El Bajío.

Figure 4.29. Clovis preform collected at Locus 8 at El Bajío.

Locus 8

Locus 8 is situated 300 m south of Locus 7. Locus 8 comprises an area of 17,000 square meters on top of a crest or mesa that is oriented northeast-southwest (Fig. 4.28). It lies to the north of one of the largest arroyo channels at El Bajío. This locus contains a scatter of artifacts and approximately 17 fire-cracked rock features. Many of the fire-cracked rock features are disarticulated but some remain in an excellent state of preservation. Several of the features appear to be surface hearths rather than subterranean roasting features (hornos). The underlying alluvium appears red in color and contains calcium

carbonate; it does not seem to be a late Holocene deposit. The Archaic and Early Agriculture period, represented by San Pedro projectile points, reflects the predominant cultural affiliation at this locus. However, a few Paleo-indian artifacts, including a distal fragment of a Clovis preform (Fig. 4.29), an end scraper, and a square-based biface were recovered at Locus 8. No test trenching was performed, but three horno features were excavated.

Locus 10

Locus 10 comprises 30,000 square meters on the rocky terrace of a low hill adjacent to Cerro de la Vuelta. The

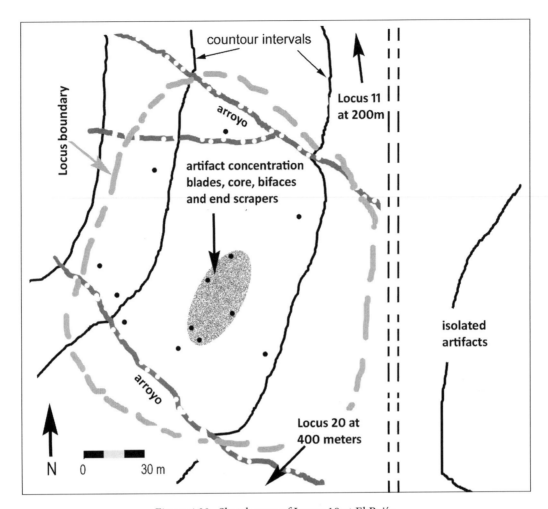

Figure 4.30. Sketch map of Locus 10 at El Bajío.

locus is situated 400 m north of Locus 20, the vitrified basalt quarry. Locus 10 is the closest unit to Cerro de la Vuelta. Although there were various artifact concentrations that could possibly represent features, detailed inspection revealed the absence of any buried contexts. The surface artifact concentrations at Locus 10 proved to be due to cattle disturbance, and the artifacts were heavily damaged by trampling. However, diagnostic Clovis artifacts were collected at Locus 10 and, in general, a light but consistent scatter of surface artifacts extends between this locus and the road at Locus 21 (Fig. 4.30). Two Clovis preforms, two bifaces displaying characteristic Clovis technology, a fragment of a fluted biface (heavily damaged by cattle trampling) that could be a Clovis point fragment, four end scrapers (Fig. 4.31), six blades, and a core were collected at Locus 10. This area appears to have few sedimentary deposits. Julio Montané and the

Figure 4.31. End scrapers from Locus 10 at El Bajío.

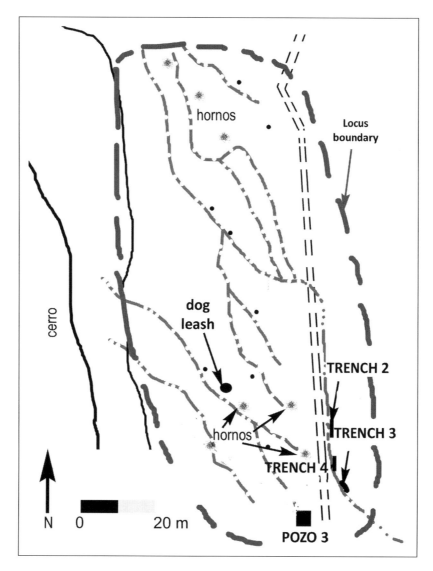

Figure 4.32. Sketch map of Locus 11 at El Bajío.

McIntyres expended much time and energy at Locus 10 during their respective investigations (Julio Montané, personal communication, 2002).

Locus 11

Locus 11 comprises an area of 710,500 square meters of a low terrace on the hill (Fig. 4.32). It is located about 200 m north of Locus 10. In contrast with Locus 10, Locus 11 presents buried deposits, and there are six horno features visible on the surface. Some of the hornos contain rocks with patina, and could possibly be of some antiquity.

Locus 11 is dissected by numerous arroyos where artifacts are exposed. No diagnostic Clovis artifacts

were collected, although several bifacial thinning flakes and fragments of bifaces with patina may have a Clovis affiliation. A well-developed stratum composed of clay-silt dark brown may be a terminal Pleistocene or early Holocene deposit that marks a brief period of intense cold and humidity. A black-mat layer was observed in the wall profile of an arroyo parallel to the road that passes in a north-south direction through the locus. Trenches Nos. 2, 3, and 4 were profiled in the arroyo close to the dirt road. Three strata were observed in these profiles (Figs. 4.33, 4.34, and 4.35). Stratum 2 is a strong and well-developed soil composed by clay and sand. Two radiocarbon dates were obtained from Stratum 2, and

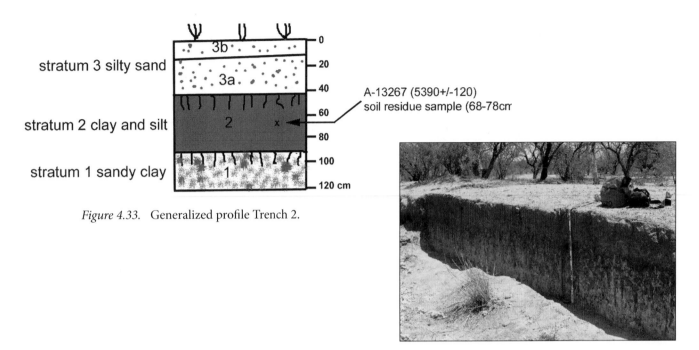

stratum 3 silty sand

stratum 2 clay and silt

stratum 1 sandy clay

A-13267 (5390+/-120)
soil residue sample (68-78cm

Figure 4.33. Generalized profile Trench 2.

Figure 4.34. East Profile of Trench 2.

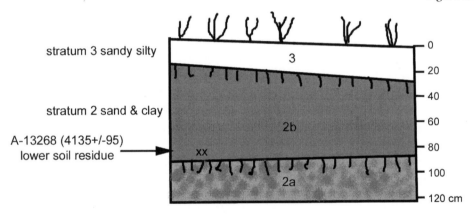

stratum 3 sandy silty

stratum 2 sand & clay

A-13268 (4135+/-95)
lower soil residue

Figure 4.35. Generalized profile Trench 4.

Figure 4.36. Horno 102 in Locus 11,
[14]C date (A-15395 = 315 ± 40).

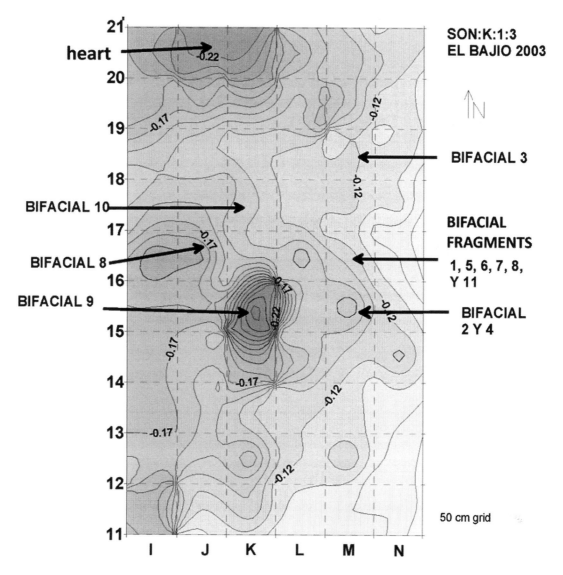

Figure 4.37. Lithic workshop at Locus 12 at El Bajío.

these confirm that a cienega formed during the middle Holocene. Soil residue from Stratum 2 in Trench No. 2 was radiocarbon dated at 5390 ± 120 B.P. (A-13267). Soil residue from Stratum 2 in Trench No. 4 was dated at 4135 ± 95 B.P. (A-13268). One horno feature was excavated at Locus 11 (Fig. 4.36). The horno has a heavy patina, and appears to be old. However, a ^{14}C sample from the roasting pit dated to 315 ± 40 B.P (A-15395).

Locus 12

Locus 12, located in the northwestern sector of El Bajío, is a small, irregularly shaped depression approximately 300 m northwest of Locus 1 (Fig. 4.37). Locus 12 consists

of a dense concentration of 638 artifacts within a 5-m by 3-m area. Artifacts collected from the surface of this locus include three fragments of square-based lanceolate bifaces, tools, numerous biface thinning flakes, and debitage, All of these artifacts were manufactured using vitrified basalt from Cerro de la Vuelta. Locus 12 was designated as a lithic workshop. The lanceolate bifaces, displaying overshot flaking, may or may not reflect a Clovis technology.

In order to conduct a controlled collection of the surface artifacts and excavate the lithic workshop, a 5-m by 3-m grid was established and divided into 50-cm by 50-cm units. All surface artifacts were collected and their point proveniences recorded. Each 50-cm by 50-cm unit

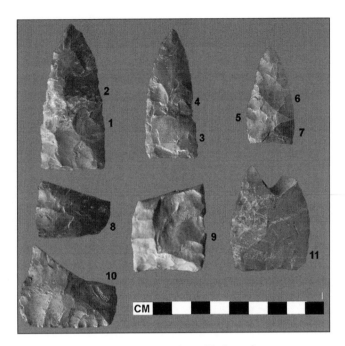

Figure 4.38. Square-based bifaces from Locus 12 workshop at El Bajío.

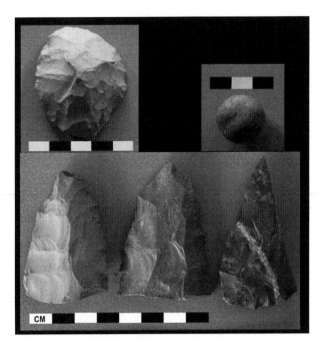

Figure 4.39. Circular scraper, grooved polished sphere, irregular bifaces, and a graver from Locus 12 at El Bajío.

was further subdivided into NE, SE, NW, and SW quadrants, producing 25-cm by 25-cm provenience units.

The lithic workshop was excavated to a depth of 22 cm. Thousands of artifacts were recovered, including biface thinning flakes and 12 square-based projectile point preforms that were broken during their manufacture. Three of the bifaces excavated at Locus 12 could be refitted (Fig.4.38). Although we have not counted the debitage flakes, we estimate that more than 4,000 artifacts were recovered during the excavation of Locus 12. We were unable to excavate this feature in its entirety during the 2003 field season, and an unknown number of artifacts still remain in the lithic workshop. Other artifacts recovered during the excavation include a pebble with an incised groove, a circular scraper, and three fragments of irregular bifaces (Fig. 4.39). Although the technique used to produce the triangular lanceolate bifaces, employing asymmetrical overshot flaking and basal thinning with several small flutes, is suggestive of Clovis technology, these artifacts cannot be positively identified as Clovis. However, at the Blackwater Draw Clovis Site, Warnica (1966:349) reported a similar point. Some of the bifaces at Locus 12 appear to represent finished tools because they display lateral and basal grinding.

The knapping feature with triangular points appears to be resting on a well-developed red paleosol that was covered by much less compacted brownish-red silt. Unit K-5 was excavated below the contact with the red soil, confirming that the artifacts are restricted to the deposits between the surface and the contact with the red soil. A hearth containing charcoal was encountered at the northern edge of the excavation but half of this feature could be excavated because it was found on the last day of the field season (Fig. 4.40). A charcoal sample produced a radiocarbon age of 1980 ± 40 B.P. (B-188544). The triangular biface reduction technique may be related to the Paleoindian lithic technology, so it is possible that the hearth postdates the workshop feature. Points from the Late Archaic or Early Agriculture period, such as San Pedro points, have been collected at El Bajío.

Locus 19

Locus 19 is situated on a small hill in the southwestern sector of the site. A vein of fine-grained basalt is exposed at the surface on the northernmost part of the hill. There are indications at Locus 19 that the inhabitants of El Bajío extracted basalt to manufacture tools. The entire upper portion of the hill is covered with artifacts. Locus 19 encompasses an area of 3,200 square meters (Fig. 4.41). Artifacts include biface fragments, thinning flakes, tested cobbles, hammerstones, and tool sharpening scars in the bedrock. In addition to the fine-grained basalt, there are

Figure 4.40. Hearth at Locus 12 at El Bajío.

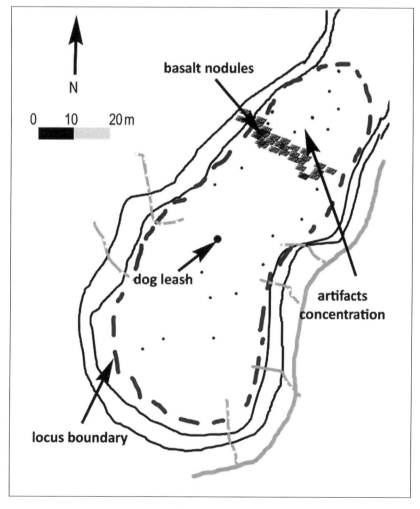

Figure 4.41. Sketch map of Locus 19 at El Bajío.

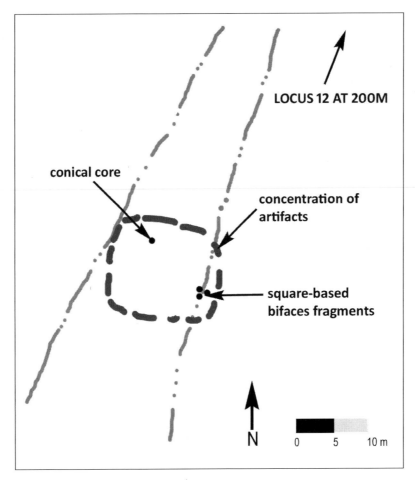

conical core

LOCUS 12 AT 200M

concentration of
artifacts

square-based
bifaces fragments

N

0   5   10 m

Figure 4.42. Sketch map of Locus 22 at El Bajío.

small (2- to 3-cm diameter) nodules of obsidian that may have been used for tool making. Although there were no Paleoindian diagnostic tools recovered in Locus 19, there were some Clovis artifacts made from obsidian and fine basalt.

Locus 22

Locus 22 is a dense artifact scatter extending over a 6-m by 8-m area (Fig. 4.42). It is located 100 m south of Locus 12, in the same small depression. The lithic artifacts at Locus 22 appear to represent a knapping station or lithic reduction workshop similar to that at Locus 12. Artifacts include a conical core, three fragments of square-based bifaces, and over 200 biface thinning flakes. Although this component is close to the present surface, it appears to be affiliated with the Paleoindian period. We did not collect artifacts at Locus 22 because we are contemplating further investigation of the locus.

El Bajío Site Summary and Conclusions of the Investigations

There is no doubt that El Bajío is one of the most important Clovis localites in Sonora. The vitrified basalt quarry at El Bajío stimulated the gathering of family groups, and provided an important resource for Paleoindian and Archaic groups in Sonora. El Bajío is the only extensive large quarry of fine stones for manufacturing tools known in Sonora. Although we did not find buried Clovis deposits during our work at El Bajío, we are confident that more extensive excavations at the site will reveal buried Paleoindian deposits. We think this because there are many intact artifacts that have not been subjected to weathering and we found a proboscidean tooth at Locus 3.

Although the vitrified basalt exposure is unquestionably the single most important resource at El Bajío, quartz crystals, red ochre, and obsidian were also important. The existence of well-defined loci at El Bajío indicates this complex site was important in Paleoindian patterns of residential mobility and land use. Although no springs or spring deposits were documented at the site, the existence of black clay deposits indicates that water accumulated in a low sink near the group of loci in the vicinity of Cerro Rojo. This area may have been fed by runoff from the pediment and small sierrita that includes Cerro de la Vuelta. Loci 3 to 6 and 15 in the middle of the site, together with Locus 7 west and north of Cerro Rojo, are the most important areas at the site. In addition to having a high potential for buried contexts, these loci suggest that this area was used repeatedly on an annual basis over a long span of time during the Paleoindian and subsequent periods. We think it is significant that El Bajío is located in a transitional zone between two different landscapes: the intervening basins of Sonora and the broad alluvial plain of the Río Zanjón that remains open terrain from El Bajío to the coast.

During the 2003 season a field strategy was implemented to collect all the diagnostic artifacts found during a systematic survey of El Bajío, including sherds, Archaic points, Paleoindian points, and other Paleoindian artifacts. To obtain a representative sample of artifacts, collections were also made at archaeological features and controlled surface collections were made in other areas of the site. The collections from El Bajío, housed at the Centro INAH Sonora, include 15,000 lithics, including flakes and debris that are impossible to affiliate to a particular period. The collection from the Paleoindian period includes 333 diagnostic tools than can be correlated to diagnostic types at Clovis sites in the United States, including collections from the Pavo Real, Gault, and Adams sites. It is significant that we did not find any late Paleoindian projectile points at El Bajío, such as Folsom, Dalton, or Golondrina points. The lack of late Paleoindian points suggests that the polyhedral cores, blades, end scrapers, and other tools at El Bajío are probably affiliated with the Clovis occupation of the site. During the 2003 season, 150 diagnostic Paleoindian artifacts were collected even though extensive collections had been made at site over the preceding 30 years. This suggests that buried archaeological features remain intact and that recent erosion is exposing artifacts. The Archaic period at El Bajío is represented by 20 points collected in 2003, the majority of which are associated with the Elko, San Pedro, and Pinto-San Jose types.

El Bajío is a complex site. Archaic components are present at the site, and the most conspicuous features are roasting pits that apparently postdate the Clovis occupation. Three radiocarbon dates obtained from El Bajío roasting pits establish that these features are dated to the late prehistoric and protohistoric periods. Nonetheless, at Ventana Cave an horno dating to about 8700 B.P was associated with fire-cracked rocks and informal ground stone (Huckell and Haynes 2003), and at the Wilson-Leonard Site hornos were dated to 9300 B.P., the earliest known hornos in Texas (Bousman and others 2002:988). It may be that some of the hornos at El Bajío date to the Paleoindian period.

El Bajío has been severely eroded, with some limited deposition. Erosional and depositional segments are distributed in a patchwork manner across the site. The presence of proboscidean tooth enamel, buried artifacts, and features indicates the existence of areas where buried Clovis contexts may be found, and supports the need for further systematic investigation at the site. Although we learned much during our work at El Bajío, our research unfortunately remains inconclusive. In part this is because we didn't have a good understanding of the distribution of terminal Pleistocene deposits at the site until the end of our single season of fieldwork. With the knowledge gained from additional radiocarbon dates obtained after our fieldwork, we think returning to the loci likely to contain Paleoindian material to search for buried contexts will be productive. Investigation of this significant Clovis site should continue.

SON O:3:1

SON O:3:1 is located on both sides of Highway 16 (La Colorada-Sahuaripa), approximately 10 km northeast of the mining town of La Colorada. The site is situated in the Río Mátape drainage basin between the Sierra de la Colorada and another mountain range. SON O:3:1 is situated on open, rolling terrain where numerous east-west trending arroyos discharge into the Río Mátape, a perennial drainage with a substantial subsurface flow. Although water may not be evident in the arroyo bed of Río Mátape, it can be easily obtained by shallow digging. At the historic Rancho El Aígame, a few kilometers east of SON O:3:1 near the Río Mátape, water is obtained from shallow wells less than 6 m deep.

SON O:3:1 extends over an eroded zone between two tributary arroyos at an elevation of 450 m above sea level. Río Mátape is in the Basin and Range physiographic province, with a Sonoran Plains Grasslands biotic community. The annual precipitation in this area is 400 mm, which supports grasses and perennial shrubs. The most prevalent grass species are *Bouteloua bothrockii*, *Aristida* sp., and *Panicum obtusum*, which grow alongside shrubby plants like ragweed (*Ambrosia* sp.), purslane (*Portulaca* sp.), and mesquite (*Prosopis velutina*). The grasslands also contain a few cacti (Brown 1994:137). Excessive exploitation of aquifers through groundwater pumping has diminished the available moisture in the subtropical grassland mosaics of the region, provoking their gradual transformation to Sonoran desert scrub. Water has existed in the basin of the Río Mátape for a long time, and there are abundant subterranean aquifers where water from the sierra has accumulated.

Javier Bustamante, an engineer who specialized in mining of graphite, discovered the site in 1971. With the participation of Manuel Robles, Javier Bustamante began to collect artifacts from the site, and he continued to do so for the next 20 years. Unfortunately, Javier Bustamante died in the winter of 2005, and his artifact collection remains in his family's hands. His collection includes two mammoth molars (Fig. 4.43), three Clovis points, several bifaces, approximately 40 end scrapers, one modified blade, and at least 100 biface thinning flakes made of quartzite, basalt and different types of chert that he found eroding from an erosional profile. Most of the lithic material was concentrated in a few areas, but not in proximity to the teeth.

I visited the site with Javier Bustamante in March 2005 and determined that the majority of Bustamante's collection was recovered from one small, well-defined and heavily eroded area. During the 2005 visit, we found an end scraper and a fluted Clovis point base in that area.

SON O:3:1 was systematically investigated because the site has an unquestionable Clovis component, the artifacts in the Bustamante collection represent a wide range of activities suggestive of a Clovis encampment, and the minimal fossilization evident on the well-preserved mammoth molars suggests the presence of late Pleistocene contexts.

Figure 4.43. Mammoth molars collected by Javier Bustamante at SON O:3:1.

The site encompasses an area 2.5 km north-south by 1.5 km east-west. We identified 28 loci, demonstrating that SON O:3:1 is a complex site that was occupied for a long period of time (Table 4.3). Ten loci had an exclusive Paleoindian affiliation, six yielded both Paleoindian and Archaic artifacts, nine produced only Archaic diagnostic artifacts, three appeared affiliated with the Early Agriculture period, and one contained ceramic artifacts. Radiocarbon samples from Loci 2, 3, and 4 yielded Early Agricultural period dates (Table 4.4). It was decided to conduct further investigations in four localities where there were possible buried Paleoindian deposits.

Table 4.3. Cultural Affiliations of the Loci Identified at SON O:3:1

Cultural Affiliation	Locus Number	Total
Paleoindian	1, 2, 3, 4, 6, 11, 12, 15, 28, 29	10
Paleoindian/Archaic	7, 14, 16, 17, 23, 24	6
Archaic	5, 8, 9, 13, 20, 21, 22, 25, 26	9
Early Agricultural	10, 18, 19	3
Ceramic	27	1
	TOTAL	29

Table 4.4. Radiocarbon Dates from SON O:3:1

Sample no.	Locus	Excavation Unit	^{14}C Date (B.P.)	Material Dated	Stratigraphic Unit
AA66509	3	Pozo 5	4009 ± 42	Charcoal	Cienega deposit
AA66497	4	Profile 1	4864 ± 74	Soil residue	Upper mud
AA66498	4	Profile 1	3558 ± 46	Soil residue	Lower mud
AA66499	2	Arroyo profile	4951 ± 55	Soil residue	Upper mud
AA66500	2	Arroyo profile	4843 ± 52	Soil residue	Lower mud

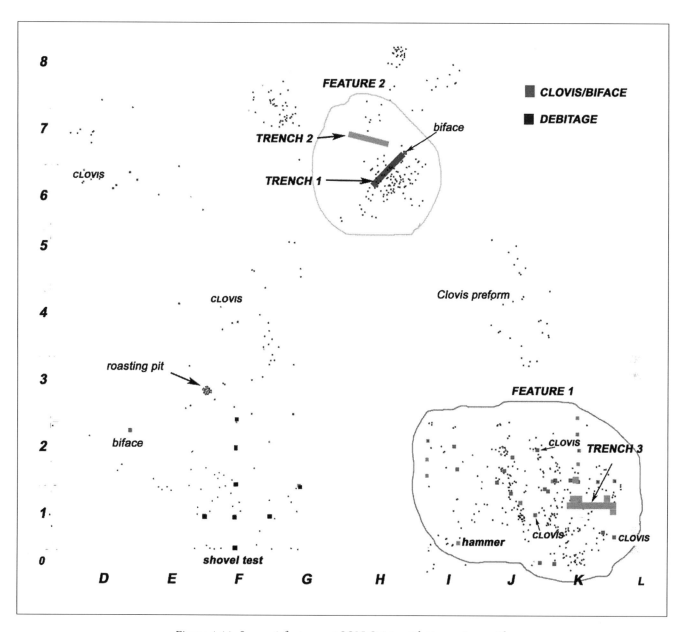

Figure 4.44. Locus 1 features at SON O:3:1, with 5-m × 5-m grid.

Locus 1 is located in the north-central area of the site. We investigated this area because there were 15 large fragments of bifaces on the surface that appeared to have been made using a Paleoindian lithic technology. Three of these bifaces showed possible channel flake removal from the base. Associated with these bifaces, were 300 lithic artifacts that included hundreds of biface thinning flakes, other flakes, and hammerstones in a 100-m by 100-m area. Two areas were defined as possible tool-making features (Fig. 4.44).

Feature 1 is located in a low-lying area in the southwest corner of Locus 1. There, 258 lithic artifacts were collected, including one complete biface and 11 fragments of bifaces, many with clear evidence of basal thinning (Table 4.5). Six of the bifaces were made using the same relatively fine red quartzite (Fig. 4.45), and one was made using high quality chert (Fig. 4.46). Hammers and abraders made from quartz crystal were also recovered (Fig. 4.47), together with hundreds of flakes and biface thinning flakes of the same raw material. The appearance

Table 4.5. Lithic Classes in Locus 1, Feature 1

Material Type	Flakes and Debitage	Biface	Core Tool	Archaic Point	Uniface	Hammer and Abrader	Total
Red quarzite	154	6		2			162
Basalt	60	4	1	2			67
Agate	3	1			1		5
Chert	7	1					8
Obsidian	3						3
Quartz crystal	7					4	11
Rhyolite	1		1				2
TOTAL	235	12	2	4	1	4	258

Figure 4.45. Red quartzite biface from Locus 1, Feature 2, at SON O:3:1.

Figure 4.47. Quartzite abrader from Locus 1 at SON O:3:1.

Figure 4.46. Chert biface from Locus 1, Feature 2, at SON O:3:1.

of surface bifaces and flakes made using the same materials suggests that the feature was recently exposed on the surface. This indicates there is a possibility of finding a buried Paleoindian context at this location. No dateable materials were found in this deposit.

Locus 2, located in the northern portion of the site, encompasses a moderate scatter of artifacts where three large Archaic basalt bifaces were collected (Fig. 4.48). Ten obsidian unifacial artifacts were observed, and three tapering stem points from the early Holocene period were also collected at this locus. Test pits were excavated in the areas presenting the highest concentrations of artifacts, exposing sediments consisting of a recent loose alluvium.

Figure 4.48. Archaic bifaces
from Locus 2 at SON O:3:1.

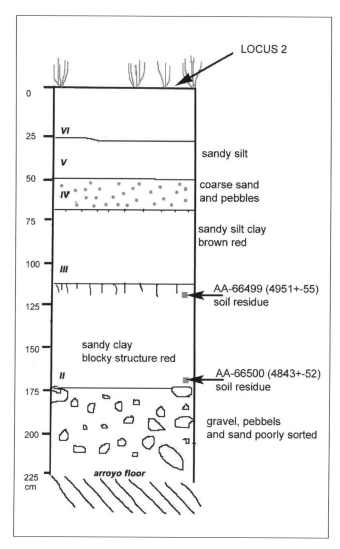

Figure 4.49. Profile of the arroyo
adjacent to Locus 2 at SON O:3:1.

An important part of our investigations at SON O:3:1 was to find intact stratigraphy that could be profiled for use in determining the geochronology of the site (Fig. 4.49). In a deep arroyo adjacent to Locality 2, we found a dark clay organic mud horizon more than a meter below the surface from which we obtained soil samples for radiocarbon dating. The lower mud gave a radiocarbon age of 4843 ± 42 B.P. (AA66500) and the upper mud an age of 4951 ± 55 B.P. (AA66499). The date obtained from the arroyo profile indicates that Locus 2 is a middle-to-late Archaic component that could contain intact archaeological features. Further investigation of this feature will be significant in understanding the Archaic period, which is poorly known in Sonora.

Locus 3, referred to by Bustamante as the KM site, includes the 70-m by 70-m area where Bustamante obtained the majority of his collection (Javier Bustamante, personal communication 2005). Three Paleoindian bifaces (Figs. 4.50 and 4.51); aproximately 40 end scrapers, many of them spurred and manufactured on blades (Fig. 4.52); and hundreds of flakes were recovered at Locus 3. During our first visit to the site, we found a Clovis point base that was fluted on both faces (Fig. 4.53). Later in the season, we found two end scrapers. A systematic survey of the entire area was conducted, and a trench (Unit 4) and a test pit (Unit 5) were excavated by hand. All the excavated deposits were screened using a 5-mm mesh. Trench 4 had a red paleosol (Bk horizon) that was heavily reworked into the more recent Holocene alluvial sediments. Unfortunately, no artifacts were found in the excavation.

Figure 4.50. Clovis preforms collected
by Bustamante at Locus 3 at SON O:3:1.

Figure 4.51. Red quartz lanceolate point collected by Bustamante at Locus 3 at SON O:3:1.

Figure 4.53. Basalt Clovis base found at Locus 3 at SON O:3:1.

Figure 4.52. End scrapers collected by Bustamante at Locus 3 at SON O:3:1.

Although no buried archaeological features of Paleo-indian age were found at this locality, excavation of Unit 5 revealed a cienega-like stratum of dark, well-developed soil composed of clay and sand (Fig. 4.54). This stratum was almost 80 cm thick. Charcoal recovered from the bottom of the dark stratum yielded a radiocarbon date of 4009 ± 42 B.P. (AA66509). The pollen profile obtained from Unit 5 was analyzed by Susana Xelhuantzi from the Archaeobotanical Laboratory of the Subdirección de Laboratorios, INAH. The pollen concentration in the samples was very low, and the sample was full of silica. However, the pollen samples from the cienega deposit contained fungi, algae, mosses, and ferns, which are consistent with a wet environment (Xelhuantzi 2008). At the bottom of the cienega soil, about 70 cm below the surface, a maize phytolith was found that is probably 4000

Figure 4.54. Test Pit 5 at SON O:3:1, showing location of pollen profile and ¹⁴C sample.

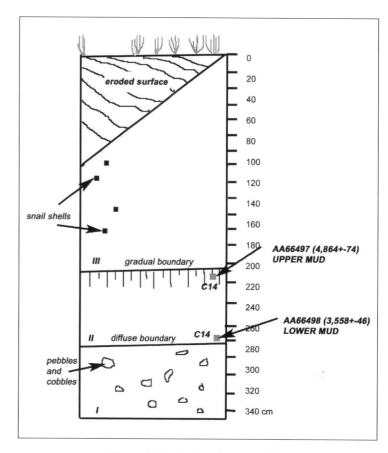

Figure 4.55. Profile of cienega-like deposit at Locus 4 at SON O:3:1.

years old. Ash, walnuts and alder pollen were observed in the samples, but none of these species are present today at the locality (Xelhuantzi 2008).

Locus 4 is situated along a drainage at the south end of SON O:3:1. The fine silt with carbonates at this locus resembles cienega deposits. At Locus 4, we recovered two fragments of an ultra-thin biface manufactured using a Paleoindian technology, along with some bison bones. Bustamante told us that he collected mammoth molars from this general area. Here, the sediments were profiled, and soil from the clayey cienega-like deposit was radiocarbon dated to 4,000 years ago (Fig. 4.55).

Summary of Investigations at SON O:3:1

In sum, SON O:3:1 is a multicomponent site with a long record of human occupation that started during Paleoindian times and extended throughout the Archaic and Early Agriculture periods. It is possible that there are some buried Pleistocene deposits left in Locus 1 and 3, where Bustamante made his Clovis collection. It is also

possible that other loci at the site contain buried deposits, but in the absence of test excavations this could not be determined. In the four stratigraphic profiles of the site that we documented, a dark brown horizon—possibly an A horizon—was observed and dated to middle Holocene times, between 5000 to 4000 B.P. The maize phytolith identified at Test Pit No. 5 in Locus 3 is associated with this period of high humidity.

At Loci 1 and 3, the presence of Clovis points, bifaces, end scrapers, blades, and bifacial thining flakes made on fine raw materials appear to represent one or more Clovis encampments. The red paleosol from the Pleistocene era probably formed the surface on which the Clovis people lived. The water table is high at SON O:3:1. At the nearby Aigame Ranch, a well is only 6 m deep. In the past, it is possible that surface water was available at SON O:3:1 several times during the year. This would have made SON O:3:1 important for the survival of animals and humans. The Clovis people at this site used locally available quartzite, basalt, and siltstone to make tools. One biface and many end scrapers in the Bustamante collection were made using a diversity of fine cherts. Twelve end scrapers in the Bustamante collection were manufactured on blades; however, no conical, tablet, or wedge-shaped blade cores have been found at the site. Although only one Clovis end scraper from the Bustamante collection was made from obsidian, this material was used to produce many of the Archaic projectile points at SON O:3:1. We found Apache tears (obsidian nodules) in the basalt hills near the site. In one of the arroyos that cut through the site we found a source of ochre or hematite in a 30-cm wide vein. We know that red pigments were important to Clovis and Archaic peoples, although we did not find any Clovis features in this area of the site. There is no doubt that SON O:3:1 was a valuable location for the hunting and gathering groups of the Paleoindian and Archaic periods. Future research at this site will yield important information for understanding the cultural development of prehistoric Sonora.

EL GRAMAL (SON N:11:20-21)

El Gramal encompasses a large site complex on the Hermosillo Plains, 60 km southwest of Hermosillo. The site lies about 18 km from the modern-day shoreline of the Sea of Cortez. El Gramal consists of a dense, multi-component artifact scatter covering more than 10 km². The artifacts are on the edge of a large playa encompassing 3 km² (Fig. 4.56), and the scatter extends several kilometers to the north and west into extensive dune fields (Fig. 4.57).

Figure 4.56. The playa at El Gramal, looking east.

El Gramal lies within the Río Sonora hydrologic basin, at an elevation of 25 m above sea level. The vegetative cover at the site is typical of the Central Coast subdivision of the Sonoran Desert (Turner and Brown 1994:212). El Gramal falls within the cactus-mesquite-saltbush vegetative community. There are six different species of columnar cacti at the site: hecho (*Pachycereus pecten-aboriginum*), cardón (*Pachycereus pringlei*), saguaro (*Carnegiea gigantea*), senita (*Lophocereus schotti*), organ pipe (*Stenocereus thurberi*), and sina (*Stenocereus alamosensis*). Various saltwater and sandy-soil tolerant shrubs also occur at El Gramal (Turner and Brown 1994:215).

Local collectors amassed a collection of 41 projectile points and bifaces dated to the Paleoindian period from five localities within El Gramal. Twenty-one of the points have classic Clovis fluting and 20 are unfluted lanceolate varieties (Gaines and others 2009a). The Paleoindian materials are generally found on the eroded flanks of the dunes adjacent to the playa margins. The dunes contain at least three buried soils, and the Clovis material seems to come from the lowest and best-developed soil that forms a resistant ledge where it is eroded. In our research, we rely on the provenience of the Paleoindian artifacts established by the private collectors who collected them. The intensive surface collection of El Gramal began in the early 1970s and continues to the present. The Paleoindian occupation is well represented at this site, as are the Archaic and Ancestral Seri periods.

Geoarchaeological Investigation

Geoarchaeological investigation of El Gramal was carried out in January and February of 2007. During this period, we only found one fluted base of a probable Paleoindian artifact on the surface. Later Archaic and Seri occupations, however, are well represented. Our field methods employed comprehensive bucket augering and limited hand trenching. Radiocarbon samples were collected and submitted to the University of Arizona NSF AMS facility. Aeolian sand samples were analyzed by the University of Washington Luminescence Laboratory using the multi-grain single-aliquot pulsed optically stimulated luminescence (OSL) method.

Loci 1, 2, and 5 are located in the dunes on the western margin of the playa. According to the collectors, a complete quartz crystal fluted point was found at Locus 1 (Fig. 4.58), as well as a chert fluted point that was resharpened into an awl or drill. These artifacts were recovered from a low-density lithic scatter on the side of a large dune (Leopoldo Velez, personal communication 2007). One

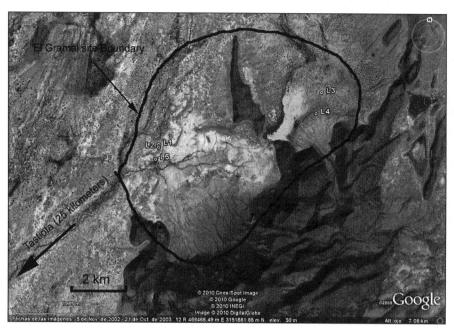

Figure 4.57. Google Earth image of El Gramal and localities. Map data © 2010 Google, INEGI, Digital Globe, CNES/SPOT Image.

Figure 4.58. Quartz crystal Clovis point from Locus 1 at El Gramal.

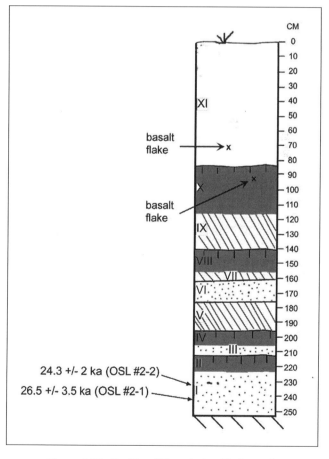

Figure 4.59. Profile of Trench 1 at El Gramal.

trench and several auger test pits were excavated at this locus. Local stratigraphy consists of interfingered sands and playa muds with a sequence of three buried soil horizons to a depth of 5.5 m beneath the surface (Fig. 4.59). We think this stratigraphy dates to the late Pleistocene and Holocene periods.

Locus 2 yielded both fluted and unfluted lanceolate points, mostly basal fragments made from local basalt and obsidian. Trenching at Locus 2 revealed

Figure 4.60. Probable fluted biface on basalt.

dune stratigraphy with two buried soils. There were intact, stratified archaeological remains throughout this sequence. Artifacts from a late prehistoric Seri occupation—sherds, groundstone fragments, shell, and flaked stone—occur within the upper deposit in a zone of recent-to-modern soil formation. The middle buried soil horizon contains lithic debitage and shell fragments indicative of a preceramic Archaic horizon. The nearby Paleoindian artifacts are thought to be associated with the basal stratum of a well-developed, buried soil.

Loci 3 and 4 are located in an expanse of low dunes and blowouts on the northeast margin of the playa. According to the collectors, both loci yielded unfluted lanceolate bifaces and projectile points. The stratigraphy in this area generally consists of shallow dune sands overlying deposits of silts, sands, and muds to a depth of six or more meters. Artifacts at Loci 3 and 4 are much more diffuse than at the other three loci, and buried remains have yet to be documented in these two areas.

A possible fluted biface fragment made using basalt was found on the surface at Locus 5 (Fig. 4.60). Subsequent geologic coring in the immediate vicinity recovered two basalt flakes at depths of 3.5 to 3.6 m (Figs. 4.61 and 4.62). This level is estimated to be 8,000 years old.

Although we did not conduct a systematic survey of El Gramal, we identified an obsidian source on a small hill to the south of Locus 5. This obsidian occurs in small 2-cm to 6-cm diameter nodules (Apache tears). The concentration of obsidian nodules extends over a 600-m by 600-m area. The presence of obsidian reduction flakes confirms the prehistoric exploitation of this raw material source. At least five Clovis points made using obsidian were picked up by private collectors at the site.

Figure 4.61. Ned Gaines and Beto Peña using an auger to dig a test pit at Locus 5 at El Gramal.

Figure 4.62. Flakes found 3.5 m below surface during testing at Locus 5 at El Gramal.

Stratigraphy and Geochronology of El Gramal

El Gramal exhibits a complex stratigraphic sequence consisting of more than 4 m of aeolian sands, alluvial silts and clays, and playa muds (Fig. 4.63). In one auger test, we excavated to a depth of 7.6 m but we did not obtain a radiocarbon sample from that unit. In general, there are seven defined stratigraphic units. From the

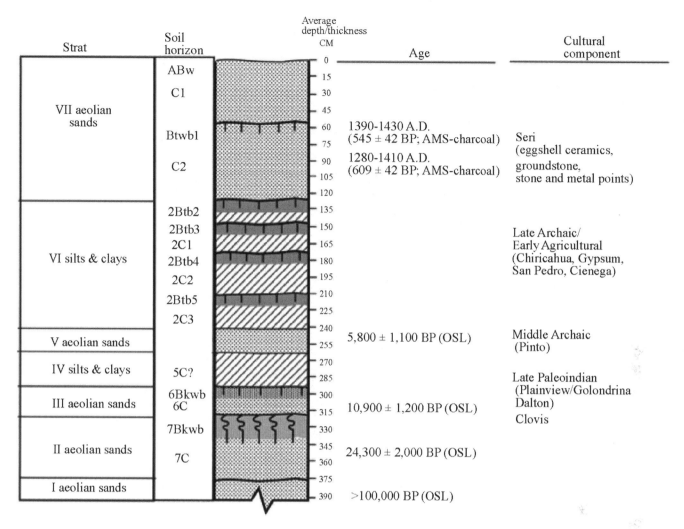

Figure 4.63. Generalized stratigraphy of El Gramal.

bottom up, they are Unit I, II, and III sands; Unit IV silts and clays; Unit V sands; Unit VI silts and clays; and Unit VII sands. Our limited testing identified in situ archaeological components in Units VI and VII. The site preserves a nearly complete record of late Quaternary aeolian and alluvial deposits spanning the last 25,000 years. This stratigraphic sequence exhibits alternating periods of alluvial and aeolian deposition, punctuated by periods of erosion, stability, and soil formation. The site has yielded surface artifacts diagnostic of nearly every phase of human occupation known in the Sonoran Desert over the past 12,000 years (Gaines and others 2009a).

Paleoindian occupation of El Gramal is evidenced by the 20 fluted points and 21 unfluted lanceolate points in a private collection, which represents more than 30 years of constant collecting. The trampling, patina, and battering seen on the artifacts indicate that they have been on the surface for a long period of time. In fact, many of the artifacts were modified by Archaic people. The lack of other diagnostic Paleoindian materials such as blades, polyhedral cores, and end scrapers may indicate that the playa at El Gramal was not used as a campsite. It could be difficult, if not impossible, to find buried Paleoindian deposits at the site. No diagnostic Paleoindian artifacts were found during our geoarchaeological investigation.

SON J:16:8

Three Clovis points are known from SON J:16:8, and there is a fourth, unconfirmed Clovis point reported for the site. SON J:16:8 is a diffuse, multicomponent site located 20 km west of Hermosillo. Two of the Clovis points reported by Manuel Robles (1974) are currently in the museum of the Universidad de Sonora, while the third point is in the hands of a collector in Bahia Kino (Fig. 4.64). Robles filled out a site card with a sketch map for SON J:16:8, and prepared a report that is on file in the Centro INAH Sonora archives. Robles' map and descriptions helped us locate the highest concentration of Paleoindian artifacts at the site.

SON J:16:8 is situated in a small basin, without evidence of recent erosion. There is no arroyo cut exposing the subsurface stratigraphy of the site (Fig. 4.65), so auguring was used to obtain stratigraphic information.

The Paleoindian materials at SON J:16:8 apparently occur along the margins of the basin. The augur testing of the buried stratigraphic contexts revealed a sequence

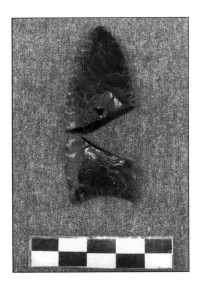

Figure 4.64. Obsidian Clovis point from SON J:16:8.

Figure 4.65. Basin at SON J:16:8, looking north.

of silt, sands, and intact clays to a depth of at least 6.5 m. The depths of the basal sediments indicate a paleotopographic basin, with the artifacts located on its margins. Although the geoarchaeological work at SON J:16:8 is preliminary, the site has been demonstrated to include buried stratigraphic deposits and the site has great potential for containing the remains of Paleoindian occupations. The basin was filled with colluvial and alluvial sediments, but we were unable to date them using OSL techniques because no material suitable for dating was encountered.

An obsidian source was identified along the southern edge of the site. The obsidian occurs in small nodules ranging between 2 and 10 cm in diameter. Two of the Clovis points collected from SON J:16:8 are made of obsidian but we did not confirm whether they were produced using the obsidian from the source at the southern edge of SON J:16:8.

FIN DEL MUNDO (SON J:6:2)

Fin del Mundo (End of the Earth) is located in a small intermontane basin about 650 m above sea level, within a chain of unnamed volcanic hills about 100 km northwest of Hermosillo. The site is exposed in an eroded landscape that drains into the Arroyo Carrizo. The valley of the Carrizo drains the intermontane basin and flows into the Río Bacoachi, which in turn flows to the south and southwest into the Gulf of California.

The plant community at Fin del Mundo is represented by a combination of Arizona Upland and Lower Colorado plant communities (Turner and Brown 1994). The area is dominated by ocotillo (*Fouquieria splendens*), creosote bush (*Larrea tridentata*), bursage (*Ambrosia deltoidea*), bush muhly (*Muhlenbergia porteri*), and several species of *Opuntia* associated with the Arizona Upland community. The dominant tree is ironwood (*Olneya tesota*), and at least two different kinds of agaves are present. Northeast of the site, there is a dense saguaro bosque (*Carnegiea gigantea*) and a dense stand of agaves.

In 1997, during a visit to the municipal museum in Carbó, Sonora, C. Vance Haynes and I observed an unfossilized mammoth femur and rib. We were told that these bones had been recovered from a ranch that was a four-hour drive from Carbó. Although the owner of the ranch invited us to visit his property, we had to decline his offer due to the time and distance involved in traveling there. A decade later, the Proyecto Geoarqueología y Tecnología Lítica de los Sitios Paleoindios de Sonora was established, and one of the principal objectives in the Spring 2007 field season was to visit all of the known localities where Paleoindian remains had been reported in Sonora. The remote ranch in the Municipio of Pitiquito, where more than 30 years earlier minimally fossilized bones of a mammoth had been found and subsequently displayed in a local municipal museum, was on our list of places to visit.

We visited Fin del Mundo on February 5, 2007. The site was used by Clovis groups that hunted and butchered proboscideans, including two juvenile gomphotheres (*Cuvieronius* sp.) as well as other Pleistocene mammals. The gomphotheres found at Fin del Mundo are significant because this animal was previously thought to have become extinct in North America around 35,000 years ago (Sánchez and others 2014).

The bones at Fin del Mundo are preserved in cienega deposits. There is an associated Clovis camp and a source of quartz crystal raw material located on top of a nearby hill. Projectile points and other artifacts at Fin del Mundo were manufactured using this raw material. Fin del Mundo is the first Pleistocene megafauna hunting or butchering site discovered in Mexico since 1957. Importantly, Fin del Mundo is the first site that we found in Sonora that has not been collected by amateur archaeologists.

The Pleistocene fauna occurs in a remnant of stratified deposits that are preserved as an "island" in an eroded landscape (Fig. 4.66). While examining exposed profiles, we observed a chalcedony chopper that had recently fallen from the wall profile from the uppermost stratum associated with the Pleistocene fauna. Shortly thereafter, a large rhyolite Clovis-style biface was found 3 m from the island. We also found the middle portion of a quartz crystal biface and a complete Clovis point of white chert 8 m south of the island (Fig. 4.67).

In four field seasons of investigations at Fin del Mundo, we determined that the complex site contains at least 10 significant localities where Pleistocene people engaged in multiple activities. These activities included acquiring lithic raw materials, tool knapping, camping, and hunting Pleistocene animals.

Locus 1

Locus 1, the most important area of Fin del Mundo, encompasses an eroded landscape with bones and artifacts exposed in a profile (Fig. 4.68). Locus 1 covers an area of roughly 100 m by 100 m. The erosional dissection of Fin del Mundo left the local basin fill exposed in head cuts and on a series of erosional islands. The bone

Figure 4.66. View of the "island" at Locus 1 at Fin del Mundo, looking NW.

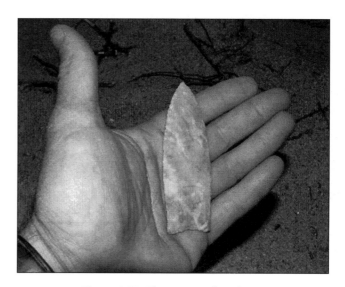

Figure 4.67. Clovis point found 8 m south of Locus 1 at Fin del Mundo.

beds, artifacts, and archaeological sediments associated with one of these islands at Locus 1 have a completely different stratigraphy than all other exposures at the site. Geomorphic and stratigraphic relations cannot be fully reconstructed across the site because erosion has removed sediments, isolating Locality 1. At Locus 1, three strata (2 to 4, bottom to top) rest on local bedrock.

Strata 3 and 4 filled a channel less than 100 m wide, of undetermined length, that cut into Stratum 2. Stratum 2 is up to 3 m thick, and is composed of pebbly-sandy clay fining upward into a sandy clay. Rare proboscidean bones were recovered from the lower portion of

Figure 4.68. Excavation at Locus 1 at Fin del Mundo.

Stratum 2. A likely equivalent to Stratum 2 forms most of the exposures surrounding Locus 1, and these deposits are at or near the surface where they are modified by soil development. On top of the soil is a carbonate layer up to 60 cm thick. The massive character, uniform density, and presence of both aquatic and terrestrial gastropods in the carbonate suggest that it was formed by a seep or spring.

Stratum 3 has a pale olive color. It is composed of unbedded, poorly sorted pebbly-sandy clay up to 1 m thick (3A), overlain by a poorly sorted sandy clay (3B).

Stratum 3 rests unconformably on Stratum 2. Bone is common throughout Stratum 3. The pebbly character of some components of Stratum 3 and the appearance of the cut-and-fill sequences indicates cyclical aggradation. The poorly sorted character of the stratum suggests variable discharge throughout deposition. These two conditions and the short transport distance indicated by the pebbles suggest deposition in spring-fed waters. The upper bone bed that was the focus of our work is in Stratum 3, which is buried by diatomite (Fig. 4.69).

Figure 4.69. Upper bone bed containing gomphothere remains in Stratum 3, Locus 1, at Fin del Mundo.

Stratum 4 is up to 1 m thick and rests unconformably on Stratum 3. The interface between Strata 3 and 4 is essentially horizontal through most of the Locus 1 island, except for the west end of the island, where the strata gradually rise. The base of Stratum 4 is a discontinuous layer of diatomite up to 10 cm thick. Most of the rest of Stratum 4 is gray, silty diatomaceous earth. The diatomite represents standing-water conditions, and the diatomaceous earth represents more marshy conditions with organic-matter production in a wet setting. This sequence is similar to the Paleoindian geoarchaeology at the Lubbock Lake and Clovis sites, as well as other localities on the Southern High Plains (Haynes 1975, 1995; Holliday 1985, 1997). No weathering was observed in upper Stratum 3, so we think the diatomite probably was deposited shortly after the upper bone bed was created.

The bone, teeth, and tusk identified in Strata 3 and 4 are from late Pleistocene mammals. The teeth are from horse (*Equus*); some bone is *Bison*. Other unidentifiable bone is from a bison-sized ungulate. Proboscidean bones and teeth recovered from all three strata were identified as either mastodon or gomphothere. All of the bone at Stratum 3, interpreted as a hunting feature, is from a gomphothere (Individual No. 2) or an unidentified proboscidean (Individual No. 1) that was the same size as Individual No. 2 and therefore probably another gomphothere. Archaeological material was found in and immediately below the gomphothere bone bed. Flakes and a unifacial tool were recovered at the stratigraphic position of the bone, resting on Stratum 3 and buried by the Stratum 4 diatomite. Additional flakes and four Clovis points were recovered less than 10 cm below the bone bed, in the upper portion of Stratum 3.

The excavations carried out at Locus 1 during four seasons revealed that a Late Pleistocene archaeological feature was preserved in situ in Stratum 3B. Semi-articulated bones from two gomphotheres were preserved, along with an occupational surface in association with 31 stone and bone artifacts (Figs. 4.70 and 4.71). During the 2011 season, three Clovis points and a 3-cm flake were found in situ within the gomphothere hunting feature, and in

Figure 4.70. Clovis points from Locus 1 at Fin del Mundo found in disturbed (A) and in situ (B) contexts.

Figure 4.71. Seven flakes and a bone artifact found in situ at Locus 1 at Fin del Mundo.

2012 an additional Clovis point was found under the gomphothere mandible. Two additional Paleoindian projectile points—a complete fluted point made of quartz crystal and a complete point made from reddish brown chert—were found near the gomphothere bones, albeit from disturbed contexts.

The artifact inventory thus includes four in situ Clovis points (three complete and one broken), 12 in situ flakes (fine retouched flakes and bifacial thinning flakes), and three bone artifacts. Nine flakes were recovered in the screen but their provenience was established within a 50-cm by 50-cm grid unit. The Clovis points, flakes, burned bone, and bone ornaments recovered at Locus 1 provide secure evidence of a human association with the gomphotheres. This assemblage suggests that Clovis

people hunted the two proboscideans in this locality. Seven Clovis points were recovered from Locus 1, including the four Clovis points found in situ within the feature, and the three Clovis points found in disturbed contexts around the "island." A complete Clovis point (No. 63177) made using local rhyolite and measuring 9.5 cm long, was found southwest of the Gomphothere No. 2 mandible. Teeth and bone fragments were found above and under the Clovis point, suggesting that the point was lost in the head and neck area of the animal. Twenty-one flakes (12 flakes in situ and nine in the screen) were recovered from the feature.

The flakes include fine retouched flakes and bifacial thinning flakes, and these were probably produced in the process of retouching various tools. The largest flake

Table 4.6. Radiocarbon Dates from Locus 1, Fin del Mundo

Sample	Stratum and Context	¹⁴C Date (B.P.)	Lab Number
Shell	4, diatomaceous earth	7840 ± 70	AA81350
Organic-rich sediment	4, diatomaceous earth	8375 ± 110	A-14837
Organic-rich sediment	4, diatomaceous earth	9030 ± 75	A-14850
Organic-rich sediment	4, diatomaceous earth	9465 ± 100	A-14836
Charcoal	4, top of diatomite	9290 ± 290	AA80085
Charcoal	4, top of diatomite	9560 ± 120	AA80671
Charcoal	4, top of diatomite	9715 ± 64	AA80084
Organic-rich sediment	3, in upper bone bed featuee	11,040 ± 580	AA83272
Charcoal	3B/3A, at 12.06 mbd, associated with a rhyolite flake	11,560 ± 140	AA100181
Charcoal (humate date)	3B/3A, at 12.10 mbd	11,800 ± 200	AA100182

measures 3.2 cm, while the smallest flake measures 0.4 cm. The flakes were found directly associated with the bone concentrations and the adjoining area. Flake No. 63448 was associated with a charcoal fragment that was dated at 11,560 ± 140 B.P., calibrated at 13,339 years ago (No. AA100181) (Table 4.6). This flake is 0.7 cm long and was made of the same rhyolite material used to produce one of the complete Clovis points (No. 63177). A burned bone and two bone artifacts were recovered from the area between the two gomphotheres. Most of the lithics were produced using local raw materials. Several points were produced using chert that is common in the channel gravels in the area.

Camp Areas and Lithic Sources at Fin del Mundo

Locus 1 is the most important locality at Fin del Mundo because it is the only known part of the site with buried Clovis deposits and tools. To date, however, we have identified 24 other loci that contribute archaeological, geological, and paleontological information. Twelve of these loci produced diagnostic Clovis artifacts. Loci 5, 10, and 21 represent an upland camping area intermittently used by Clovis people for several years. These camping areas are found in an arc 500 to 1,000 m around Locus 1. The extensive lithic scatters in the camping areas include 25 point preforms, 38 end scrapers, 39 large blades, and seven blade cores and core tablets (Figs. 4.72, 4.73, and 4.74).

Figure 4.72. Clovis artifacts from camping areas surrounding Locus 1 at Fin del Mundo.

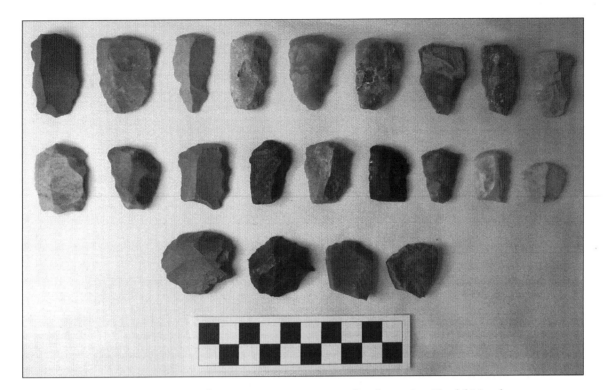

Figure 4.73. Scrapers from camping areas surrounding Locus 1 at Fin del Mundo.

Figure 4.74. Blades from camping areas surrounding Locus 1 at Fin del Mundo.

Locus 25 is a quarry area where the people who used Fin del Mundo acquired lithic raw material to manufacture tools (Table 4.7). Locus 5 (n=88), Locus 1 (n=10), and Locus 10 (n=10) contained many diagnostic Clovis artifacts. Other loci at Fin del Mundo contain flakes, cores, unifacial artifacts, and bifacial artifacts, but we do not know if these artifacts are of Clovis age. We excavated 20 test pits at Locus 5 and Locus 10 to search for subsurface deposits but none were found in these areas.

Auger tests at Locus 21 indicate that buried stratified surfaces exist at this locus, and we plan to carry out more extensive excavations in this area of Fin del Mundo.

A complete Clovis point and a medial fragment of a Clovis point recovered from Locus 1, along with many more tools from Locus 5, were manufactured from quartz crystals. The complete Clovis point specimen is perfectly transparent and is a veritable work of art, with the flake scars creating a prism displaying the colors of

Table 4.7. Lithics from Locus 25, Fin del Mundo

Locus	Blade	Conical Core	Core Tablet	Clovis Preform	Clovis Point	Scraper	End Scraper	Total
1				2	7	1		10
2					1			1
5	28	3	2	16	6	10	23	88
8					1	1		2
9					1			1
10	2			6	1		1	10
14						1		1
17	1			1			1	3
21				1				1
22				1			1	2
25	8	15						23
TOTAL	39	18	2	27	17	13	26	142

the rainbow (Fig. 4.70 A). A hill with enormous veins of quartz situated around the lower slope, which we call Cerro del Cuarzo, lies 5 km west of Fin del Mundo. The quartz at Cerro del Cuarzo occurs in varying purities, but all of it displays hair-like filaments of the mineral rutilio, and this provides a distinctive signature for this source (Fig. 4.75). Preliminary reconnaissance at Cerro del Cuarzo identified at least three lithic workshop areas with thousands of pieces of quartz debitage.

Figure 4.75. Quartz from Cerro del Cuarzo.

Summary

Our discovery of a gomphothere (*Cuvieronius* sp.) at Fin del Mundo is the first time this Pleistocene proboscidean has been found in association with Clovis artifacts at a hunting site in North America. This find appears to indicate that the paleoenvironment of Sonora permitted more growth of warmer-weather plants than in other places in the northern latitudes. We think Sonoran Clovis bands traveled long distances over a large territory in their hunting and gathering activities, and that these bands interacted with other family groups to carry out communal activities that included the exchange of mates and resources.

Until excavation of Fin del Mundo, the Clovis occupation of Sonora was not documented with absolute dates. Radiocarbon dates at Locus 1 at Fin del Mundo derived from charcoal above the gomphotheres and from succinids, or terrestrial gastropods, below the gomphotheres bracket the age between ~12,130 and 9,700 ^{14}C years B.P. A radiocarbon date from charcoal recovered within the gomphothere feature provided an uncorrected date of 11,560 ± 140 (AA100181). This establishes Fin del Mundo among the earliest sites in the Clovis chronology.

The Fin del Mundo Clovis groups apparently used local and regional raw materials of varying quality for the majority of their tool production. One Clovis point was manufactured from a locally available quartz crystal.

Local fine basalt and rhyolite are also common materials used in Clovis points at the site, as well as various sources of cherts. The use of the local raw material indicates that the Clovis groups spent some time in the area in activities that were not solely associated with proboscidean hunting. Our investigations revealed that Fin del Mundo is a complex site with at least 10 important archaeological loci where Pleistocene people were engaged in multiple activities, including acquiring lithic raw materials, tool knapping, camping, and hunting Pleistocene animals.

Fin del Mundo, with its 25,000 year-long stratigraphic record and archaeological features, is an important site for investigating environmental change during the late Pleistocene and early Holocene, Paleoindian subsistence and regional interaction, the role humans may have played in the extinction of the Pleistocene fauna, and how the first people adapted to the Sonoran region. This site thus contributes to our knowledge of the peopling of North America and Mexico.

EL AGUAJITO (SON K:15:1)

El Aguajito is located approximately 40 km from Hermosillo. This site has been heavily gleaned by private collectors for more than 30 years, an activity that continues today. Private collections include at least a half-dozen late Paleoindian artifacts (Gaines 2006), as well as a fluted Clovis point base and hundreds of Archaic projectile points (Fig. 4.76). The site setting is in a transition zone between the Plains of Sonora and the parallel ranges and valleys of Sonora to the east. The surface has suffered from substantial erosion and once-buried features are now exposed (Fig. 4.77). We briefly investigated El Aguajito during the winter 2007 field season.

El Aguajito consists of a continuous distribution of lithic artifacts and fire-cracked rock extending over an area of 5 square kilometers. Research at the site focused upon characterizing the stratigraphy and determining the age of the four strata of organic dark clays that might be related to late Pleistocene black mats. The stratigraphic deposits consist of a possible layer of volcanic ash resting atop calcareous clays and silts that exhibit four separate layers of black clays (Fig. 4.78). An horno of probable San Pedro phase affiliation rests upon the most recent of these cienega deposits, suggesting an age no older than the middle Holocene for this stratum. Radiocarbon dates obtained from charcoal and the organic soils confirmed this date, and indicate a geochronology for the middle

Figure 4.76. Projectile Point from El Aguajito.

Figure 4.77. El Aguajito, looking west.

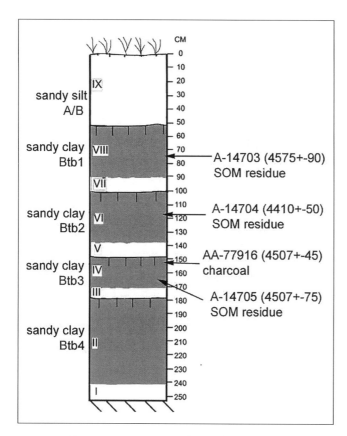

Figure 4.78. Stratigraphy at El Aguajito, showing location of ¹⁴C samples.

Figure 4.79. Fluted points from Rancho Bojorquez in the Velez Collection.

and late Holocene (ca. 4700 B.P.). Sediments at El Aguajito appear to be related to a period of increased humidity that occurred at the onset of the Holocene (Martin 1963).

Although El Aguajito does not appear to contain buried deposits associated with the late Pleistocene or early Holocene, the numerous horno features, manos, metates, and Archaic projectile point styles, along with other lithic tools and debitage, make this site appear to be a significant locality for investigating the development of the Early Agriculture period in northwestern Mexico.

LAS PEÑITAS (SON O:12:1)

Las Peñitas was reported by Javier Bustamante in 1972. The site is located 20 km southeast of the abandoned Buenavista granite mine, accessed off of Highway 16 (La Colorada-Sahuaripa). According to Bustamante, the site is located on the bajada of a mountain in the Valle de las Peñitas, situated between an arroyo and a type of desert pavement. There, Bustamante collected a complete white chert Clovis point with fluting on both faces, several

scrapers, and a conical blade core. Bustamante described this site as being a raw-material procurement site. Several bifacial thinning flakes of the same white chert that was found at Las Peñitas were observed at SON O:3:1. We considered it imperative to relocate Las Peñitas but we were not able to find the site.

RANCHO BOJORQUEZ AT KM17

We learned of this site from Dr. Leopoldo Velez, one of the Hermosillo collectors. According to Velez, five Clovis point bases have been collected from this site, three of which are in his possession (Fig. 4.79). The site is located on the highway to Sahuaripa at the kilometer 17 marker, where there is an exit to the south for Rancho Bojorquez. The site is situated on flat terrain in the Plains of Sonora, and has been heavily modified by agricultural activities, cattle grazing, and extensive erosion. A systematic survey determined that this site consists of a light but continuous distribution of lithics, ceramics, shell, manos, and metates. Some of the artifacts may have a Paleoindian affiliation but we were unable to identify a single diagnostic Paleoindian artifact. At least three arroyos dissect the site. Examination of the profiles exposed in arroyo walls revealed that the drainages were cut down to granite bedrock, and that the deposits above the bedrock were composed of a loose, silty alluvium, probably of recent origin. No potential late Pleistocene or early Holocene contexts were observed.

CUEVA EL TETABEJO

Cueva El Tetabejo is located in the Sierra Libre, within the large site of La Pintada, 60 km south of Hermosillo. The cave at this site measures 20 m wide, 12 m deep,

Figure 4.80. Clovis point from Cueva
El Tetabejo in private collection.

and 12 m high, with the mouth oriented at 200 degrees, providing a view to the south.

Walter W. Taylor and José Luis Lorenzo carried out excavations at Cueva El Tetabejo (SON O:5:6) in 1956, with the explicit objective of locating Paleoindian contexts. Today, the remains of their grid can still be seen. Although Taylor and Lorenzo failed to locate Clovis contexts, one of the Hermosillo artifact collectors has a distal fragment of a fluted Clovis point from Cueva El Tetabejo that was made using purple chert (Fig. 4.80). This artifact was apparently obtained from looting of Cueva El Tetabejo that occurred in 1985. The cave appears to contain stratified deposits and merits further study. Recently, Manuel Gramiel, an archaeologist with the team investigating La Pintada, discovered that the field notes and excavated materials from Cueva El Tetabejo are probably curated at the Smithsonian Institution, in Washington D.C.

CHINOBAMPO

Chinobampo is where Pleistocene-age humans were first discovered in Sonora. This discovery was made in January 1937 at Rancho Chinobampo, 20 km south of Navajoa. During the "Pleistocene Mammals" project sponsored by the Frick Laboratory of the American Museum of Natural History, Howard Scott Gentry and John C. Blick encountered a human cranium within a stratified deposit at Chinobampo that was composed of caliche and silt of probable Pleistocene age. This deposit

also contained the remains of camel, horse, and wolf. The cranium was removed and transported to New York. In March 1937, Gentry and Blick returned to Chinobampo to re-examine the site. During their fieldwork, they extracted a stratigraphic block sample of the deposits that weighed approximately 23 kg and contained bone and charcoal (Blick 1938). In December 1938, Gordon Ekholm and Carl Sauer visited Chinobampo, offering the observation that if the skull had been removed from the deposits described by Blick, there was indeed a high probability of a late Pleistocene context (Ekholm 1937:46). Donald Lehmer (1949b) revisited the Chinobampo during his Sonora Project in 1949 but was unable to relocate any Pleistocene deposits. Lehmer noted, however, that Archaic artifacts were present in the general area.

In 2007, we were able to locate the site, which is situated on the Arroyo Chinobampo within the Rancho de Chinobampo that the Navarro family has owned since 1957. The Navarro family was unaware of Blick and Gentry's discovery in 1937. The Arroyo Chinobampo offers a permanent water flow. Approximately 100 m from the ranch houses, at the point where there is a prominent curve in the arroyo, there is a 2-m high exposed face composed of hard, well-developed carbonates. This exposure extends along the arroyo for approximately 20 m. It appears likely that that these deposits represent the remnants of a lake. Although no test excavations were conducted to examine buried deposits, a close examination of the exposure revealed a small fragment of bone embedded in the carbonate deposits. Based upon Blick's descriptions, this is unquestionably the locale described in 1937 (Blick 1938). No diagnostic Paleoindian artifacts were encountered, although an Archaic period site was observed farther downstream. Future systematic investigations to determine the nature of these deposits are planned.

UNDERSTANDING THE CLOVIS OCCUPATION OF SONORA

My research demonstrates that Sonora began to be populated in Late Pleistocene times. The Clovis occupation is well represented in the northern half of Sonora, in the Sonoran Desert area around the city of Hermosillo. There, the landscape includes three principal zones. These zones include the Llanos de Hermosillo, a more or less flat landscape filled by alluvium that slopes gently down to the west-southwest into the Gulf of California. It is probable that lakes and playas existed seasonally in the Llanos de Hermosillo during the late Pleistocene. To the east of the Llanos de Hermosillo are intervening small basins that constrain biotic communities. The third zone is the Sierra Madre Occidental with high altitude resources. These three landscapes provided Paleoindian groups with a rich mosaic of diverse environments that supported animals and plants.

Water, animals, plants, and raw materials for making stone tools constitute indispensable resources for hunters and gatherers, and Sonora provided all these resources for the Paleoindian groups that made it their land. The paleoeviromental proxy data that we have indicate that at the end of the Pleistocene, Sonora was a good place to live. Wet and cool summers and wet and warm winters established the desert grasses that were grazed by herbivores, including mammoths, gomphotheres, deer, and horses. Although the Sonoran Clovis people used local lithic raw materials to make Clovis points and tools, the vitrified basalt source at Cerro de la Vuelta at El Bajío was an important resource with regional use.

Fin del Mundo, located in the Río Bacoachi basin with a spring-fed pond, was an authentic oasis. The pond at Fin del Mundo attracted animals, including large Pleistocene mammals. Clovis people hunted gomphotheres at Fin del Mundo and camped around the pond. They also exploited quartz and rhyolite outcrops in the vicinity of the site for making tools.

El Bajío and Fin del Mundo are approximately 600 m above sea level, matking them the highest Paleoindian sites known in north-central Sonora. Although we do not have an environmental reconstruction for these sites, a pine-oak woodland with some shrubs may have existed at the end of the Pleistocene.

SON N:11:20 and SON J:16:8 are located in the Llanos de Sonora near the Gulf of California, at an elevation of 25 to 50 m above sea level, At the end of the Pleistocene, playas and lakes were present in this area, and the environment probably was open grassland with a few trees. The two Clovis sites known in this area appear to be hunting localities where Clovis points were lost.

SON O:3:1 and Rancho Bojorquez are located in the southwestern portion of the Llanos de Hermosillo where the intervening basins begin. SON O:3.1 is located in the Río Matape basin, 300 m above sea level, where springs and seasonal cienegas are present. The environment of this area at the end of the Pleistocene probably was grassy rolling hills with oaks. SON O:3:1 is composed of two camp areas, apparently of Clovis age.

After seven years of investigations, we are beginning to understand the basic aspects of Paleoindian settlement patterns in Sonora. Paleoindian land use was multifaceted and included an extensive territory where the hunters exploited elemental and important resources. The Llanos de Hermosillo was the center of one of the Clovis territories; Paleoindian sites there are large and small, and there are a substantial number of isolated Clovis points as well. Paleoindian groups in the Llanos de Hermosillo had access to an important lithic raw material quarry, permanent sources of water, access to coastal resources, and a large territory with seasonally available animals, plants, and water sources.

Sonora provided a rich, new territory for the Clovis people. The region had a good climate and a diversity of food resources that allowed Clovis groups to stay and successfully settle the land. Radiocarbon dates from Fin del Mundo indicate that the Clovis occupation of Sonora is at least 600 years earlier than the Paleoindian use of Murray Springs in southern Arizona, making Fin del Mundo one of the earliest Paleoindian sites in North America. The expansion and interaction of Clovis people in Sonora has proven to be more complex than we previously thought.

CHAPTER FIVE

Clovis Lithic Technology at El Bajío

Stone Sources, Variation, and Interaction

Lithics are the most important artifact category for understanding the oldest human behavior (Andrefsky 2009:65). In many early sites stone tools and debitage are the only artifacts that survive decomposition. Lithic technological organization refers to the manner in which people organize their lives and activities with regard to the production and use of stone tools. In the study of hunter-gatherer groups, lithic technological organization provides a way to investigate local forager adaptive strategies and, at a larger scale, human land use related to environmental, social, and historical contexts (Andrefsky 2009).

The human groups that inhabited Sonora at the end of the Pleistocene left us very little evidence of their lifeways. We therefore rely on their lithic technological organization to provide information about adaptive strategies. The reduction sequence of the stone tools allows us to observe the transformation of tools during their procurement, production, use, and maintenance (Shott 1986:34). Although toolmakers may have had a mental template of the type of artifact that they wanted to make, the raw material packet size, abundance, and quality determined the kind of tool that could be produced (Bleed 1986; Bradbury and Franklin 2000). According to Shott (1986), hunter-gatherers who practice high residential mobility produce fewer but more versatile tools, and those tools are associated with a wider range of tasks. These more versatile tools evince heavier resharpening and curation when compared to formal, non-versatile tool types (Shott 1986:40).

CLOVIS TOOL KITS

The Clovis culture is recognized for its characteristic bifacial point. Marie Wormington (1957:263) defined it as a lanceolate-shaped point with flutes that originate at the base and extend no more than halfway up to the tip. Traditionally, this fluted projectile point has been the principal—or the only—diagnostic criterion to categorize an archaeological context or an assemblage as Clovis (Bradley and others 2010:2). The accentuation of a single artifact form is inevitable when an isolated point is the only find, or when it is the only artifact found in a kill site (Bradley and others 2010; Bever and Meltzer 2007).

Since the 1980s, research on the Clovis complex has greatly intensified. The discovery of new sites and the refinement of dating, sourcing, excavation, and analytical techniques have led to new and emerging explanations with notable variations in Clovis assemblages (Bradley and others 2010; Collins 1999a, 2002, 2003; Gingerich 2007; Huckell 2007; Sánchez and Carpenter 2009; Prascuinas 2008; Smallwood 2011:3; Waters and others 2011). Where once it was argued that Clovis—and especially the diagnostic Clovis fluted point—was rather homogenous from coast to coast (Haynes 1982), most archaeologists now believe that Clovis can no longer be viewed as a monolithic cultural phenomenon (Bever and Meltzer 2007:65). Adopting this perspective, variation and regionalization is expected in the Clovis archaeological context, and the idea that Clovis points are the sole diagnostic artifact can no longer be supported.

Following Bradley and others (2010:1), artifacts from Clovis sites commonly consist of large flaked stone tools in the form of distinctive fluted spear points, various types of scrapping and cutting tools, and, on rare occasions of good preservation, bone, antler, and ivory tools (Lepper and Bonnichsen 2004). Stone tools were made with distinct and unique technologies that were unvarying throughout the Clovis range, in spite of varied environments and landscapes (Bradley and others 2010:1).

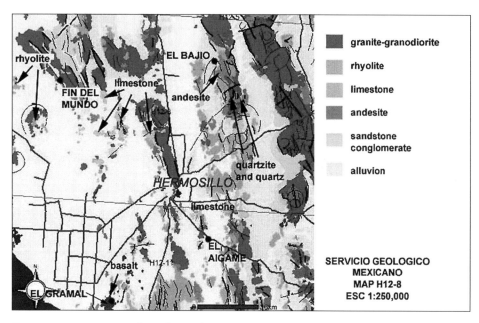

Figure 5.1. Raw materials in the study area. Map data from Sistema Geologico Mexicano.

The typical Clovis tool kit is represented by biface cores, retouched biface flakes, point preforms, Clovis points, blade cores, denticulated blades, end scrapers on blades, and utilized blades (Bradley and others 2010:1; Huckell 2007; Waters and others 2011).

Over more than 40 years, several thousand stone tools and pieces of debitage were collected from the surface of El Bajío Clovis site. The site includes an extensive lithic quarry and 10 Clovis loci representing campsites and special activity areas distributed over a 4-square-kilometer area. Although we have been unable to find buried deposits at El Bajío, the vast and diverse collection of tools that have been collected at the site provide an ideal collection for studying Clovis lithic technology organization. A total of 333 stone tools from El Bajío were classified as belonging to the typical Clovis tool kit. We were able to make these determinations by comparing the El Bajío collection to recent Clovis technology studies (Bradley and others 2010; Waters and others 2011). The presence of patination on tools was used as an ancillary attribute to define the Clovis artifact collection at the site.

Regionalization and dependence on local resources appear to be a fundamental part of the cultural adaptation of the Clovis people of Sonora. Because there were geological sources with fine lithic materials, tools were produced using local materials with medium-to-fine textures. Many of these materials are volcanic rocks, which are more difficult to flake than chert. An overview of the lithic sources available for the Clovis people in Sonora is presented next.

SONORAN RAW MATERIAL SOURCES FOR TOOL MAKING

The regional patterns and attributes of Late Pleistocene sites in Sonora make it clear that Clovis groups probably do not represent a single homogeneous adaptation. Clovis groups appear to have had assorted economic strategies and varied mobility patterns related to differing environments, resources, and social contexts. Hunter-gatherer mobility patterns and land use depended on the location of essential resources. Water sources and raw materials for tool making were fundamental assets that had an impact on hunter-gatherer adaptative strategies. In particular, access to raw materials suitable for tool production probably determined mobility strategies that were unrelated to food procurement (Fig. 5.1). The time and energy invested in procuring raw materials and tool production also directly affected the time available for subsistence activities (Kuhn 1991:250).

El Bajío Vitrified Basalt Quarry at Cerro de la Vuelta

The El Bajío quarry at Cerro de la Vuelta was the only massive and extensive raw material source for tool making used by Paleoindian people in Sonora. At least 98 percent

Figure 5.2. Google Earth image of basalt quarry at El Bajío. Map data © 2009 Google, INEGI, Digital Globe, CNES/SPOT Image.

of the lithic artifacts documented at El Bajío were derived from this source. Cerro de la Vuelta and nearby hills with a northwest-southeast orientation, apparently were formed by volcanic eruptions. The hills are composed primarily of medium-texture basalts that intrude into the granite pediment of the Sierra San Jerónimo along a northeast-southwest axis (Fig. 5.2). This basaltic eruption formed a *bajo*, or playa-like landform, where El Bajío is located. Cerro de la Vuelta is the most northwestern hill formed by the volcanic activity. Although we were able to find vitrified basalt of medium quality in the hills around Cerro de la Vuelta, the vitrified basalt most suitable for tool making is concentrated on the southern section of the hill.

On the southern slope of Cerro de la Vuelta, near the summit, there is an extensive outcrop of vitrified basalt. This outcrop is associated with enormous lithic waste material dumps that extend for more than 20 m, along with fragments of cores, blanks, biface preforms, hammerstones, and abraders. The principal quarry area extends over a hectare. The vitrified basalt occurs in prismatic and subprismatic blocks, and, although the quality of the raw material with regard to the production of flaked stone tools is unpredictable, the overall quality goes from good to supreme. Some blocks are fine-grained

and good for tool making; others have abundant internal fractures or inclusions of olivine crystals of varying sizes, or both. The raw material color is extremely variable, ranging from a cream color to jet-black. Once flaked, the material develops a surface patina, so the artifacts at the site variously display a thick yellow glaze patina, a thinner greenish patina, or a grey patina.

This Cerro de la Vuelta quarry appears to have been exploited principally during the Paleoindian and Archaic periods. In the only locality where ceramics were documented (Locus 20), we observed that the lithic artifacts were manufactured from waterworn cobbles of basalt, rhyolite, and diorite, with a notable absence of vitrified basalt.

Obsidian Sources

Small sources of obsidian are common in Sonora. The small obsidian nodules that are commonly referred to as Apache tears were observed on almost every site we visited. These nodules, associated with andesite and basalt, may have been used by Paleoindians.

At El Bajío, an obsidian source was located on a hill north of Cerro de la Vuelta. On that hill, the obsidian occurs in the form of small nodules that were between

2 and 7 cm in diameter. Nodules no larger than 50 mm were observed within a 100-m by 100-m area at the top of another small, nearby hill. On a hill at the south end of SON J:16:8, there is an obsidian source with small nodules ranging between 2 and 10 cm in diameter. At SON N:11:20, an obsidian source was located on a small hill south of Locus 5. This obsidian source occurs in a 600-m by 600-m area and consists of small nodules that are to 2 to 6 cm in diameter. The presence of obsidian reduction flakes at SON N:11:20 confirms the prehistoric exploitation of this raw material source. Apache tear sources are distributed all over the Sierra Libre southeast of Hermosillo and have been the focus of research by a group of geologists of the Geology Department at the Universidad de Sonora (Jesus Vidal, personal communication 2010).

Quartz Crystal Sources

At El Bajío, Cerro Rojo is located in the center of the site. This hill contains quartz crystal and iron oxide deposits. Bifacial retouch debitage produced using quartz crystal and a possible Clovis point tip of quartz were collected at Cerro Rojo.

Five kilometers west of Fin del Mundo, there is a hill with enormous veins of quartz situated around its lower slope. The quartz material occurs in varying purities but all of displays hair-like filaments of the mineral rutile, which provides a distinctive signature for this source. Preliminary reconnaissance identified at least three lithic workshop areas with thousands of pieces of quartz debitage at Fin del Mundo. A complete Clovis point and a medial fragment of a Clovis point recovered from Locus 1 at Fin del Mundo, along with many more tools from Locus 5, were manufactured from quartz crystal that probably came from the quartz vein on the nearby hill, which we refer to as Cerro del Cuarzo.

Fine Rhyolite Quarry

The Sierra Madre Occidental parental materials are extrusive rhyolites, and these types of rocks are widely distributed. At the locality of Upanguaymas we discovered a quarry of a fine rhyolite with artifacts and debitage. At least four Clovis points from different localities were manufactured using rhyolite (see Gaines and others 2009b). At Fin del Mundo, rhyolite was widely used to fabricate bifaces.

Quartzite Cobbles from Arroyos

There are many artifacts at SON O:3:1 made from quartzite. The quartzite cobbles common in the local arroyos at the site may be the source of raw material used to produce artifacts. Two Clovis points at Fin del Mundo, as well as many artifacts at Locus 5, were made from quartzite. It is probable that the source of quartzite at Fin del Mundo is local. Quartzite outcrops occur south of El Bajío.

Chalcedony and Chert Sources

All the cryptocrystalline silicates that have a genesis from sedimentary parental material are in this group. Cherts undergo multiple phases of genesis and configuration of minerals during their formation, making it difficult to determine their provenience (Foradas 2003; Andrefsky 2009). The chert sources in Sonora probably underwent a relatively isolated genesis due to silica precipitation from unique sources, such as a volcanic vent pushing through a sedimentary limestone deposit. Although it will be difficult to find chert quarries because they are typically small, once they are found it will be easier to determine their geochemical properties. Many different classes of chert and chalcedony were used for making Clovis points, end scrapers, and blades in Sonora. We did not find any sources of chert during our investigations but limestone is present between Fin del Mundo and El Bajío. A geological survey to find chert sources is needed.

SONORAN CLOVIS LITHIC TECHNOLOGY

The Clovis tool kit includes the lanceolate Clovis point with its distinctive basal flute; large prismatic blades; conical, wedge-shaped cores; delicate end scrapers; and a variety of unifacial and bifacial tools, including gravers, that were manufactured from blades and flakes (Bradley and others 2010:1; Haynes 1980, 1987; Stanford 1991). The most diagnostic characteristic of the Clovis tool kit is the skilled reduction process used by the makers of Clovis tools. Using mostly percussion, they achieved sophisticated and distinctive attributes such as the overshot flaking and fluting that are evident in the tools. After Clovis, no other groups that inhabited Sonora developed sophisticated flaking lithic industries similar to Clovis. This makes the Clovis industry relatively easy to recognize and separate from later industries. Late Paleoindian tool kits are virtually unknown from the southernmost regions of the Sonoran Desert. The subsequent Archaic lithic industries in northwestern Mexico and the southwestern United States are more expeditious, and there are relatively few formal tools in the assemblages (Carpenter and others 2002; Sánchez and Martinez 2001).

Table 5.1. Patination on El Bajío Stone Tools

Munsell Code	Color Name	Patina Thickness
GLEY 23/10G	Bluish black	No patina
5Y 3/1	Very dark gray	Very little patina
5Y 6/1	Gray	Some patina
2.5Y 6/2	Light brownish gray	Medium patina/biological process
2.5Y 7/2	Light gray	Medium -heavy patina
10YR 5/4	Yellowish brown	Heavy patina/biological process
10YR 7/4	Very pale brown	Heavy patina/biological process

Rock Patina on El Bajío Basalt Tools

The natural color of the vitrified basalt from El Bajío quarry is bluish black (GLEY 23/10G) and very dark gray (5Y 3/1), with olivine and other large crystals. The majority of the Clovis diagnostic artifacts collected from the surface show a thick patina. The patination present on El Bajío artifacts is not only a luster, it is a dense surface cover that transformed the artifact texture and physical appearance of the rock. In some tools the patina penetrates all the way to the core of the tool. It is possible that the El Bajío patina is a combination of physio-chemical and biological processes that developed over a long period of time. Nonetheless, the components of the soil matrix and weathering played an important role in patina formation on the tools.

To measure the amount of patina contained in an artifact, the Munsell Color Chart was employed (Table 5.1). The biological processes of patina formation produced patinas with more red colors than the physio-chemical processes; these patinas needed more time to develop. The thickness of the patina on the El Bajío stone tools sometimes was used in this study in combination with some technological attributes as an indicator of antiquity. A systematic study of patina on artifacts at El Bajío needs to be developed to fully understand their formation process. Significantly, patination is not present on the Archaic projectile points from the site.

The Sample and the Analytical Method

Clovis projectile points have been the central topic of many studies (Agenbroad 1967; Bamforth 2009; Buchanan and Collar 2007; Anderson and Gillam 2000; Gains and others 2009b; Huckell 1982, 2004; Northon and others 2005). The variety of Clovis artifacts comprising the Clovis tool kit, however, has received less study (Bradley and others 2010; Collins 1999a; Waters and others 2011). According to Huckell (2007:186), Clovis lithic technology can be best understood as a system comprised of four different production subsystems: biface, flake, blade, and expedient. Each subsystem begins with raw material procurement and passes through various manufacturing or reduction stages that terminate in finished tools. The subsystems are not isolated from each other and they may start with the same blank (Bradley and others 2010:1). After tools are produced, they often undergo a series of transformations until they are discarded (Andrefsky 2009:66).

Lithic studies on non-projectile point Clovis diagnostic tools are rare, perhaps due to the fact that usually few lithics are found in Clovis sites. The El Bajío collection is unique because of the quantity of lithics collected from the site, numbering around 14,000 artifacts. All of the artifacts come from the surface, however, making it difficult to assign them to a particular chronological complex. This study uses existing literature to identify lithics that have been reported from Clovis sites. Previous researchers considered these artifacts to be diagnostic of the Clovis techno-complex. The degree of patina is also used as a tool for determining the antiquity of artifacts. The study presented here relies upon the published literature available regarding Clovis technology (Bradley 1991; Collins 1999a, 1999b, 2003; Crabtree 1966; Gramly 1990; Green 1963; Huckell 2007; Sanders 1990).

El Bajío has been collected for more than 40 years. Investigations and artifact collections at the site were made by Manuel Robles in the 1960s and early 1970s, by Marion McIntyre and Kenneth McIntyre in 1975, and by Julio César Montané between 1978 and 1980.

Table 5.2. Clovis Lithic Industry from El Bajío

Collection or Locus	Blade Industry	Unifacial Industry	Biface Industry	Misc. Cores	Hammers	Total
Montané	59	47	42	6		154
M-Cerro Rojo		26	3			29
Locus 1			1			1
Locus 2			1			1
Locus 4	7		20			27
Locus 5	12	4	2			18
Locus 6	9	2		1	3	15
Locus 7	17	5	3	2		27
Locus 8		1	2			3
Locus 10	10	2	4			16
Locus 12	2	1	15		1	19
Locus 15			1			1
Isolated	6	2	12	2	1	23
TOTAL	122	90	106	11	5	334

Unfortunately, none of these researchers produced reports or other documentation of their investigations. Although these earlier projects produced extensive artifact collections from surface finds and subsurface excavations, there is virtually no information regarding the horizontal or vertical provenience of the artifacts.

Julio César Montané collected at least 10 boxes of artifacts. Although little is known about the provenience of his artifacts, his collection provides us with an important source of Clovis diagnostic materials. The investigations carried out by the Proyecto Geoarquelogía and Tecnología Litica de los Grupos Paleo-Indios de Sonora in 2003 collected artifacts with precise provenience information, although the majority of the artifacts were collected from the surface. Between the Montané collection and the 2003 collection, there is a significant sample of 334 Clovis artifacts (Table 5.2). The only tools recovered from a subsurface provenience were at Feature 1 in Locus 12, a knapping station where square-base bifaces were manufactured. The analysis is divided into three industries and two miscellaneous tool classes: a blade industry (n=122), a unifacial industry (n=90), a bifacial industry (n=106), and expedient miscellaneous cores (n=11) and hammers (n=5).

The Montané collection comprises 183 tools and the 2003 collection contains 150 Clovis diagnostic artifacts.

Being able to collect 150 Clovis diagnostic tools from El Bajío in 2003 was an impressive achievement because people have been collecting at the site for a long time. This attests to the importance of the site in studying Paleoindian archaeology. Only 12 diagnostic Archaic projectile points were found in 2003, indicating that the Archaic occupation of the site was less extensive than the Paleoindian occupation.

CLOVIS BLADE TECHNOLOGY

In 1963, F. E. Green defined and described "Clovis blades" as a new artifact type associated with the Clovis complex. Seventeen Clovis blades were recovered from a gravel pit at the Clovis site in Blackwater Draw, north of Portales in eastern New Mexico (Green 1963). The simple definition of a blade is a piece of chipped stone that is at least twice as long as it is wide (Bordes 1967). Although blades can occur fortuitously during flake-core reduction, Clovis blades are the product of a distinctive blade technology (Collins 1999a). Clovis blade technology is common in central and southeastern Texas at the Pavo Real, Keven Davis, and Gault sites (Collins 1999a:4, 1999b, 2003; Haynes 2002:110; Tankersley 2004:55). The blade technology strategy is diagnostic of Clovis groups.

As far as we know, later Paleoindian groups—including Folsom, Plainview, and Dalton—did not have a blade technology.

Blade technology refers to the knowledge, strategy, activities, and equipment used in the intentional production of blades. This process involves preparing a core to extract blades (Collins 1999a:9). In Mesoamerica, during the Classic and Postclassic periods (A.D. 600 to A.D. 1521), an obsidian blade technology was an essential lithic technological process for tool making, and this technology was controlled by Mesoamerican states to fabricate blades for mass production. The blades and manufacturing byproducts were sold to large cities such as Teotihuacan, Tula, and the Gran Tenochtitlan. The physical control of obsidian quarries by states was fundamental in managing the production and distribution of tools (Pastrana 1998). Ten thousand years earlier, bands of Clovis hunters and gatherers fabricated blades employing a technology similar to the later Mesoamerican one. Clovis blade technology is common at Clovis sites in Texas, and is present at Blackwater Draw in New Mexico, Murray Springs in Arizona, and Adams in Kentucky, as well as at other Paleoinidan sites (Collins 1999a).

Blade technology is an efficient use of stone in terms of total length and cutting edge produced for a given mass of raw material (Collins 1999a; Pastrana 1998). Blade knappers' biggest concerns are the angle of flaking and the amount of force they deliver into the core. Blades can be produced by direct percussion with a sharp blow if the core is held with one hand or with a foot; a second person may also hold the core. To initiate reduction from a blade core it is necessary to have an acute angular edge that establishes a platform. If a core lacks a suitable natural face, a ridge can be produced by bifacial flaking, and the flakes that are removed during this procedure are referred as crested blades. The first blades removed from the core will contain much of the natural cortex. As more blades are removed from a core, the face constantly changes as the relationship between the core face and the platform also changes (Collins 1999a).

If the angle between the platform and the face of the core is near 90 degrees, it is possible for the toolmaker to move around the entire circumference of the core removing blades, leaving an exhausted conical shaped core as a result. Damage to the platform sometimes occurs, and although this can be repaired by flaking the platform and face, eventually the damage reaches a point were no more blades can be detached. If sufficient mass remains, a new platform can be made by completely removing the old platform by a single large flake from the side; the mass removed is known as a core tablet flake. In many cases, the blades obtained from conical cores have narrow platforms that are curved because the angle between the platform and the face is approximately 60 to 70 degrees (Collins 1999a).

Another type of core produced by Clovis people for obtaining blades was the wedge-shaped core. The blades produced from a wedge-shaped core have a more acute angle than those from conical cores. Wedge-shaped cores generally have a narrow face and a multifaceted platform. Maintenance of platforms on these cores is much simpler than that needed for other cores, and consists of trimming an acute bifacial edge. Wedge-shaped cores can have opposing platforms. The blades obtained from wedge-shaped cores are not curved (Collins 1999a:51). Following Collins (1999a), blades are divided into three groups: cortical blades, non-cortical blades with prior blade scars, and prismatic blades.

THE SONORAN CLOVIS BLADE INDUSTRY

Clovis blade technology is an important component of the El Bajío lithic collection. A total of 122 artifacts representing all the stages of Clovis blade technology have been collected from the site, including conical cores (n=3), core tablet flakes (n=5), wedge-shaped cores (n=9), crested blades (n=9), cortical blades (n=12), non-cortical blades with prior blade scars (n=22), prismatic blades (n=49), flakes for core rejuvenation (n=6), and platform maintenance flakes (n=7) (Table 5.3). All the artifacts of the blade subsystem were fabricated on El Bajío basalt, with the exception of three chert blades.

Conical Cores

In 2003, three conical core fragments were collected at El Bajío from three loci. These conical cores are broken, and they all have faceted platforms. One conical core with a multifaceted platform was collected from El Bajío by Manuel Robles in the 1960s (Table 5.4; Fig. 5.3). This core measures 90 mm in length, and is curated at the Museo de la Universidad de Sonora, in Hermosillo.

Core Tablet Flakes

Core tablet flakes are associated with the repair of the platform in conical cores (Fig. 5.4). Five core tablet flakes are part of the El Bajío collection. Four tablet flakes were collected by Montané in 1979, and one was found in Locus 5 during fieldwork in 2003 (Table 5.5).

Table 5.3. Clovis Blade Industry Artifacts from El Bajío

Artifact Types	Montané Collection	Locus 4	Locus 5	Locus 6	Locus 7	Locus 10	Locus 12	Isolated	Totals
Conical cores		1		1	1				3
Core tablet flakes	4		1						5
Wedge-shaped cores	5		1	2		1			9
Crested blades	5			1	3				9
Cortical blades	9		1	1			1		12
Non-cortical blades	12	3	2		2	3			22
Prismatic blades	18	3	5	4	8	6	1	4	49
Blade core error recovery flakes	2		1		1			2	6
Platform mainten-ance flakes	4		1		2				7
TOTAL	59	7	12	9	17	10	2	6	122

Table 5.4. Conical Cores from El Bajío

Bag Number	Locus	Condition	Weight (g)	Length (mm)	Width (mm)	Thickness (mm)	Raw Material (Munsell Color)	Platform
37733	6	Core fragment	66	53	52	35	Bajío basalt with patina (5y 5/2)	Faceted
45469	4	Core fragment	95	38	48	38	Bajío basalt with patina (5y 5/2)	Multifaceted
45415	7	Core fragment	148.5	30	61	56	Bajío basalt with patina (5y 5/1)	Faceted

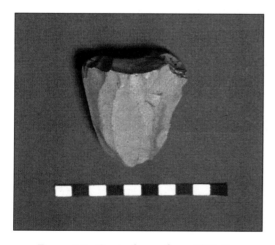

Figure 5.3. Conical core from El Bajío.

Figure 5.4. Core tablet flakes from El Bajío.

Table 5.5. Core Tablet Flakes from El Bajío

Bag No.	Collection or Locus	Condition	Weight (g)	Length (mm)	Width (mm)	Thickness (mm)	Raw material (Munsell Color)	Exterior Face
1101	Montané	Complete	22.1	46	35	30	Bajío basalt with patina (5y 5/2)	Multifaceted
141	Montané	Complete	35.2	72	32	22	Bajío basalt with patina (2.5y 5/2)	Faceted
1096	Montané	Complete	170	81	78	40	Bajío basalt with patina (2.5y 7/2)	Multifaceted
199	Montané	Fragment	25.8	44	33	16	Bajío basalt with patina (5y 5/2)	Multifaceted
37739	Locus 5	Complete	24.5	49	43	25	Bajío basalt with patina (2.5y 6/2)	Cortical

Table 5.6. Wedge-Shaped Cores from El Bajío

Bag No.	Collection or Locus	Condition	Weight (g)	Length (mm)	Width (mm)	Thickness (mm)	Raw Material (Munsell Color)	Cortex	Platform
140	Montané	Complete	153.8	82	67	33	Bajío basalt with patina (2.5y 5/2)	30%	Multifaceted
35432	Montané	Distal	100.6	60	54	39	Bajío basalt with patina (5y 5/2)	No	Faceted
35440	Montané	Complete	81.4	58	57	20	Bajío basalt with patina (2.5y 5/2)	30%	Cortex
37550.2	Locus 6	Complete	71.5	62	49	29	Bajío basalt with patina (5y 5/2)	No	Cortex
45397	Locus 10	Fragment	54.5	52	43	25	Bajío basalt with patina (5y 5/2)	25%	
37550.2	Locus 6	Complete	147	75	52	35	Bajío basalt with patina (5y 5/1)	No	Cortex
195	Montané	Fragment	62	31	61	32	Bajío basalt with patina (5y 6/2)	40%	
695B	Montané	Fragment	72	54	60	24	Bajío basalt with patina (5y 6/1)	No	Faceted
37007	Locus 5	Fragment	60.5	51	49	18	Bajío basalt with patina (2.5y 5/1)	20%	Cortex

Wedge-Shaped Cores

Wedge-shaped cores for blade production have a right angle between the platform and the core. These cores have a narrower and flatter face than conical cores, with a multifaceted platform. Blades were only obtained from one face. The opposite face is terminated by bifacial flaking or retains original cortex. Platform management of wedge-shaped cores is much simpler than that of conical cores, consisting of trimming an acute bifacial edge.

Nine wedge-shaped cores are in the El Bajío collection (Table 5.6). All are exhausted cores, with platforms that are faceted or cortical, and many of them retain the original cortex on their faces. The complete cores (n=4) have lengths that range from 58 mm to 82 mm. The productivity of these cores is much lower than that of the conical variety; however, the maintenance of the platform and face is much simpler.

Table 5.7. Crested Blades from El Bajío

Bag No.	Locus	Condition	Weight (g)	Length (mm)	Width (mm)	Thickness	Raw Material (Munsell Color)
695B	Montané	Complete	18.7	79	24	12	Bajío basalt (2.5y 7/4)
1098	Montané	Complete	22	60	30	15	Bajío basalt (5y 6/2)
193	Montané	Complete	28	59.5	26	21	Bajío basalt (2.5y 6/2)
695B	Montané	Complete	20.5	60	25	18	Bajío basalt (2.5y 7/4)
35448	Montané	Complete	45.8	87	31	17	Bajío basalt (5y 6/2)
45311	Locus 7	Distal	38	78	30	18	Bajío basalt (2.5y 7/3)
37546	Locus 6	Medial	11.5	54	18	8	Bajío basalt (5y 6/2)
37557	Locus 7	Terminal	22	5.6	2.6	16	Bajío basalt (5y 6/3)
45413	Locus 7	Complete	21.5	51	26	18	Bajío basalt (5y 6/3)

Table 5.8. Platform Preparation Flakes

Bag No.	Collection or Locus	Condition	Weight (g)	Length (mm)	Width (mm)	Thickness (mm)	Raw Material Munsell Color)	Exterior Face
695B	Montané	Complete	41.7	73	59	9	Bajío basalt (5y 6/2)	Faceted
695B	Montané	Complete	46.8	57	70	12	Bajío basalt (5y 6/2)	Faceted
1087	Montané	Complete	64.2	71	70	13	Bajío basalt (2.5y 6/3)	Faceted
195	Montané	Split	15	60	30	9	Bajío basalt (5y 6/2)	Faceted
45412	Locus 7	Complete	49	57	62	12	Bajío basalt (2.5y 7/3)	Faceted
45508	Locus 7	Complete	12	55	38	6	Bajío basalt (2.5y 5/1)	Faceted
37608	Locus 5 - ele1	Complete	31	55	50	7	Bajío basalt (10yr 5/3)	Faceted

Crested Blades

Crested blades are mostly used in maintenance of conical cores (Collins (1999a:19). Nine crested blades of the El Bajío basalt are part of the collection, six are complete and three are fragments (Table 5.7; Fig. 5.5).

Platform Preparation and Rejuvenation Flakes

Distinctive flakes are produced during the maintenance and rejuvenation of core platforms. The dorsal side of these flakes is distinctive because they show the scars of the multifaceted platform of the core. The rejuvenation of the core platform produced by the subtraction of flakes is less intrusive than the core tablet flakes, and they probably are the first choice of a knapper for fixing the platform of a core. If this remedy fails, removal of the core tablet will be the next step. Seven platform preparation flakes are part of the El Bajío collection (Table 5.8).

Figure 5.5. Crested blades made from El Bajío basalt.

Table 5.9. Blade Core Error Recovery Flakes from El Bajío

Bag No.	Collection or Locus	Condition	Weight (gr)	Length (mm)	Width (mm)	Thickness (mm)	Raw Material (Munsell Color)
35428	Montané	Complete	10.5	35	27	10	Bajío basalt (2.5y 5/2)
1043	Montané	Complete	15.5	30	38	7	Bajío basalt (5y7/2)
37551	Isolated 12	Complete	36	46	39	14	Bajío basalt (5y 4/2)
37542	Isolated 12	Terminal	19.5	75	28	8	Bajío basalt (5y 5/2)
37556.2	Locus 7	Complete	2.5	48	16	5	Bajío basalt (5y 5/1)
37608	Locus 5 -ele1	Complete	31	28	55	11	Bajío basalt (10yr 5/3)

Blade Core Error Recovery Flakes

When a blade hinges or a step fracture occurs during blade core reduction, it creates an impediment to further blade removals (Collins 2003:116). Occasionally, this obstacle can be removed by driving a blade beneath the errant spot in the same alignment. In other cases it is necessary to run a flake across the face of the core. Many times the flake's exterior retains the hinged scar. Six error recovery flakes are in the El Bajío collection (Table 5.9).

Primary Cortex Blades

Primary cortex blades represent the initial blades that are obtained from the core. Twelve primary cortex blades are contained in the El Bajío collection (Table 5.10). Ten are complete blades, and two are proximal fragments. The primary flakes retain 50 to 70 percent of the cortex, and they have at least one cortical facet. The blades show faceted (n=6), multifaceted (n=2), and cortical (n=3) platforms. The lengths of the complete blades are between 57 mm and 135 mm, and their widths are between 25 mm and 60 mm. With the exception of three primary cortex blades made using Bajío basalt, all the primary cortext blades have varying degrees of patina. The majority of the blades are flat, but three of them present some curvature. The degree of curvature is measured as the change in course of the fracture between the proximal and distal end of the blade interior (Collins and Lohse 2004:120). At least five blades in this group present macroscopic use-wear scars along one or two edges, indicative of scraping and cutting tasks. The use-wear scars of these artifacts, recovered from the surface, are covered with patina.

Non-Cortical Blades with Prior Blade Scars

The El Bajío collection includes 22 non-cortical blades or blade fragments with prior blade scars (Table 5.11). Seven blades are complete; three are proximal fragments. The complete blades vary between 45 mm and 86 mm in length. Their widths range from 17 mm to 41 mm. Eight blades in this group bear macroscopic use-wear scars along one or two edges, indicative of scraping and cutting tasks. The use-wear scars on three blades recovered from the surface are covered with patina.

Prismatic Blades

Prismatic blades are specialized flakes removed from a prepared core where the blades are at least twice as long as they are wide and they exhibit more than one parallel blade scar on their dorsal surface. These blades have a prismatic, triangular or trapezoidal cross section. Forty-nine prismatic blades and blade fragments are in the El Bajío collection (Table 5.12, Figs. 5.6 and 5.7). The majority of these blades have trapezoidal cross sections. Twenty-three of the blades are complete, with lengths between 40 mm and 123 mm. The width of these prismatic blades falls between 16 mm and 40 mm. All of them are made on the Bajío Basalt, with the exception of three blades that were manufactured on different kinds of cherts. One prismatic blade was made with the same kind of chert as observed in an artifact collected at Fin del Mundo. One large prismatic blade indicates bipolar flaking represented by opposite protuberant bulbs. Most blades in this group have faceted platforms. Sixteen blades exhibit macroscopic use-wear scars along one or two edges, indicative of scraping and cutting tasks. The use-wear scars on the blades, collected from the surface, are covered with patina.

Table 5.10. Primary Cortex Blades from El Bajío

Bag No.	Collection or Locus	Condition	Weight (g)	Length (mm)	Width (mm)	Thickness (mm)	Facets	Raw Material (Munsell Color)	Cortex	Degree of Curvature	Platform	Macro Use-Wear
1031	Montané	Complete	82.5	135	53	12	2	Rhyolite	40%	—	—	—
695B	Montané	Complete	18.5	66	23	10		Bajío basalt (2.5y 6/2)	70%	—	Faceted	—
35445	Locus 4	Complete	39.2	80	45	11.5	1	Bajío basalt (2.5y 6/2)	45%	—	Multi-faceted	+
35430	Montané	Complete	26.5	85	27	11		Bajío basalt (2.5y 6/2)	70%	—	Faceted	+
35448	Isolated 3	Complete	45.8	86	32	19	1	Bajío basalt (2.5y 7/3)	50%	—	Multi-faceted	—
195	Montané	Proximal	37	51	38	18	2	Bajío basalt (2.5y 7/3)	30%	10	Faceted	—
35440	Montané	Complete	161	130	64	—	2	Rhyolite	25%	—	Cortex	+
695B	Montané	Proximal	60	48R	60	16	1	Bajío basalt (5y 6/2)	50%	—	Cortex	+
695B	Montané	Complete	39.5	68	25	16	1	Bajío basalt (5y 6/3)	50%	10	Faceted/cortex	—
37544	Locus 6	Complete	34	62	46	12	2	Red/yellow chert (5yr 4/3)	60%	10	Faceted	+
45573	Locus 12-ele2	Complete	29	57	20	8	1	1 Bajío basalt (10yr 5/3)	30%	—	Faceted	—
37608	Locus 5	Complete	51	98	30	12	1	Bajío basalt patina (2.5y 5/1	50%	15	—	—

Figure 5.6. Prismatic Blades from El Bajío.

Figure 5.7. Prismatic Blades from El Bajío.

Table 5.11. Cortical Blades with Prior Scars from El Bajío

Bag No.	Collection or Locus	Condition	Weight (g)	Length (mm)	Width (mm)	Thickness (mm)	Facets	Raw Material (Munsell Color)	Degree of Curvature	Platform	Macro Use-Wear
1038	Montané	Distal	33.5	81	30	12	1	Bajío basalt (5y 6/3)		—	+
695B	Montané	Distal	12.1	46	31	9	1	Bajío basalt (5y 7/2)		—	+
35430	Montané	Distal	10.4	45	23	11	1	Bajío basalt (2.5y 6/2)		Much patina	+
1812	Montané	Distal	19.9	55	29	16	1	Bajío basalt (2.5y 6/2)		—	+
35429	Montané	Medial	6.1	31	22	0.7	1	Bajío basalt (2.5y 6/2)		—	+
1096	Montané	Proximal	5.2	29	25	7	1	Bajío basalt (2.5y 6/2)		Cortex	+
1840	Montané	Complete	59	86	36	16	1	Bajío basalt (2.5y 7/2)		Cortex	—
35449	Montané	Distal	26.5	64	29	11	1	White chert		—	—
695B	Montané	Complete	11.5	45	24	10	1	Bajío basalt (2.5y 6/2)		Faceted	—
35448	Montané	Complete	35	75	33	12	2	Chert cream and white.*		—	—
695A	Montané	Proximal	30	36	41	11	1	Bajío basalt (2.5y 6/2)		Faceted	+
695B	Montané	Complete	7.6	46	29	7	1	Bajío basalt (2.5y 6/2)		Faceted and cortex	—
37540	Locus 5	Distal	53.5	78	38	16	1	Bajío basalt (5y 5/2)	8	—	—
37529	Locus 4	Complete	30	66	33	22	1	Bajío basalt (2.5y 6/1)		Faceted	+
37629	Locus 4	Complete	9.5	51	17	7	1	Bajío basalt (gley 1 3/n)		—	—
37534	Locus 4	Distal	25	60	27	15	1	Bajío basalt (5y 6/2)		—	—
37561.1	Locus 7	Distal	14.5	43	38	10	1	Bajío basalt (2.5y 7/3)		—	—
37561.1	Locus 7	Distal	72.5	92	38	20	1	Bajío basalt (2.5y 7/3)		—	—
45312	Locus 10	Medial	1.5	18	16	4	1	White chert with black lines (2.5y 7/1)		—	—
45391	Locus 10	Complete	15	51	30	9	1	Bajío basalt (5y 5/2)	6	—	—
37574	Locus 10	Medial	11.5	50	28	17	1	Bajío basalt (5y 5/2)		—	—
37608	Locus 5 (Feature 1)	Proximal	19	41	34	8	1	Bajío basalt (10yr6/2)		—	—

Note: * This piece is similar to one found at Fin del Mundo.

Table 5.12. Prismatic Blades from El Bajío

Bag No.	Collection or Locus	Condition	Weight (g)	Length (mm)	Width (mm)	Thick-ness (mm)	Raw Material (Munsell Color)	Degree of Curvature	Protub-erant Bulb	Platform	Macro Use-Wear
695A	Montané	Complete	66.8	108	35	17	2.5y 7/2	5	—	Faceted	+
695b	Montané	Medial	1.8	17	15.5	4.5	Chert	—	—		
35430	Montané	Medial	45	72	36	17	5y 6/2	—	—		+
35430	Montané	Proximal	18.5	56	26	10	5 y 5/2	—	+	Faceted	+
35430	Montané	Complete	44.3	88	32	11	5y 5/2	—	+		+
695B	Montané	Medial	5.5	24	27	5.5	5y 7/2	—	—		
695B	Montané	Proximal	26.5	51	29	11	2.5y 6/2	—	+	Faceted	
695B	Montané	Proximal	14	35	35	8	5y 6/2	—	+	Faceted	+
35435	Montané	Complete	68.5	83	36	20	10yr 7/4	—	—	Cortical	
	Montané	Complete	94	112	35	21	10yr 5/4	—	Bipolar	Faceted	+
1847	Montané	Complete	102	106	38	21	2.5y 6/2	—	+	Faceted	+
	Montané	Complete	77.2	123	36.5	15	10yr 5/4	—	—	Faceted	.+
35428	Montané	Complete	38.6	72	31	15	10yr 7/4	—	+	Faceted	
695A	Montané	Complete	—	59	20	15	2.5y 6/2	—	—		
1031	Montané	Complete	22.6	76	27	12.5	2.5y 6/2	—	—	Faceted	Reclam-ation
695B	Montané	Complete	5	48	16	7	5y 6/2	—	—	Faceted	+
695B	Montané	Complete	39.2	105	40	12	2.5y 6/2	8	+	Faceted	+
695B	Montané	Complete	34.2	81	39	10	2.5y 7/4	7	—	Faceted	
37672	Isolated	Complete	36.8	73	36	12	2.5y 7/4	15	+	Faceted	
37542	Isolated	Complete	39	82	30	14	5y 6/2	6	—		
45305	Locus 6	Medial	6.5	40	18	8	10yr 6/3	—	—	Cortical	+
45305	Locus 6	Distal	10.3	53	25	9	5y 3/1	—	—		+
37730	Locus 6	Proximal	50.5	69	40	15	5y 5/1	—	—	Faceted	
37542	Isolated	Terminal	89.5	79	36	24	5y 5/1	10	—		
37538	Locus 5	Complete	54.8	111	38	12	5y 6/2	10	—	Faceted	
37624	Locus 4	Complete	12.5	60	26	6	5y 5/1	—	+	Faceted	
37540	Locus 5	Complete	44	72	38	14	2.5y 6/2	—	—	Cortical	
37729	Locus 6	Proximal	17	35	30	12	5y 6/2	—	+	Faceted	
37530	Locus 4	Distal	7.5	28	30	7	5y 7/2	—	—		
37530	Locus 4	Distal	19.5	34	38	15	5y 7/2	14	—		

continued

Table 5.12. *(continued)*

Bag No.	Collection or Locus	Condition	Weight (g)	Length (mm)	Width (mm)	Thickness (mm)	Raw Material (Munsell Color)	Degree of Curvature	Protuberant Bulb	Platform	Macro Use-Wear
37561.1	Locus 7	Complete	22	58		22	2.5y 6/1	—	+	Faceted	No
45317	Locus 7	Distal	17.5	50	22	9	5y 5/1	14	—		
45504	Locus 7	Proximal	18.5	46	29	8	2.5y 7/3	—	+	Faceted	+
45420	Locus 7	Proximal	74	81	46	16	5y 6/2	—	—	Faceted	+
45506	Locus 7	Terminal	25.5	24	32	12	Purple/ white chert	—	—		
37555	Locus 7	Proximal	1.5	16	18	4	Gray chert	—	—		
37561.1	Locus 7	Distal	42	5	34	13	5y 6/3	—	13		+
37560	Locus 7	Distal	37.5	85	30	13	10yr 7/4	—	12		
45447	Locus 12	Distal	11	34	30	12	10yr 5/3	—	10		
45314	Locus 10	Distal	6	35	20	5	5y 5/2	—	—		Trampling
45392	Locus 10	Distal	9.2	72	30	9	5y 5/2	—	—		Trampling
37574	Locus 10	Complete	19.5	60	30	9	5y 6/2	12	—	Faceted	Trampling
45394	Locus 10	Proximal	13	44	29	8	5y 5/1	—	—	Faceted	Trampling
45315	Locus 10	Complete	22.5	62	25	11	5y 6/2	—	—		
45395	Locus 10	Complete	53	75	38	25	5y 6/2	—	+	Cortical	Trampling
37657	Isolated	Proximal	23	47r	28	12	5y 6/1	—	—	Faceted	+
37608	Locus 5-ele1	Complete	61	40	29	7	10yr 5/3	—	—	Faceted	
37608	Locus 5-ele1	Distal	13.5	28	28	14	2.5y 5/1	—	—		
37608	Locus 5-ele1	Complete	36	70	34	11	10yr 6/2	13	—		

UNIFACIAL TECHNOLOGY

A uniface is a specific type of stone tool that has been flaked on one surface only. Scrapers are unifacially retouched tools with a steep, obtuse-angled edge that is suitable for a number of tasks, including scraping hides, planing wood or bone, and cutting like a knife (Whittaker 1994). A total of 90 unifacial tools are part of the El Bajío lithic collection, including flakes, blades, and core fragments (Table 5.13). End scrapers in the Bajío collection include 28 lateral scrapers, 10 composite scrapers, four denticulate lateral and composite scrapers, three tortoise back scrapers, 10 unifacially retouched gravers, and five notched tools. Julio Montané collected the largest concentration of unifacial artifacts from a single locality in 1979. These unifacial artifacts came from a surface concentration of tools in the northern sector of Cerro Rojo, a small hill located in the middle of the El Bajío site (Julio Montané, personal communication 2003). Twenty-six unifacially retouched tools were collected from this locality.

End Scrapers

End scrapers are diagnostic Paleoindian tools. In the United States, they are important temporal indicators, like

Table 5.13. Unifacial Tools from El Bajío

Tool Type	Montané Collection	Montané-Cerro Colorado	Locus 5	Locus 6	Locus 7	Locus 8	Locus 10	Locus 12	Isolated	Totals
End scrapers	14	9		1	1	1	2		2	30
Side scraper	19	7	2	1	3					32
Composite scraper	3	3								6
Denticulate	1	1	1		1					4
Gravers	6	3	1							10
Notched tools	4	1								5
Circular scrapers		2						1		3
TOTAL	47	26	4	2	5	1	2	1	2	90

Figure 5.8. End scrapers from El Bajío.

Figure 5.9. End scrapers from Fin del Mundo.

projectile points (Collins 2003; Frison 1991). End scrapers are diagnostic of all Paleoindian components, including Clovis, Folsom, and Plainview, because they are not present in Archaic complexes in Sonora and Arizona. End scrapers are triangular, about 5 cm in length. Many of them have a spur at the intersection of the lateral edge and the distal end. Many spurs are broken off of the end scrapers, presumably from use (Morrow 1997). Paleoindian end scrapers were almost certainly hafted. Hafted scrapers have been found in the state of Coahuila, Mexico, in dry caves, including Cueva de la Candelaria and Cuatro Cienegas. Although the Coahuila scrapers are of much later age (A.D. 0 to 1400) it is possible that the Paleoindian scrapers were hafted in the same way as these examples.

A total of 30 end scrapers are present in the El Bajío collections, 13 of which are made on prismatic blades and 17 on flakes (Table 5.14). Twelve scrapers were made on fine cryptocrystalline cherts that are not locally available (Fig. 5.8). At least two of the chert end scrapers were made on the same cherts used to make two end scrapers and blades at the Fin del Mundo site (Fig. 5.9). Furthermore, an end scraper made on a red chert resembles the material used to make an end scraper recovered at Murray Springs in Southern Arizona (C. Vance Haynes Jr., personal communication 2003).

Fourteen end scrapers exhibit one or two spurs, protuberances made by notching. One spur was formed by a burin spall. The spurs are located at the intersection of the lateral edge and the distal end, and they probably functioned as leather punches. Eight scrapers have the spur on the left side; four have the spur on the right side; and two scrapers have double spurs. The majority of the El Bajío end scrapers were probably hafted. Fifteen

Table 5.14. Attributes of End Scrapers from El Bajío

Bag No.	Collection or Locus	Raw Material	Munsell Color	Made On	Attributes	Length (mm)	Width (mm)	Thickness (mm)	Function Angle	Spur (dorsal aspect)	Hafting Marks
141	Montané	Bajío basalt	10yr 7/3	Blade	Step termination	45.9	32.3	9.5	40	No	20 mm from the base
1027	Montané	Bajío basalt	2.5y 6/2	Flake		24.3	21.5	4.9	20	Left	
1027	Montané	Bajío basalt	10yr 7/3	Flake	Was hafted	30	18.1	5.6	20	No	Snap
1069	Montané	Gray chert	gley 1 4/n	Flake		28.8	23.6	15.6	40	Left	Snap
1079	Montané	Bajío basalt	2.5y 7/4	Flake	Was hafted	30.9	48.5	12.2	45	No	Snap
1096	M-rojo	Bajío basalt	10yr 7/4	Flake	Was hafted	20.5	34.2	11.3	25	No	Snap
1096	M-rojo	Pink, heat-treated chert*	10r 6/3	Flake	Was hafted	28.0	27.5	8.6	70	1	Snap
1272	Montané	Bajío basalt	2.5y 5/2	Flake	Heavily fragmented	64.1	56.2	12.5	25	No	No
1847	Montané	Bajío basalt	2.5y 6/3	Flake	Step termination	51.1	36.9	17.1	55	Left	18 mm from the base
35428	M-rojo	Bajío basalt	2.5 y 6/2	Flake	Was hafted	32.8	28.4	8.0	25	No	19 mm from the base
35428	M-rojo	Bajío basalt	10yr 10/4	Flake	Step termination	59.3	42.0	16.5	30	Burin flake	No
35428	M-rojo	Bajío basalt	5y 7/2	Flake	Was hafted	38.4	32.8	10.8	30	No	12 mm from the base
35428	M-rojo	Bajío basalt	5y 7/1	Blade	Was hafted	40.0	35.1	9.0	20	Left	10 mm from the base
35428	M-rojo	Bajío basalt	2.5y 6/2	Flake		54.0	69.4	16.7	30	No	No
35428	M-rojo	Brown chert	5y 6/1	Flake	Was hafted	27.6	25.2	15.4	50	Right	10 mm from the base
35429	Montané	Brown chert	10yr 6/1	Flake	Step termination and hafted	39.1	39.2	13.8	40	No	10 mm from the base

Table 5.14. *(continued)*

Bag No.	Collection or Locus	Raw Material	Munsell Color	Made On	Attributes	Length (mm)	Width (mm)	Thickness (mm)	Function Angle	Spur (dorsal aspect)	Hafting Marks
35442	Isolated	Yellow chert	10yr 7/6	Blade	Hafted	32	29.6	6	23	No	Snap
35447	Isolated	Orange chert	7.5y 5/8	Blade	Hafted	19.8	25	4.1	20	Left	Snap
695A	Montané	Bajío basalt	2.5y 7/2	Blade	Hafted	31	22	6.2	25	2	Snap
695B	Montané	Bajío basalt	2.5y 6/3	Blade	Hafted	32.0	30.5	7.8	30	No	18 mm from the base
695B	Montané	Yellow chert*	2.5y 5/4	Flake	Step, hafted	27.6	29.0	6.9	40	Right	12 mm from the base
1069	Montané	Bajío basalt	10yr 7/10	Blade	Hafted	40	32	11	30	No	12 mm from the base
35435	Montané	Purple chert	10r 5/2	Flake	Hafted	36	31	13	45	No	11 mm from the base
695B	Montané	Bajío basalt	2.5y 6/1	Blade	Hafted	20	20	3.5	20	No	Distal end fragment
37549b	Locus 6	Red chert**	10r 4/4	Blade	Hafted	37	21	6	20	Right	17 mm from the base
45460	Locus 8	White chert	10yr 8/1	Flake	Hafted	34	32	8	25	No	Snap
37556	Locus 7	Bajío basalt	5y 6/2	Blade	Hafted	41	26	7	25	No	17 mm from the base
45398	Locus 10	Bajío basalt	5y 6/2	Blade	Step, hafted	49	28	11	40	Right	22 mm from the base
37574	Locus 10	Pink, heat-treated chert*	2.5yr 5/4	Blade	Step, hafted	45	28	8	40	Left	25 mm from the base
35428	M-rojo	Bajío basalt	5y 6/2	Blade	Hafted	39	31	5	20	Left	14mm from the base

Key: M-rojo = Montané-Cerro Rojo.

Note: *same material as found at Fin del Mundo.
**same material as found at Murray Springs.

of them have notches in their sides near the base that appear to be hafting marks. In 10 specimens the distal end of the tool snapped, probably when they were hafted. Twelve end scrapers have poorer workmanship on their lateral edges than on their distal ends, indicating that they were retouched or curated while hafted.

Side Scrapers

Side scrapers may be made on blanks that are blades or flakes (Whittaker 1994:27). The retouched side may be either the left edge or the right edge, or even on both edges, in which case it would be called a double side scraper. Side scrapers are further defined by the shape of their retouched edges as being concave, straight or convex. Thirty-two side scrapers are part of the El Bajío collection (Table 5.15). Side scrapers are not age diagnostic tools because they are common during Paleoindian times and during the Holocene. The analysis of the El Bajío collection, however, indicated the side scrapers may be of Paleoindian age. Some of them are manufactured on blades, and a group of them was found with end scrapers at the locality of Cerro Rojo. This may indicate their use in the same activity. Most of the side scrapers exhibit a heavy patina.

Most of the side scrapers are made on flakes and three were manufactured on blades. Six side scrapers were made using a non-local chalcedony or chert raw material, one was made using a quartz crystal that was probably local, and the rest were made using the local vitrified basalt. Fourteen backed scrapers were classified as backed side scrapers. According to Gramly (1990), a backed scraper is a side scraper that has an edge that is comfortable and safe for gripping opposite to the cutting edge. The back may have been created intentionally or may have resulted from a natural plane present in the rock. At least four backed scrapers have a spur located at the intersection of the lateral edge and the distal end. Two spurs were manufactured by notching and two were produced by a burin spall. Julio Montané collected seven side scrapers form a locus near Cerro Rojo in the center of the site, and four of these are backed side scrapers. The most interesting backed side scraper is a specimen made using an 81-mm thick flake of a totally transparent quartz crystal, bag number 1094 (Fig. 5.10).

Composite Scraper

Composite scrapers are defined as unifacial tools with a continuous invasive medium-to-steep retouch in multiple edges (Sliva 1997). The six composite scrapers in

Figure 5.10. Side scraper from El Bajío made from quartz crystal.

the El Bajío collection were all made on flakes (Table 5.16). Five of these scrapers were made using Bajío basalt and one was made using an orange chert. Composite scrapers are not diagnostic of a particular time period or lithic complex in the southwestern United States or northern Mexico. Although composite, denticulate, and circular scrapers are common in Archaic assemblages, we consider the collection from El Bajío to have a Paleoindian affiliation. This is because the scrapers have a thick patina, and they were spatially associated with Paleoindian assemblages.

Denticulate Scrapers

Denticulate scrapers have a morphology that displays one or more edges worked into multiple notched shapes, much like the toothed edge of a saw. These tools might have been used as saws, most likely for meat processing and plant processing (Whittaker 1994). Four denticulate scrapers are present in the El Bajío collection (Table 5.17). Two of these are side scrapers and two are end scrapers, one of which presents a spur.

Circular Scrapers

Circular scrapers are also known as discoidal scrapers. They are usually based on a flake that has a circular shape, with retouch completely around the periphery. In many cases circular scrapers are resharpened and reworked end scrapers (Gramly 1990:14). Three examples of cicular

Table 5.15. Side Scrapers from El Bajío

Bag No.	Collection or Locus	Raw Material	Color	Length (mm)	Width (mm)	Thickness (mm)	Weight (g)	Functional Angle	Spur	Other Attributes
1281	Montané	Bajío basalt	10yr 7/4	42.4	44.2	18.1	33.4	40	1	Backed
695B	Montané	Bajío basalt	10yr 6/2	60	46	20	61.9	45	1	Backed
1094	Montané	Quartz crystal	transparent	81.0	50.0	21.5	106.9	30	1	Backed
1079	Montané	Bajío basalt	10yr 8/4	49.5	42.4	25.1	52.3	45		Backed
35430	Montané	Bajío basalt	5y 5/2	67.6	49.8	24.9	56.1	20		Backed
695A	Montané	Bajío basalt	10yr 7/3	29.3	53.5	11.8	20.9	50		Backed in blade
142	Montané	Bajío basalt	2.5y 8/2	44.2	38.4	13.8	27.8	30	1	Backed
1034	Montané	Red chert	2.5 yr 5/4	48.9	41	17.6	31.4	45		Backed
35430	Montané	Red chert	7.5yr 4/3	47.1	33.1	20.6	34.8	70	1	Backed
35429	Montané	Brown chert	10yr 6/4	27.9	43.1	14.5	19.9	45		Backed
192	Montané	Bajío basalt	5y 7/1	34.9	42.8	6.9	25	23		
1069	Montané	Bajío basalt	10y 7/3	49.4	31	16	33.4	40		
35440	Montané	Bajío basalt	10yr 8/1	61.7	78.2	22.8	105.3	50		
35429	Montané	Bajío basalt	2.5y 6/3	42.5	27	12.8	19.8	25		
695A	Montané	Brown chert	10yr 6/3	31	33.8	15.1	17.5	50		
1069	Montané	Brown chert	10yr 4/1	47	36	10	25	30		
142	Montané	Orange chert	10yr 5/4	46.5	31	6	9.2	20		
142	Montané	Pink chert	10r 6/1	30.6	52.9	7.2	14.1	25		
1096	M-rojo	Bajío basalt	10yr 7/4	42.1	31	11	17.5	25		Backed
1095	M-rojo	Bajío basalt	10yr 6/3	54	42	14	44.7	30		Backed
35428	M-rojo	Bajío basalt	2.5y 7/1	39.3	32.1	5.5	16.4	50	1	Backed
35428	M-rojo	Bajío basalt	2.5y 7/3	55.3	39.4	16.0	42.3	70		Backed
35428	M-rojo	Bajío basalt	5y 6/1	51.4	41.2	15.7	34.5	80		
35428	M-rojo	Bajío basalt	10yr 5/2	58	33.4	14.6	28	35	1	
1096	M-rojo	Bajío basalt	2.5y 7/1	39.5	34	13	36.2	30		
37007	Locus 5- e1	Bajío basalt	2.5yr 5/4	31	55	50	7	25		
37555	Locus 7	Bajío basalt	5y 6/2	72	38	15	47.5	20		
37563	Locus 7	White chert	10y 8/2	12	20	5	2.5	25	1	
37540	Locus 5	Bajío basalt	2.5y 5/3	74	61	16	87.5	20		

Key: M-rojo = Montané-Cerro Rojo.

Table 5.16. Composite Scrapers from El Bajío

Bag No.	Locus	Raw Material	Munsell Color	Length (mm)	Width (mm)	Thickness (mm)	Weight (g)	Functional Angle
141	Montané	Bajío basalt		55.3	39.4	16	42.3	40
1096	M-rojo	Bajío basalt	10yr 7/4	46.4	44.0	19.4	47.7	80
35428	M-rojo	Bajío basalt	5y 7/1	45.3	30.3	12.2	17.4	50
35428	M-rojo	Bajío basalt	2.5y 6/1	42.8	33.9	13.6	19.2	40/50
695A	Montané	Bajío basalt	5y 5/1	42.1	33.0	18.0	26.6	40-70
695B	Montané	Orange chert	7.5yr 5/6	23.2	43.1	9.5	10.2	50-40

Key: M-rojo = Montané-Cerro Rojo.

Table 5.17. Denticulated Scrapers from El Bajío

Bag No.	Collection or Locus	Raw Material	Munsell Color	Made On	Length (mm)	Width (mm)	Thickness (mm)	Weight (g)	Scraper Type	Spur
35428	M-rojo	Pink chert	2.5y 6/1	Flake	31.0	20.0	6.0	24.1	End	Broken
1069	Montané	Bajío basalt	2.5y 7/1	Flake	44	18	11	10	Side	
45470	Locus 5	Bajío basalt	2.5y 7/4	Flake	93	74	16	107	End	
45414	Locus 7	Bajío basalt	2.5y 6/3	Flake	39	25	12	15	Side	

Key: M-rojo = Montané-Cerro Rojo.

Table 5.18. Circular Scrapers from El Bajío

Bag No.	Collection or Locus	Raw Material	Munsell Color	Length (mm)	Width (mm)	Thickness (mm)	Weight (g)
35428	M-rojo	White chert	2.5y 8/1	46.4	32.7	22	24.4
35428	M-rojo	White chert	2.5y 8/1	44.3	41.1	12.3	22.2
45565	Locus 12-e1	Bajío basalt	10yr 6/4	51.8	45.3	14.2	31.3

Key: M-rojo = Montané-Cerro Rojo.

scrapers are part of the El Bajío collection (Table 5.18; Fig. 5.11). All of these were made on flakes that have their bulbs of percussion flaked away.

Notched Tools

Notched tools are artifacts that have one or more narrow concavities on their edges that have been created using unifacial retouch. They are similar to scrapers but have a tightly circumscribed working edge. The notches on these tools may have been used to plane shafts of small diameter in the manner of spoke shaves (Gramly 1990:34; Sliva 1997:43). The five notched tools in the El Bajío collection are made on flakes (Table 5.19).

Figure 5.11. Circular scraper from Locus 12 at El Bajío.

Table 5.19. Notched Tools from El Bajío

Bag No.	Collection or Locus	Raw Material	Munsell Color	Length (mm)	Width (mm)	Thickness (mm)	Weight (g)	Spur
142	Montané	Bajío basalt	2.5y 5/1	51	42	22	46.3	X
1252	Montané	Bajío basalt	5y 6/2	49.7r	67	23.04	77.6	
35440	Montané	Bajío basalt	2.5y 6/2	65.3	54.2	18.6	63	
695B	Montané	Bajío basalt	2.5y 5/2	62	48	21	67.5	
37560	Locus 7	Pink chert	10r 4/4	28	22	6	25	X

Table 5.20. Gravers from El Bajío

Bag No.	Collection or Locus	Raw Material	Munsell Color	Length (mm)	Width (mm)	Thickness (mm)	Weight (g)	Retouch	Boring (mm)	Hafted
1018	Montane	Bajío basalt	10yr 6/2	37.4	30.5	10.2	12.5	Notches and retouch flaking	17 x 10	Yes
1069	Montane	Bajío basalt	7.5yr 6/3	20.3	41.08	12.4	7.8	Retouch flaking	13 x 11	No
1031	Montane	Bajío basalt	2.5y 7/4	3.1	14	15	6.5	Retouch flaking	14 x 15	Yes
695b	Montane	Bajío basalt	10yr 7/3	60	48	18	56.2	Retouch flaking	112 x 10	No
696	Montane	Bajío basalt	5y 7/2	48	34	9	16.5	Burin	Burin	Yes
1099	Montane	Bajío basalt	5y 6/3	100	45		18	Graver retouch flaking	25 x 15	No
1095	M-rojo	Bajío basalt	2.5y 7/2	45.2	39	17.1	30	Notches and retouch flaking	14 x 12	No
35428	M-rojo	Bajío basalt	2.5y 8/3	67.7	46.2	17.7	38.4	Notches and retouch flaking	3	No
35428	M-rojo	Chert, pink	2.5y 6/1	54.0	23.0	15.0	19.6	Notches (big and massive)	14 x 13	
37528	Locus 4	Bajío basalt	5y 6/1	52	30	14	24.5	Notches	15 x 11	No

Key: M-rojo = Montané-Cerro Rojo.

Gravers

Gravers are implements used for perforation. They are flakes that were transformed by unifacial flaking or notching to produce a sharp point. Gravers are sometimes referred to as borers or perforators (Collins 2003:131; Gramly 1990; Sliva 1997:44). Sliva (1997) identifies the ethnographically documented functions of this type of artifact for punching leather; boring wood, bone, and antler; and graving wood, bone, and antler. Nine of the 10 gravers in the El Bajío collection were made using flakes, and one was made using a core fragment (Table 5.20). The gravers are not uniform, and at least three of them apparently were used as hafted tools. One graver was fabricated by removing a burin spall.

BIFACIAL TECHNOLOGY

A biface is a two-sided stone tool that displays flake scars on both sides. A profile of the final product tends to exhibit a lenticular shape. These tools are an essential part of the Clovis lithic technological system (Collins 2003; Gramly 1990; Huckell 2007). Bifaces undergo a specialized production phase that is distinct from the use phase (Andrefsky 2009:74). Six groups of bifaces from El Bajío are discussed (Table 5.21). These include primary bifaces (n=16), secondary bifaces (n=36), Clovis preforms (n=15), Clovis points (n=2), square based bifaces (n=33), bifacial gravers (n=2) and overshot flakes (n=2). The manufacture of projectile points is an important part of the biface reduction at the site. However, other

Table 5.21. Bifacial Industry, El Bajío

Biface Type	Montané	M-rojo	Locus 1	Locus 2	Locus 4	Locus 5	Locus 7	Locus 8	Locus 10	Locus 12	Locus 15	Iso-lated	Totals
Primary	6	1			5	1	1					2	16
Secondary	18	2		1	6		1		2	4		2	36
Clovis preforms	2				5	1	1	1	2		1	2	15
Clovis points					1							1	2
Square-base points	14		1		3			1		9		5	33
Gravers										2			2
Overshot flakes	2												2
TOTALS	42	3	1	1	20	2	3	2	4	15	1	12	106

Key: M-rojo = Montané-Cerro Rojo.

Table 5.22. Primary Bifaces from El Bajío (all Bajío basalt)

Bag No.	Collection or Locus	Munsell Patina Color	Condition	Weight (g)	Length (mm)	Width (mm)	Basal width (mm)	Thickness (mm)	Retouch Type
142	Montané	5y 6/2	Complete	81.5	73.3	51.5	41.3	19	
1068	Montané	2.5y 7/3	Complete	50.9	68.1	45	35.2	16	
1840	Montané	gley2 4/5	Complete	20.8	51.7	51.7	2.7	1.4	
1840	Montané	hue2.5 6/2	Complete	43.1	66.2	46	35	18	Overshot
35429	Montané	2.5y 6/1	Complete	45.4	76.5	37.3	32.5	14.2	Overshot
695B	Montané	5y 6/2	Basal	40	43	53	33	16	
35428	M-rojo	5y 5/2	Split	28.7	68.2	—	—	1.5	Overshot
35443	Isolated	5y 6/2	Basal	82.8	60.8r	57.5	41.7	2.4	Overshot asymmetrical
37542	Isolated 12	2.5y 6/4	Basal	203	84.1r	66	52	40.2	
37555	Locus 7	5y 6/2	Split	51	57	41	—	20	
37538	Locus 5	2.5y 6/4	Basal	16.1	75.9r	78.9	65	20	Overshot
35445	Locus 4	5y 6/1	Complete	76.5	80.5	47.1	32	21.3	
35445	Locus 4	5y 6/2	Basal	93.8	58.4R	69	59.2	16.9	
37528	Locus 4	gley1 3/n	Basal	67	62	60	16	—	Overshot
37529	Locus 4	5y 6/2	Basal	80.8	62.6r	51.9	40	2	Overshot
37530	Locus 4	5y 6/2	Distal	27.7	30	50	—	12.5	Overshot

Key: M-rojo = Montané-Cerro Rojo.

Figure 5.12. Primary bifaces from El Bajío.

Figure 5.13. Secondary bifaces from El Bajío; the lower row is ready for channel flaking.

bifaces were made that were not related to point manufacture but were likely intended for use as knives, gravers, and other kinds of tools employed in the daily camp activities. All of the bifaces, except for one square-based biface, were manufactured using the local vitrified basalt.

Primary Bifaces

Following Huckell (2007:191), primary bifaces exhibit several large expansive scars where flakes were removed in a selective fashion. Primary bifaces are irregular in shape and thickness, and they have a generally oval shape with very little differentiation between the proximal and distal ends. There are 16 primary bifaces in the El Bajío collection, eight complete and eight fragments (Table 5.22; Fig. 5.12). Eight bifaces retain overshot flake scars. Overshot flaking consists of removing a large single flake that terminates near the opposite margin of the biface or removes part of it (Huckell 2007). There is a high probability that the eight primary bifaces with overshot flaking were to be transformed into Clovis spear points. The remaining bifaces were likely going to be transformed into knives.

Secondary Bifaces

Secondary bifaces represent formal tools in which the tip and the basal ends have been established. The flaking exhibits smaller and more closely spaced scars than those associated with primary bifaces (Huckell 2007:192). A total of 36 secondary bifaces have been collected from El Bajío, including six complete artifacts, 14 basal fragments, and 16 distal fragments (Table 5.23; Fig. 5.13). All of these artifacts have concave bases and a side configuration that expands from the base. Eight secondary bifaces present overshot flaking scars that create an asymmetrical ridge

in one face, with an asymmetrical ridge on the opposite side in the other face. It is probable that the bifaces displaying overshot flaking were going to be transformed into Clovis points, while the rest were likely going to be transformed into other tools. For example, one complete biface (No. 35445) with symmetrical overshot flaking appears to be a knife preform.

Clovis Points and Preforms

Clovis is recognized for its characteristic bifacial point, a type defined by Wormington (1957:263). Clovis points were undoubtedly used as spear points (Gramly 1990; Collins 2003). More has been written about fluting of Clovis points than any other lithic retouch techniques. Fluting is an unusual technique that was used early in the development of tools in North America. Fluting probably had a practical function in thinning the base for easier hafting, but fluting is not a necessity and in some points fluting was carried to extremes of perfection (Whittaker 1994:234–235). Projectile points are among the few artifacts that were produced for a well-planned activity; the shape must approximate a mental template for the symmetry and the efficiency of the point (Andrefsky 2009). Seventeen Clovis preforms and Clovis points are part of the El Bajío collection.

Table 5.23. Secondary Bifaces from El Bajío

Bag No.	Collection, Locus, or Isolate	Raw Material	Munsell Color	Condition	Weight (g)	Length (mm)	Width (mm)	Basal Width (mm)	Thickness (mm)	Retouch Type
1031	Montané	Bajío basalt	5y 6/2	Basal	25.3	43.2	46	28	11	Overshot
35430	Montané	Bajío basalt	5y 6/1	Basal	40.4	52.6	48.7	22.4	23	
35430	Montané	Bajío basalt	5y 6/2	Basal	42.8	47.4	47	23.7	14	Overshot
1847	Montané	Bajío basalt	5y 6/3	Basal	10.3	32.5r	34	13	8	
695B	Montané	Bajío basalt	2.5y 8/3	Basal	55.1	46.6r	63.8	43.6	18	Overshot asymmetrical
695B	Montané	Chert	X	Distal	6.5	35r	26.5	27.2	6	
142	Montané	Bajío basalt	2.5y 5/1	Basal	16.2	33.7r	41.2	17.3	8	
1840	Montané	Bajío basalt	5y 5/1	Basal	12.3	28.7	49.9	18.7	18	
197	Montané	Bajío basalt	2.5y 6/2	Distal	7.7	32.5		—	6	
1069	Montané	Bajío basalt	5y 6/3	Distal	19.6	37.2	$50	—	11	
1069	Montané	Bajío basalt	2.5y 6/4	Distal	7.5	48.3	x	—	6	
35430	Montané	Bajío basalt	5y 6/3	Medial	53.8	72.5r	44		12	Overshot asymmetrical
1847	Montané	Bajío basalt	5y 6/2	Distal	28.1	46.6	41.5		16	Overshot asymmetrical
695B	Montané	Bajío basalt	5y 6/3	Distal	42.7	55.8r	46.4		16	Overshot asymmetrical
139	Montané	Bajío basalt	2.5y 7/3	Distal	13.1	39.5	37.5r		7.8	
140	Montané	Bajío basalt	2.5y5/1	Distal	46.1	60.5	49.5	—	12	Overshot asymmetrical
35430	Montané	Bajío basalt	5y 6/3	Medial	48.6	56.3r	48	—	12	Overshot asymmetrical
35430	Montané	Bajío basalt	5y 6/2	Basal	15.9	28.7r	48.5	22.5	11	Overshot and basal thinning
35428	M-rojo	Bajío basalt	2.5y7/3	Distal	22.5	55r	35	—	12	
1096	M-rojo	Chert red	10r 4/6	Complete	9.5	28	29		8	

Table 5.23. *(continued)*

Bag No.	Collection, Locus, or Isolate	Raw Material	Munsell Color	Condition	Weight (g)	Length (mm)	Width (mm)	Basal Width (mm)	Thickness (mm)	Retouch Type
37542	Isolate 12	Bajío basalt	5y 6/2	Basal	42.4	45.5r	50	14	15	Overshot asymmetrical
37542	Isolate 12	Bajío basalt	gley24/5B	Basal	19.2	30.5	36.5	23.5	13	
45566	Locus 12-ele2	Bajío basalt	5y 5/1	Distal	23.7	49	35	No	13	Overshot asymmetrical
45567	Locus 12-ele2	Bajío basalt	5y 4/1	Distal	7	41	27		7	
45571	Locus 12-ele2	Bajío basalt	2.5y 6/2	Distal	25	51	40		12	Overshot asymmetrical
45575	Locus 12-ele2	Bajío basalt		Distal	6	33r	25		6	Overshot
37670	Locus 10	Bajío basalt	5y 6/2	Basal	73.8	78	52	35	12	Overshot asymmetrical
37574	Locus 10	Bajío basalt	2.5y 7/3	Split	114	98	38		25	
37558	Locus 7	Bajío basalt	5y 6/2	Medial	7.1	50	17		6	
35445	Locus 4	Bajío basalt	5y 5/1	Complete	83.7	112	45	35.5	13	Overshot symmetrical
35445	Locus 4	Bajío basalt	5y 5/1	Basal	35.4	49.5r	48.6	18.2	10	Overshot asymmetrical
35445	Locus 4	Bajío basalt	2.5Y 6/3	Basal	25.3	38.5	43	29.5	14	Overshot asymmetrical
37624	Locus 4	Bajío basalt	5y 6/2	Complete	62.5	68	54		17	Overshot asymmetrical
37634	Locus 4	Bajío basalt	5y 6/2	Complete	43	53	41		14	Overshot asymmetrical
37632	Locus 4	Bajío basalt	5y 6/2	Split	38.5	66	36	28	14	Overshot asymmetrical
37516	Locus 2	Bajío basalt	X	Basal	27.8	40.3	42	26.6	13	

Key: M-rojo = Montané-Cerro Rojo.

Table 5.24. Clovis Preform Attributes, El Bajío Collection

Bag No.	Collection, Locus, or Isolate	Bajío Basalt Patina Color (Munsell)	Condition	Length (mm)	Width (mm)	Basal Width (mm)	Thick-ness (mm)	Retouch Type	Flute Length (mm)	Flute Width (mm)
695B	Montané	gley2 3/10b	Basal	30.5r	42.3	33.7	11.5	Basal fluting, overshot	28.5	16.5
695A	Montané	2.5y 7/4	Basal	50r	50.5	30	14.7	Basal fluting both sites, overshot	31/38	17.5/19
37667	Isolate 9	2.5y 6/4	Basal	47.3	36	24	10	Basalt fluting, overshot	20	16
35449	Isolate	5y 7/1	Basal	55.7	56.9	20.2	13.8	Basalt fluting, overshot	55	25.3
35086	Isolate	2.5y 4/1	Basal	63r	42.3	30	12	Basalt fluting , overshot	43	21
37819	Locus 15	5y 6/1	Basal	37.4	49.2	22.3	18.9	Basal fluting	33.5	15.5
37668	Locus 10	2.5y 6/3	Distal	45	32		10	Basal fluting	43	20
45313	Locus 10	10yr 6/3	Medial	43	30		12	Basal fluting	38	18
37566	Locus 8	5y 6/3	Basal	52	36.7	31.4	8.8	Basalt fluting , overshot	25.5/30	19.6/14.4
37559	Locus 7	5y 5/2	Basal	41	46	46	12	Basal fluting, overshot	16	21
37740	Locus 5	5y 7/2	Medial	34	39		10	Basal fluting		
35075	Locus 4	5y 5/2	Basal	51r	40	37.2	11	Basal fluting both sides, overshot	30/39.1	26/24
35086	Locus 4	2.5y 5/1	Basal	49r	41	28.1	11.5	Basal fluting, overshot	38	18.2
35086	Locus 4	2.5y 6/2	Basal	41r	41	26	7.5	Basal fluting both sides, overshot	38/36	25/18
35086	Locus 4	2.5y 7/2	Basal	73.4r	55	44	13.2	Basalt fluting	67	28

Clovis Preforms

Fifteen Clovis preforms that were broken or discarded during the manufacture are in the El Bajío collection (Table 5.24; Figs. 5.14 and 5.15). All have convex bases and sides that expand from the base. Ten of the Clovis preforms have an asymmetric overshot pattern that forms an unbalanced ridge on one or both faces. They exhibit basal fluting early in the manufacturing process to thin the biface. Early fluting has been seen in collections from other sites but it was extensively used at El Bajío.

Clovis Points

Measurements were obtained for two Clovis points from El Bajío (Table 5.25). One finished Clovis base was found in 2003 (Fig. 5.16); another complete Clovis point was documented at the Museo Municipal de Carbó (Fig. 5.17). At least a dozen more Clovis points have been collected at the site. All the Clovis points collected at El Bajío were manufactured using El Bajío basalt, with the exception of one Clovis base collected by Julio Motané that was made using obsidian.

Figure 5.14. Clovis preforms with channel flutes from El Bajío.

The complete Clovis point at the Carbó Museum has small fluting on both sides, and grinding at the base and sides (Fig. 5.17). This point, produced using El Bajío basalt, does not exhibit the characteristic patina seen on all the other artifacts at El Bajío. The collector of the point has been deceased for more than 15 years and nobody knows the provenience of the point.

Square-Based Bifaces

Thirty-three lanceolate or triangular, square-based bifaces were collected at El Bajío (Table 5.26). They have sharp

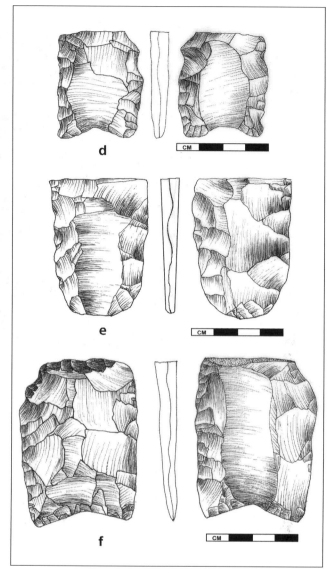

Figure 5.15. Drawings of the Clovis preforms d, e, and f illustrated in Figure 5.14.

Table 5.25. Clovis Points from El Bajío

Bag No.	Locus	Bajío Basalt Patina Color (Munsell)	Condition	Length (mm)	Width (mm)	Basal Width (mm)	Thick-ness (mm)	Flute Length (mm)	Flute Width (mm)	Flaking Type	Grinding
37628	4	gley1 4/10b	Basal fragment	30.8	38.7	23.5	7	22.5/22.5	13.2/13.1	Fine retouch	Basal and lateral
Carbo		2.5y 7/3	Complete	88	29	27	7	20/22	10/8	Small channel flake	Basal and lateral

Figure 5.16. Clovis base found at El Bajío in 2003.

Figure 5.18. Square-based bifaces excavated at Locus 12 at El Bajío.

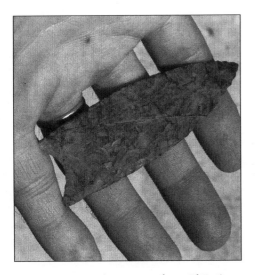

Figure 5.17. Clovis point from El Bajío at the Museo Municipal de Carbó.

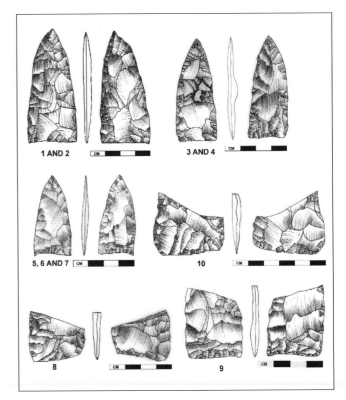

Figure 5.19. Drawings of square-based bifaces from Locus 12 at El Bajío.

corners and more-or-less straight sides (Figs. 5.18 and 5.19). A Clovis-like reduction process was carried out to manufacture these square-based bifaces. The blade of the biface was reduced by overshot flaking to facilitate hafting of the tool, and several channel-like flakes were removed from the base of the tool. The square-based bifaces from El Bajío are comparable to Plainview points; however, overshot flaking and use of direct percussion for reduction of the bifaces appear to indicate that these artifacts are more likely correlated with a Clovis technology.

Table 5.26. Square-based Points and Knives from El Bajío

Bag No.	Collection, Locus, or Isolate	Bajío Basalt Patina Color (Munsell)	Condition	Length (mm)	Width (mm)	Basal Width (mm)	Thickness (mm)	Retouch Type	Flute Length (mm)	Flute Width (mm)
1280	Montané	2.5y 6/2	Basal	X	X	43	9.3			
1840	Montané	2.5 5/3	Complete	64.8r	36	36	8	Overshot asymmetrical	22	11
35431	Montané	gley2 3/10b	Basal	46.5	X	37.5	5.5	Overshot asymmetrical	X	X
695A	Montané	5y 6/1	Basal	23.6r	44	34.4	13	Fluting both sides, overshot	26/25	18/20
139	Montané	gely1 3/n	Basal	31.8r	35	41	9	Fluting and overshot	21	15
139	Montané	gley2 4/10bg	Basal	40.3	27.6	34.3	6.4			
139	Montané	gley1 4/5gy	Basal	34	39	33	6	Fluting and overshot	27.5	16.6
139	Montané	Rhyolite	Basal	39	29.8	28	9.1	Bifacial thinning	X	X
1831	Montané	gley1 6/10gy	Basal	28.7r	29.6	28	16.4	Fluting and overshot	14	14
1831	Montané	5y 6/2	Basal	27r	19.5	22	4.8	Bifacial thinning		
1831	Montané	Chert	Basal	42.3r	32	31	8.4	Fluting and overshot	17.3	20
695B	Montané	gley1 3/10gy	Basal	45.5	38.6	33	11.5		X	X
139	Montané	gley2 3/10b	Basal	41.3r	40.4	X	7	Fluting 2 faces	27/26.5	12/13
695B	Montané	gley2 3/10bg	Basal	39.3	30	34.4	8	Fluting 2 faces overshot	15/16	13/12
37681	Isolate 14	gley2 5/10g	Basal	38.2r	34	41	7	Fluting and overshot asymmetrical	24	12.3
35449	Isolate	gley25/10bc	Basal	36.5	37.5	34.6	8	Overshot	X	X
37693	Isolate	5y 6/2	Basal	4.7r	3.1	3.1	1.12			
37843	Isolate	gley1 4/5y	Basal	36.5	X	42	7	Fluting	15	18
37917	Isolate	5y 6/2	Basal	42	X	39	7.5	Overshot, basal/lateral grinding		

continued

Table 5.26. (continued)

Bag No.	Collection, Locus, or Isolate	Bajio Basalt Patina Color (Munsell)	Condition	Length (mm)	Width (mm)	Basal Width (mm)	Thickness (mm)	Retouch Type	Flute Length (mm)	Flute Width (mm)
45541	Locus 12-e1	5y 4/2	Basal	40	38		8	Overshot asymmetrical	No	No
37962	Locus 12-e1	5y 4/2	Distal	41	30		7		No	No
2 fragments m15-m16	Locus 12-e1	5y 4/2	Complete	71	30	32	7	Fluting and overshot asymmetrical	17/21	11/14
2 fragments m15-18	Locus 12-e1	5y 4/2	Complete	64	26	26	7	Fluting and overshot asymmetrical	13	11
3 fragments in m16	Locus12-e1	5y 4/2	Complete	48	24	24	5	Overshot asymmetrical	No	No
45549	Locus 12-e1	5y 4/1	Distal	41r	29		7	Overshot		
45545	Locus 12-e1	5y 4/1	Basal	51	43	36	11	Overshot	20	24
45548	Locus 12-e1	5y 4/1	Basal	16r	38	34	8	Fluting and overshot	14	9
45551	Locus 12-e1	5y 5/2	Basal	40r	43	48	8	Fluting and overshot	18	22
37569	Locus 8	gley1 3/10gy	Basal	41.5r	41.4	37.2	9	5 flakes forming the fluting	21.4	17
35445	Locus 4	gley2 3/10b	Basal	21.5	X	42	8.1	Fluting	X	20
37632	Locus 4	gley1 4/n	Basal	40r	38		10	Overshot		
37636	Locus 4	5y 5/2	Complete	50	30	30	7			
37504	Locus 1	gley2 4/5bg	Basal	3.4		33	5	Several flakes make the fluting	18/19	

In six examples the sides sharply contract toward the tip, making a triangular-shaped point. Five bifacess exhibit straight sides with equivalent base and maximal widths. Eleven bifaces have sides that expand from the base. Some square-based bifaces are broken in a transverse angle that appears to indicate that at least some of them were not hafted and probably were used as knives rather than projectile points. Two of the bifaces have grinding on the base and sides. A comparison of the basal width and the maximum width of the specimens indicates that only five tools have a wider base than the maximum width of the shaft. The rest of the bifaces exhibit parallel sides and bases similar to Clovis points. Square-based points and knives are not part of the traditional Clovis lithic repertoire; however, at El Bajío these artifacts seem to be related to Clovis technology. James Warnica (1966:249) reported three similar square-based points from gray sands that he attributed to Clovis.

Locus 12 at El Bajío is a tool-making station that was partially excavated in 2009. The people who used this work area specialized in producing lanceolate square-base bifaces. Nine of these artifacts were recovered, including four complete bifaces and five fragments. Thirty biface fragments that may be refitted in the future, and 4,000 retouched flakes, were also recovered at this locus.

Bifacial Drills

Two bifacially retouched drills were collected at El Bajío. Both drills were found in Feature 2 at Locus 12. They appear to have been made from flakes that were byproducts of the manufacturing process of the square base bifaces. The two examples have a central drill 20 mm long and it is likely that they were hafted (Fig. 5.20).

Overshot Flakes

Two overshot flakes were found in the Montané collection (Table 5.27; Fig. 5.21). They are flakes with a step termination. On the exterior faces there are long scars with an asymmetrical ridge consistent with overshot flaking.

MISCELLANEOUS CORES AND CORE-TOOLS

Eleven miscellaneous cores of probable Paleoindian association were collected from El Bajío (Table 5.28). Compared with the other three industries, these micellanous cores represent a more informal tool-making process. Three single platform nuclei, three multiple platform cores, two bifacial cores, two core fragments, and one single platform core converted into a plane are

Figure 5.20. Bifacial drills from El Bajío.

Table 5.27. Overshot Flakes from the Montané Collection

Bag No.	Raw Material (Munsell Color)	Length (mm)	Width (mm)	Thickness (mm)	Weight (g)
695B	Bajío basalt (2.5y 5/2)	49	28	7	8
695B	Bajío basalt (5y 5/2)	48	48	8	19

Figure 5.21. Overshot flakes from the Montané collection.

Table 5.28. Miscellaneous Nuclei from El Bajío

Bag No.	Collection, Locus, or Isolate	Raw Material	Munsell Color	Lithic Class	Length (mm)	Width (mm)	Thickness (mm)	Weight (g)
1031	Montané	White chert	2.5y 7/1	Core fragment	38	18	13	12.5
695A	Montané	Brown chert	10yr 4/3	Multiple-platform core	45	40	18	45
1069	Montané	El Bajío basalt	2.5y 5/3	Single platform core	80	64	33	176.5
35441	Montané	El Bajío basalt	5y 6/3	Bifacial core	50	64	20	81
140	Montané	El Bajío basalt	5y 5/3	Multiple-platform core	84	46	25	109.4
140	Montané	El Bajío basalt	5y 5/3	Multiple-platform core	63	42	20	70.3
37682	Isolate 14	El Bajío basalt	2.5y 5/1	Single platform core	62	58	41	151.6
37542	Isolate 12	El Bajío basalt	5y 6/2	Single platform core	74	61	28	210
45416	Locus 7	Red chert	5yr 5/3	Bifacial core with one spur*	38	33	15	18.5
37549	Locus 6	Black chert	5y 4/1	Core fragment	31	18	13	6
45505	7	El Bajío basalt	2.5y 5/2	Plain core	50	58	33	568

Note: * Same pink chert as found at Fin del Mundo.

Table 5.29. Hammers and Abraders from El Bajío

Bag No.	Locus or Isolate	Raw Material	Artifact Type	Length (mm)	Width (mm)	Thickness (mm)	Weight (g)
37541	Isolate 2	Granite	Hammer and abrader	68	56	31	167.5
37548	Locus 6	Quartz crystal	Hammer and abrader	83	79	47	305.5
37550	Locus 6	Dense basalt	Hammer	74	63	37	293
37545	Locus 6	Lutite	Hammer and abrader	73r	4		147.5
45552	Locus 12- ele 1	Rhyolite	Abrader fragment	61r		28	60

including in the assemblage. Three of the cores are chert, the rest are El Bajío basalt. Flakes obtained from these nuclei were transformed into scrapers and another tools. One exhausted bifacial core that was transformed into a graver tool was made on the same distinctive pinkish chert used to make an end scraper and blade found at Fin del Mundo.

HAMMERS AND ABRADERS

At the Cerro de la Vuelta quarry (Locus 22) many hammers and abraders were observed but they were not collected. However, five hammers and abraders were collected from Locus 6 and Locus 12, and one was collected

Figure 5.22. Hammers from the Cerro de la Vuelta quarry.

from an isolated context (Table 5.29; Fig. 5.22) Tool making was an important activity at Loci 6 and 12, where there are at least two knapping stations. Three tools combined a hammer and an abrader.

SONORAN CLOVIS LITHIC TECHNOLOGICAL ORGANIZATION

The manner in which toolmakers and tool users organized their lives and activities with regard to lithic technology was observed at El Bajío. The only large quarry of fine lithic materials known in Sonora is located at Cerro de la Vuelta, which is part of the El Bajío site complex. However, cobbles from arroyos and cores from small sources of material suitable for making tools are distributed all over Sonora. The restricted size and quality of the raw material from these sources constrain the kinds of artifacts that can be manufactured. At large sources of raw material, the toolmaker has more freedom in the design of the artifacts, and the shapes made are consequently more uniform. If mobile human groups found a large source of lithic raw material, they probably made this resource an important part of their exploitation strategy. More work needs to be carried out at El Bajío, and more intact archaeological contexts need to be located. Nonetheless, based upon the analysis of the stone tool assemblage, I propose some preliminary inferences regarding the Clovis lithic technological process, the activities carried out at the site, the land use of the Sonoran Clovis groups, and the relationship between the Clovis assemblage from Sonora and other regions.

Site Localities and Specialized Activity Areas

To date, Julio Montané has collected the greatest number of artifacts at El Bajío. Unfortunately the provenience of the artifacts he collected is mostly unknown, with the exception of his collection made at the north side of Cerro Rojo, or Cuarzo. Artifacts from that provenience were bagged together. In 2003, we documented Clovis artifacts at 10 loci, although most of the Clovis artifacts came from six of these areas (Loci 4, 5, 6, 7, 10, and 12; see Fig. 4.3). There were differences in the types of artifacts found at different loci (Table 5.30). The Cerro Rojo Locus appears to be a specialized area of hide and woodworking; 26 scrapers were concentrated in this area. Nine end scrapers, seven side scrapers, denticulate tools, and circular scrapers were found at that locus. The scrapers at Cerro Rojo were used and curated, and the locality

appears to have been a special activity area unrelated to tool manufacture.

A distributional pattern was observed in the artifacts found at Loci 4, 5, and 6, which are close to each other. Locus 4 contained many bifacial tools; in the northern area of the locus three secondary bifaces were found together. These three bifaces were probably cached or stored. Bifaces were produced and used in Locus 4. Loci 5 and 6 showed a specialization in blade production; five blade cores were collected at these loci, as well as 13 blades. Feature 1 at Locus 6 was a concentration of artifacts in a 3-m by 6-m area. Sub-angular blocks at Locus 6 were brought from the quarry. Core fragments and flakes for the preparation of blade cores and blades, as well as at least five finished blades, were present at Locus 6.

Locus 7 appears to have been a campsite where daily activities were carried out. Ten blades were recovered from the locus, all of which have use-wear damage. End scrapers on blades were also present at Locus 7, as well as bifacial tools. Clovis artifacts were well preserved at the locus and apparently were recently exposed. Further investigations need to be carried out at this locality.

Locus 10 also appears to have been a campsite. Ten blades and two end scrapers were collected at the locus. These artifacts had been damaged by animal trampling. Granite bedrock is exposed on the surface of Locus 10 so it will be difficult to find intact deposits at this locality. Apparently, the Clovis points collected by Manuel Robles were obtained from this locus (Julio Montané, personal communication 2003).

Locus 12 was a specialized activity area where El Bajío square-based points were produced. This workshop is located within a 5-m by 3-m area containing nine square-base bifaces, 20 biface fragments, and 4,000 bifacial thinning flakes.

Based upon the distribution and types of the lithic artifacts at El Bajío, it is possible to propose that the site was more than just a quarry for tool making. Although tool making was the principal and most important activity at the site, there were also a series of campsites at El Bajío where various activities were carried out. The artifacts from the campsites show evidence of abundant use and curation. Many of the artifacts were modified and converted into other tools with additional functions such as gravers or notchers. More studies at El Bajío are necessary to understand this complex site and learn more about the forager strategies of Clovis groups in Sonora.

Table 5.30. Distribution of Clovis-era Artifacts Found at El Bajío

Artifact Type	Montané	M-Cuarzo	Locus 1	Locus 2	Locus 4	Locus 5	Locus 6	Locus 7	Locus 8	Locus 10	Locus 12	Locus 15	Iso-lated	Total
Primary bifaces	6	1			5	1		1					2	16
Secundary bifaces	18	2		1	6			1		2	4		2	36
Clovis preforms	2				5	1		1	1	2		1	2	15
Clovis points					1								1	2
Square base bifaces and points	14		1		3				1		9		5	33
Gravers											2			2
Conical cores					1		1	1						3
Core tablet flakes	4					1								5
Wedge-shaped cores	5					1	2			1				9
Crested blades	5						1	3						9
Primary cortex blades	9					1	1				1			12
Blades with one sub-paralel blade scars	12				3	2		2		3				22
Blades with two subparalel blade scars	18				3	5	4	8		6	1		4	49
Blade core error recovery flakes	2					1		1					2	6
Platform mantenance flakes	4					1		2						7
End scrapers	14	9					1	1	1	2			2	30
Side scrapers	19	7				2	1	3						32
Composite scrapers	3	3												6
Denticulates	1	1				1		1						4
Gravers	6	3				1								10
Notched tools	4	1												5
Circular scrapers		2									1			3
Hammers							3				1		1	5
Overshot flakes	2													2
TOTAL	148	29	1	1	27	18	14	25	3	16	19	1	21	323

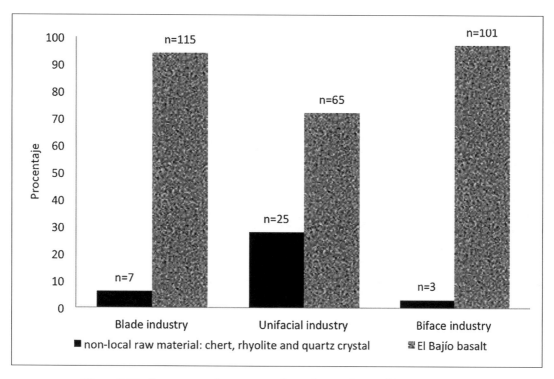

Figure 5.23. Percentage of raw materials used in tool assemblage at El Bajío.

Sonoran Clovis Forager Group Interaction and Land-Use

The lithic technological organization of Paleoindian sites in Sonora provides insight into the interaction between human groups and the use of land by the first occupants of the region. Less than 2 percent of the artifacts at El Bajío were made from raw material other than El Bajío basalt. Twenty-eight percent of the unifacially flaked end scrapers and side scrapers were manufactured using various chalcedonies or cherts; however, only 3 percent of the bifacial tools and 6 percent of the blades were manufactured using non-local raw material, mostly chert (Fig. 5.23). Because El Bajío is a quarry that produced stone to make all types of tools, I suggest that the artifacts made using non-local raw material indicate interactions between hunter-gatherer groups.

A regional survey focused on lithology is needed to guide research investigating interactions among the occupants of different sites. In looking at a geological map of the region, it is evident that raw materials are concentrated in discrete locations. El Bajío basalt is distributed close to the El Bajío site; two sources of rhyolite are located close to Fin del Mundo, and a basalt source is located close to SON N:11:20. South of El Bajío in

the mountains between the Río San Miguel valley and the Río Zanjón alluvial plain, there is a complex array of fissures contain metamorphic materials of different ages. Between El Bajío and Fin del Mundo, there is a concentration of old limestone, where chalcedony and chert might have been found.

Five different kinds of cherts, identified at a macroscopic level, were used to manufacture scrapers at El Bajío. Four of these cherts were also used to produce four artifacts at Fin del Mundo. The use of the same raw materials in tools at El Bajío and Fin del Mundo appears to indicate that forager groups interacted in communal activities where scrapers were exchanged.

It is odd that the raw materials for manufacturing Clovis points and bifacial tools are not shared between the sites. At Fin del Mundo, the majority of bifaces were made of rhyolite, and the Clovis points are made using chert, quartz crystal and quartzite. We have yet to find a biface at Fin del Mundo that was manufactured using El Bajío basalt. All the bifaces, Clovis points, and preforms at El Bajío were made using the local basalt. According to Andrefsky (2009:69), projectile points have discrete production and use phases; they are the only tools that have to be made with precision. The shape and technological characteristics of points determine the efficiency of the projectiles. It is possible that each hunter made their own projectile points in order to control all the attributes for better success during hunting.

TECHNOLOGICAL INFERENCES AND COMPARISONS WITH OTHER CLOVIS INDUSTRIES

Three major Clovis industries were distinguished at El Bajío: (1) a blade industry (n=122 artifacts); (2) a biface industry (n=104 artifacts); and (3) a uniface industry (n=90 artifacts). A small, informal core-flake industry may be related to the uniface industry (n=10 artifacts).

Biface Industry

According to Collins (1999:45), biface production was ubiquitous and remarkably uniform over the entire continent during the Clovis period. The El Bajío site fits into this pattern. A comparison of the width of primary bifaces, secondary bifaces, and Clovis preforms indicates that primary bifaces were transformed into Clovis preforms and secondary bifaces that served as blanks for additional types of tools. The secondary bifaces were reduced by removing broad extensive flakes and overshot flakes; bifacial flake removal was performed in a serial fashion. Once the knapper established an appropriate lateral and longitudinal cross section, the fluting began (Crabtree 1966; Huckell 2007). Channel flakes were obtained by creating small platforms in the basal edge by making a straight, beveled edge or by making a small platform or nipple. The El Bajío bifacial industry is comparable to that of other Clovis sites, including Adams, Murray Springs and Gault.

There is a unique projectile point or knife form at El Bajío. These are the square-based points that are lanceolate to triangular in shape and retouched in the same manner as Clovis points with overshot flaking. Twenty-four of the square-based points have sharp straight corners, and on five of them both sides contract towards the tip. It is possible that five square-based bifaces represent knives instead of projectiles, but the remainder appear to be projectile points. Although we do not know if the square-based points are contemporaneous with Clovis points, they have also been reported by James Warnica (1966:249) in association with Pleistocene-age gray sands at a Clovis site. There is a possibility that the square-based points may be late Paleoindian in age.

In contrast to the square-based points, Clovis preforms at El Bajío have convex bases. A convex base is fundamental for fluting and it is common at the Gault site (Dickens 2007). The square-based points at El Bajío never had a convex base, and early in their manufacturing process the base was plain with straight and sharp corners. The base was thinned by removing three or four small flutes, so a concave base was unnecessary. Square-based points have been recovered from several sites in Sonora. At Fin del Mundo, four square-based points were made using rhyolite.

Blade Industry

The basalt at the Bajío quarry occurs in sub-angular blocks that naturally contain acute angles and ridges that make the preparation of blade cores easier. The Paleoindian tool makers at El Bajío prepared cores by removing crested blades and forming ridges. Multifaceted platforms were the most common way to prepare the cores. The longest complete blade is 135 mm; however, there are blade fragments about 108 mm long in the collection that most likely were derived from blades of about 200 mm in length. An assessment of the three types of blades—cortical, non-cortical and prismatic—revealed that they are part of the same reduction process. The cortical blades are longer and wider, while the tabular or prismatic blades are shorter and slimmer. Nine of the 23 prismatic blades have the curvature typical of Clovis blades. One third of the blades from El Bajío are fragments that exhibit heavy patina in the broken ends. This suggests that they were broken during use. Some blades were used without any further modification, and some were transformed into end scrapers.

Blade technology is an important part of the Clovis contexts at several sites in North America. True blades have never been found in association with Folsom or other late Paleoindian assemblages; for that time period they are considered to be unique to Clovis technology (Collins 1999a). At Murray Springs, Arizona, Huckell (2007:205) reported 13 blades. Most of the blades at Murray Springs presented a prepared platform, and they were unifacially retouched. From Blackwater Draw, New Mexico, Green (1963) reported 17 blades, presumably part of a cache at the site. At the Adams Site in Kentucky, Sanders (1990) reports 2,000 blades, as well as conical and wedge-shaped cores. The Gulf Coastal Plain in Central Texas is the region with the highest number of reported Clovis blade artifacts. The Gault, Pavo Real, Kincaid, and Keven Davis Cache sites contained Clovis blades, conical and wedge-shape cores, core tablets, and other lithics associated with blade making technology

(Collins 1999a, 2003; Hester 2003). At the El Bajío Clovis site, all of the various types of artifacts associated with blade technology have been found. El Bajío represents the most important locality outside of central Texas with evidence of Clovis blade technology.

End Scrapers

In the Sonoran collection, end scrapers are considered to be a significant diagnostic Paleoindian tool, one that is important to understanding the interactions among Clovis groups. Twenty-five percent of the scrapers at El Bajío are made of fine non-local materials that were also used at other sites. The artifacts collected by Julio Montané at the north end of Cerro Rojo appear to indicate that the area was a locality where specialized activities related to hide and woodworking took place.

End scrapers have been found associated with Clovis assemblages, as well with later Paleoindian sites that include Folsom, Plainview, and Dalton contexts. At El Bajío, late Paleoindian assemblages have not been identified. Approximately half of the end scrapers were made on Clovis prismatic blades, making them quite distinctive. The end scrapers from El Bajío are similar to those found at Murray Springs in Arizona, Fin del Mundo in Sonora, and Pavo Real in Texas.

FINAL CONSIDERATIONS

The lithic technological organization at El Bajío indicates that the Cerro de la Vuelta quarry was the most important landmark in the region for Clovis groups. The quarry produces sub-angular blocks that are easy to reduce, and the high-quality vitrified basalt from the quarry is good for tool making. At present, Cerro de la Vuelta is the only known large quarry of fine materials in Sonora. Its importance is reflected by the numerous campsites and workshops that occur in the area up to 4 km from the quarry.

At El Bajío, blades were manufactured using conical cores and wedge-shaped cores. The blade industry is thus comparable to the Pavo Real, Gault, and Adams sites, all of which are quarry sites. The blades at El Bajío are comparable to the blades found at Murray Springs because many of them were modified into end and lateral scrapers. The Clovis preforms with long and deep flutes made in the early stages of the manufacturing process appear to be a local technological marker of the El Bajío tool industry. This attribute is not exclusive, however; it also occurs at the Adams site in Kentucky, where early fluting is common. Early fluting may be related to the hardness of the raw material, but experiments are needed to confirm this hypothesis. It is also possible that more early fluting is found at quarries than other sites because the bifaces were discarded at the site, making them more visible to archaeologists.

There is no doubt that the El Bajío artifact collection is one of the most important Clovis assemblages in western North America. Future research in Sonora, including intrasite investigations, regional studies that investigate the relationship between sites, and experiments pertaining to lithic technology, will greatly contribute to our knowledge of the Late Pleistocene Clovis occupation of the continent.

CHAPTER SIX

Defining the Late Pleistocene Clovis Occupation in Sonora

The archaeological record of the Late Pleistocene occupation of Mexico is poorly known and somewhat confusing. This makes it difficult to propose a model for the human colonization of Mexico. The only two secure dates of Pleistocene age that we have in Mexico outside of Sonora are the human skeleton from El Peñon III, which has been radiocarbon dated at 10,755 ± 75 B.P. (OxA-10112), and the Tlapacoya skeleton, which has been dated at 10,200 ± 65 B.P. (OxA-10113) (Gonzalez and others 2003:381; Gonzalez, Jiménez, and others 2006:69). These dates suggest that at least a few people were in the Basin of Mexico 12,000 years ago. Tracking diagnostic artifacts of Pleistocene age—Clovis, Folsom, and Plainview—into Mexico is a difficult task because only the states of Sonora, Chihuahua, Baja California, Hidalgo, Jalisco, and Nuevo León have more than four projectile points affiliated with Paleoindian times.

Sonora presents a remarkably pristine setting for studying the late Pleistocene occupation of North America and Mexico. The early archaeological record is stunning in terms of its relative abundance of Paleoindian remains. The investigations carried out in the past 10 years demonstrate the quantity and extent of Pleistocene archaeological materials. Rapidly deflating surfaces, due in part to overgrazing, might be one reason that these sites are extraordinarily visible. Nevertheless, the Sonoran landscape, along with the essential resources required by Paleoindian groups to succeed, contributed to making this region an attractive place for pioneering human groups.

Based upon current research presented in this monograph, I offer propositions for defining the Late Pleistocene Clovis occupation of Sonora. Clovis land use patterns, subsistence strategies, organization of labor, chronology, and social interaction and integration are reviewed in this final chapter.

LAND-USE PATTERNS

One of the most startling aspects of Clovis culture is its extensive geographic distribution, which covers all of North America south of the Continental ice sheets (G. Haynes 2002; Tankersley 2004; Willig 1991). The general style and technological attributes of Clovis projectile points are consistent over all the areas where they appear. The ubiquity of Clovis has been explained as a trait dispersed by humans as they migrated through North America (Anderson 1991, 1996; Fiedel 2004; Goebel and others 2008; G. Haynes 2002; Kelly 1996; Kelly and Todd 1988; Martin 1973; Meltzer 2002, 2004).

Two models have been proposed to explain the geographical extent of Clovis. The "high-technology forager" model (Kelly 1996) assumes that Clovis people migrated into an unpopulated country through the ice-free corridor in western Canada, preadapted with the necessary skills and tools to hunt large Pleistocene mammals (Kelly and Todd 1988). Under pressure from a rapidly changing environment, the Clovis predisposition for hunting allowed small groups to quickly move across the land, following familiar resources and avoiding setbacks caused by diminished local food sources and patchiness (Kelly 1996).

The "staging-area" model (Anderson 1991, 1996) explains the spread of Clovis technology by means of human migrations—but at a much slower pace than the high-technology model. According to Anderson (2005, 2013), resource-rich locations became staging areas where discrete populations concentrated activities and settled for years or even generations, periods much longer than that predicted by the high-technology model.

The archaeological Clovis record of Sonora supports the "staging-area" model. The majority of Clovis points from Sonoran sites were made using local raw material sources of varied quality. Clovis points are not easy to manufacture, and the quality of raw material is fundamental for the toolmakers. The use of local raw materials may indicate that Clovis groups stayed at sites for long periods of times, or that they visited the same sites recurrently as a part of their land-use strategy. Periodic or annual visits enabled Clovis people to explore and test the lithic sources for tool making, and come to know which rocks were good for making Clovis points and artifacts.

The Clovis groups that inhabited the Llanos de Hermosillo and surrounding areas exploited an extensive territory of approximately 25,000 square kilometers over a diverse landscape that included the Central Gulf Coast, Lower Colorado River valley, and Plains of Sonora. The central Gulf Coast and the Llanos de Hermosillo constitute a low-lying land with occasional mountains peaks between 20 to 100 m above sea level. During the Pleistocene, extensive but shallow playas and lakes formed intermittently during the year. In the river valleys, cienegas formed near the alluvial fans. The semipermanent water supply supported a variety of plants and animals.

The weather in the Sonoran Desert at the end of the Pleistocene was warm and humid in the winter, and cool and wet in the summer, Along the coastal plains, the characteristic plant community was probably chaparral with yucca. The characteristic plant community in the interior valleys and bajadas was pinyon pines, junipers and oaks, along with a series of grasses, agaves, and prickly pears (Van Devender 2007).

Extensive Clovis campsites, hunting areas, stone procurement areas, and wild resources indicate that the territory was used repeatedly. Clovis economic strategies were organized in a large and pristine landscape that contained a great variety of animals and plants. Our investigations suggest that Clovis people had a sophisticated knowledge of the region that allowed them to use a variety of raw materials for tool making, including different sources of chert, quartzite, quartz crystal, rhyolite, obsidian, and basalt.

Our research revealed 12 sites that were used by different Clovis groups. El Bajío appears to have been an important locality situated at the edge of the Llanos de Hermosillo and the Río San Miguel valley, a natural north-south corridor. Our investigations suggest that Cerro de la Vuelta, part of the El Bajío site complex, was the most important and extensively used source of lithic material in the region. Access to suitable raw material for tool making is an essential resource for hunter-gatherers, and can determine mobility strategies unrelated to food procurement. At El Bajío, family groups congregated predominantly for tool making activities, but the extensive camp areas and localities containing only one type of artifact appear to indicate that other specific activities were also carried out at the site, including the manufacture of clothing and shoes.

Fin del Mundo, in the Bacoachi Basin north of the Llanos de Hermosillo, is in an area with an important source of subsurface water that formed seasonal cienegas. These cienegas would have attracted many animals—an ideal place for hunting. Clovis people also used the lithic sources available at and nearby the site.

SON O:3:1, located in the southeastern corner of the Llanos de Hermosillo, is composed of two camp areas. It is probable that, during the Pleistocene, several spring-fed cienegas existed at this site. The cienegas supported open grasslands where proboscideans and other big mammals ranged. Although one or two artifacts made from El Bajío basalt were found at SON O:3:1, most of the artifacts were made using local stone found in arroyos and other nearby small sources.

We documented two Clovis sites in the Llanos de Hermosillo, SON N:11:20 and SON J:16:8. These sites appear to be hunting localities. They contain only broken and worn-out Clovis projectile points, and no camp sites have been found at them. The fundamental resources for hunter-gatherer groups, which are permanent water and lithic raw material for tool making, are indispensable in a given territory. The Llanos de Hermosillo and surrounding areas offered the Clovis groups both of these necessary resources.

The El Bajío quarry site probably was persistently used by Clovis groups, and they left a considerable amount of debris and tools over a 4-square kilometer area. One of the important activities carried out at El Bajío was the manufacture of blades. About 100 blades have been collected at the site. The manufacture of bifaces and Clovis points is also well represented at the site. Five blades and two core rejuvenation tablet flakes collected at Fin del Mundo (about 150 km away) were made using El Bajío vitrified basalt. The presence of El Bajío basalt tablet flakes indictate the interaction and integration between the people who used the two sites.

In sum, the settlement pattern recognized in Sonora indicates that Clovis groups had multiple economic strategies. Big game hunting was one of the most important subsistence activities, but it was risky and had a high percentage of failure. Activities relating to collecting plants and hunting small animals were more reliable than big game hunting on a daily basis. The Clovis groups in Sonora developed a sophisticated settlement pattern and land-use system that was determined by the location of lithic sources for tool making, water sources, large prey animals, and a mosaic of edible plants and small animals. Exploitation of an extensive territory, together with the excellent climate that existed in the Sonoran Desert at the end of the Pleistocene, allowed Clovis groups to remain in the same region for long periods of time.

SUBSISTENCE STRATEGIES AND ORGANIZATION OF LABOR

Traditionally, Paleoindian scholars assumed that all Clovis groups were specialized high-tech hunters of proboscideans and other big Pleistocene mammals, and this this assumption may be an appropriate interpretation for some regions in Northern North America that had tundra-like climate and vegetation during the late Pleistocene. The Sonoran Desert region, however, had an optimal climate at the end of the Pleistocene, with warm and wet winters and cool and wet summers. This supported a chaparral-like environment with yucca stands, pinyon, juniper, oak, agave, prickly pear, and a variety of grasses. The variety of plants and animals that the Clovis people encountered in Sonora surely were incorporated into their diet.

Using ethnographic data about hunter-gatherers, Binford (1980, 1990) and, more recently, Kelly (1995) have shown that effective temperature (ET) is a reliable index for modeling aspects of past adaptations. ET provides a direct measure of plant productivity and an indirect measure of animal productivity (Bettinger 1991:65; Hill 2001:10). The equator has an ET of 26, and the Poles have an ET of 8. Although there are no modern analogs for Paleoindian groups, the dimensions of past and present hunter and gatherers are broadly shaped by similar constraints and conditions, and the ET index may be used with caution to interpret the adaptions of past societies (Hill 2001:12).

In Clovis times, the difference in the ET between the Northern Plains (ET 9) and the Sonoran Desert region (ET 15) suggests that Clovis groups living at the Sonoran Desert were able to rely upon plants and small animals throughout the year. According to packrat midden and pollen records, the plant repertoire available as foodstuffs was abundant in the Sonoran Desert, including pinyon, oak, juniper, agave, prickly pear, acacia, saguaro, and other cacti. Although, our research in Sonora has not yet found a Clovis age archaeological feature with plant remains, an agave charcoal in a feature of Clovis age (UCIAMS-12859, 10,095 ± 30) recently was found at Isla Cedros in Baja California Norte by Matthew R. Des Lauriers (2011:168). The ET index of the Sonoran Desert, together with the edible plant repertoire and direct evidence of consumption of agave at Isla Cedros, support the existence of multiple economic strategies for the Clovis groups at the Sonoran Desert.

There is no question that hunting large game was an important activity in the life of Clovis people. Hunting megafauna, however, is a risky activity with a low success rate that had to be complemented with other activities. Hunting was a multidimensional phenomenon, and did not occur in isolation from other subsistence activities (Kelly 1995; Waguespack 2003:109). The actual killing of large animals may have been a male activity, but the labors of women and other non-hunters may have played major roles in hunting as well (Wuadespack 2003:109). All members of the society were involved in tasks relating to hunting, such as making shoes and clothes, manufacturing tools, butchering, and preserving the meat.

Clovis social organization probably entailed family groups with a minimal size of 25 to 40 members. However, the homogeneity of Clovis points, the sharing of artifacts between groups, and the sharing of raw materials appear to indicate that family groups maintained strong ties with extended Clovis populations at a regional level.

CLOVIS CHRONOLOGY AND MIGRATION TO SONORA

Secure dating of Clovis archaeological contexts in Sonora has been difficult. Although large Clovis collections and sites have been known for Sonora since the 1960s, intact archaeological contexts with datable material were not found until 2012. The lack of stratified deposits at the majority of the Sonoran Clovis sites makes it impossible to have an adequate sample of well-dated materials. Fin del Mundo contains stratified deposits, but for five years we were unable to date the archaeological context. In 2012, however, we obtained three charcoal samples from the gomphothere archaeological feature that date this site to 11,550 B.P. (13,390 cal B.P.) (Sánchez and others 2014).

When peoples moved down the west coast of North America and reached the end of the Baja California peninsula, land literally ran out. Unless they had watercraft capable of making the crossing to Mexico across the 100-km open water gap that existed 15,000 years ago, and were aware of the possibility of land across the water, they would have had to turn back to the north. Moving north along the eastern side of Baja, unless they island hopped over to Sonora near the northern end of the Gulf in the vicinity of Isla Ángel de la Guarda and Tiburón Island, they would have encountered the mouth of the Colorado River. Some populations may have chosen to follow this large waterway into the interior, while others, continued down the western coast of Sonora, where they would have eventually reached Central and South America. Sonora is thus a critically important area in the peopling of the Americas.

CLOVIS INTERACTION AND INTEGRATION BETWEEN REGIONS

Current investigations in Sonora have permitted us to reconstruct tentative Clovis settlement patterns. Clovis groups used an extensive territory about 25,000 square kilometers in size in and around the Llanos de Hermosillo. A variety of site types are present in this area, including lithic procurement sites, lithic workshops, megafauna hunting sites, encampments, and an extensive distribution of isolated Clovis projectile points. Clovis caches are common in the United States, where more than one hundred of them have been reported. There are no Clovis cache sites in Sonora, however, and they do not appear to have been an important part of the settlement pattern. Although, the largest and most important Clovis sites in Sonora are located in the Llanos de Hermosillo area, Clovis points also have been found between Caborca and Trincheras, and along the Río Sonora in Mexico and the San Pedro River in southern Arizona.

The Clovis archaeological record in southern Arizona is represented by 150 isolated Clovis points, two small sites containing a handful of artifacts, and a series of sites that are distributed in a compact area extending along 31 km of the San Pedro River Valley, including Naco, Lehner, Murray Springs, Escapule, and Navarrete. The San Pedro sites represent punctual events of short duration related to megafauna hunting activity (Haynes and Huckell 2007).

Murray Springs can be compared to Fin del Mundo because both sites have hunting features and associated camp areas. However, Murray Springs represents only one event, while Fin del Mundo was visited several times (Sánchez and others 2014). The exploitation of the local source of quartz crystal at Fin del Mundo appears to indicate that Clovis groups had an extensive knowledge of resources as a result of their constant use of the region.

Geoarchaeological investigations on the Mexican side of the Río San Pedro were unsuccessful in producing an archaeological record similar to that in Arizona. A study by Gaines (2006) produced a half-dozen isolated projectile points in private collections and one small site composed of one Clovis point and two other artifacts. Apparently the Mexican side of the San Pedro River experienced periods of deposition and erosion that destroyed the late Pleistocene depositional history. The lack of a robust Clovis archaeological record in the Río San Pedro in Sonora limits the direct comparison between Arizona and Sonora.

The Clovis occupation of Sonora is distinguished from that of Arizona and New Mexico because of the presence of the large quarry site at El Bajío. Lithic raw material procurement is of fundamental importance within a given territory. The El Bajío quarry functioned as a communal locality for regional groups that was visited and used several times a year. Annual residential mobility probably was planned to take into account the El Bajío lithic source, along with localities with permanent water.

The gomphotheres found at Fin del Mundo are puzzling because they have never been found at any other archaeological site in North America. It is probable that Clovis groups in Sonora encountered fauna and flora that they had never seen before, along with a better climate. These conditions likely prompted them to inhabit Sonora. The Sonoran Clovis occupation is a testimony that multiple regional Clovis adaptations emerged with specific responses to plants, animals, and resources.

Despite the relatively few investigations conducted to date, Sonora seemingly presents an extraordinarily high density of Clovis sites and isolated finds, especially when compared with the adjacent regions of Arizona, and the remarkable paucity of evidence from Chihuahua and Sinaloa. The evidence that we have indicates that Sonora served as a corridor for the migration of the first Americans.

THE CLOVIS RECORD IN THE REGIONS SURROUNDING SONORA

With the objective of placing the state of Sonora within a framework of late Pleistocene human occupation, an overview of the Paleoindian record of the regions surrounding

Sonora is presented here. Currently, the existence of a pre-Clovis or pre-terminal Pleistocene occupation has not been confirmed within Arizona, New Mexico, or Texas. The few sites that have been proposed as pre-Clovis are problematic and remain equivocal (Faught and Freeman 1998; Haynes 2002; Huckell 2004; Mabry 1998a).

Arizona

The state of Sonora has many similarities with the state of Arizona. They share the same desert, and the human adaptations to this environment are similar during the entire history of the region (Mabry 2008). The Clovis sites on the San Pedro River in southeastern Arizona, including mammoth kill sites, bison kill sites and camp sites, are well understood. They have an unusually complete record of late Quaternary depositional, pedological, and erosional events, and a complete series of radiocarbon dates (Haynes 1991, 1993, 2000a, 2000b, 2007; Huckell 2004, 2007; Taylor and others 1996). These San Pedro River sites are located only a few kilometers north of the international border between Arizona and Sonora.

Two sites located outside the San Pedro River valley have been reported in Arizona (Huckell 1978, 1982, 2004). In 1976 and 1981, Bruce Huckell carried out limited excavations at the Silktassel Site, north of Phoenix, where a Clovis occupation is represented by a Clovis point, two end scrapers, a blade, a graver, and debitage (Huckell 1978, 1982:3). He recently returned to the site and found one additional blade. According to Huckell, the Silktassel site has suffered much erosion and the land has been burned at least once (Bruce Huckell, personal communication 2009). At the multicomponent site AZ Y:8:100 (ASM), located northwest of Ajo, SWCA Environmental Consultants found Clovis materials, although more work needs to be done to determine the precise nature of the Clovis occupation (Huckell 2004:94). Beside these sites, there are 150 solitary Clovis points reported in the state. These isolated Clovis finds are from the surface, and are distributed in the Sonoran Desert area and Colorado Plateau (Agenbroad 1967; Huckell 1982, 2004; Northon and others 2005).

The San Pedro River Valley in southeastern Arizona is a unique place with good preservation that provides evidence of the different activities carried out by Clovis groups. Sites include mammoth, horse, and bison kill sites, butchering areas for processing meat, and areas for knapping stone tools. At some sites, these different activities overlapped (Haynes 2007; Huckell 2007). Fortunately, the San Pedro sites are preserved in a complex stratigraphic framework, with deposits that preserved events and archaeological contexts that were buried for 13,000 years. The archaeological record of the San Pedro Valley sites is summarized in the Table 6.1.

The San Pedro sites were excavated by various people between 1957 and 1973. C. Vance Haynes, Jr., was instrumental in conducting superb geoarchaeological investigation of the sites and their environs. The Clovis activities represented at the sites included hunting and butchering of megafauna, manufacture of butchering tools, and curating or resharpening of tools during use. The knapping stations are well defined and concentrated in discrete features, although they are in proximity to the Pleistocene animal bones (Huckell 2007). The researchers deduced that the events represented at the San Pedro River sites were of short duration, and it is possible that they represented the activities of a single group (Haynes and Huckell 2007).

In Arizona, Clovis was followed by the Folsom complex of Late Paleoindian age; however, the two complexes do not share the same spatial distribution. Folsom is well represented on the Colorado Plateau in Arizona, but appears to have been absent from the Sonoran Desert (Faught and Freeman 1998). Huckell (1982) reported 20 Folsom points for the state of Arizona, with 12 located in the St. Johns area on the Colorado Plateau. One unique late Paleoindian site reported in Arizona is the Badger Springs site in the northeastern part of the state, which dates to 9,000 cy B.P. (Hesse and others 1998, 2000). There, a child cremation and several Badger Spring lanceolate points without flutes were documented. These points are clearly related to Angostura, Agate Basin, and Foothill Mountain types.

At Ventana Cave, Huckell and Haynes (2003) reported a Sulphur Springs component containing contracting stem projectile points, fire-cracked rocks, and informal ground stone. This component dates to about 8700 B.P. The Sulphur Springs complex was considered as part of the Cochise culture previously defined by Sayles and Antevs (1941). At Whitewater Draw in the San Pedro Valley, the Sulphur Spring lithic assemblage is represented by informal ground stone and fire-cracked rock. In 1985, Michael Waters (1986) reinvestigated the sites described by Sayles and Antevs and obtained 10 radiocarbon dates from different features, all of which dated between 8100 and 9000 B.P. Based upon the increased manipulations of plants, as represented by ground stone and roasting pits, the Sulphur Spring complex may represent an adaptation of the Paleoindian hunters to a more Archaic subsistence

Table 6.1. The Clovis Archaeological Record of the San Pedro Valley

Site Name	Site Type	Artifacts	Pleistocene Fauna	C-14 Dates	Time Context of Discovery	Citations
Naco	Kill site	8 complete Clovis points	Single mammoth		Navarrete family 1951	Haury and others 1953; Haynes 2007:1
Lehner	Kill site, processing	13 Clovis points; flakes, unifacial tools, 2 hearths; 1 shallow roasting pit	12 mammoths, bison, camel; roasting pit with bear and rabbit bones.	11,160 from a hearth, and 12 from a Clovis stratum 10,949 ± 40	Ed Lehner 1955	Haury and others 1959; Mehringer and Haynes 1965; Haynes 1982, 2007
Escapule	Kill site	2 Clovis points	Partial mammoth		Luis Escapule 1960	Hemmings and Haynes 1969; Haynes 2007
Leikem	Kill site	1 Clovis point	Two mammoths		Slim Leiken 1964	Haynes 2007
Navarrete	Hunting	1 point proximal fragment, 1 possible bone tool	Two mammoths, 50 m upstream from Naco		Marc Navarrete 1973	Huckell 1981; Haynes 2007
Murray Springs, areas 1, 2, and 3	Mammoth kill, butchering	1 Clovis point, tip of 2 others, several stone tools, 66 thinning flakes, and possible bone artifacts	Two disarticulated mammoths, mammoth tracks, horse, 2 bison, and canids	Charcoal date of 11,150 B.P.	Murray Springs project 1966-1972	Hemmings 1970; Haynes 2007
Murray Springs, area 3	Kill site, knapping areas	1 unifacial cutting tool, used flakes, cobble hammers, 9,467 pieces of debitage, 1 mammoth bone shaft tool	Nearly a complete mammoth, 2 bison, canids, rodents		Murray Springs Project 1971	Hemmings 1970; Haynes 2007; Huckell 2007
Murray Springs, areas 3 and 4	Multiple bison kill site, knapping area, processing area	9 Clovis points, 3 bifaces, 2 unifacial retouch flakes, 4 utilized blades and flakes, 2 cobble hammers, 1,560 pieces of debitage, 3 hearths	Multiple bison, peccary, and horse	10,760 ± 100	Murray Springs Project 1968-1969	Hemmings 1970, 2007; Haynes 2007; Huckell 2007
Murray Springs, area 5	Clovis camp and horse butchering	2 Clovis bases, 2 bifaces, 1 preform, unifacial retouch blade, pebble hammers, 1,030 pieces of debitage	Horse		Murray Springs Project 1967	Hemmings 1970, 2007; Haynes 2007; Huckell 2007

pattern that is characteristic of the nascent Sonoran Desert (Huckell 1996).

New Mexico

The Clovis and Folsom type sites, the landmarks of Paleoindian archaeology, are located on the Southern Great Plains of eastern New Mexico. Several sites in New Mexico contain a complete array of Paleoindian and Early Archaic occupations (Holliday 1997, 2005). Blackwater Draw and Mockingbird Gap are the important Clovis sites in New Mexico. Approximately 350 Clovis points have been documented in the state, the majority of them from Socorro County (Hamilton 2008; Paleoindian Database of the Americas 2014).

In 1927, Carl Schwachheim, working with paleontologists Harold Cook and Jesse Figgins, excavated a complete specimen of a *Bison antiquus* of late Pleistocene age from what became known as the Folsom site in northeastern New Mexico. They discovered a beautiful lanceolate fluted projectile point (Folsom style) between two ribs of the animal, thus proving that humans interacted with Pleistocene megafauna in the Americas (Cook 1927, 1928; Figgins 1927).

In 1933, Edgar B. Howard was shown Blackwater Draw—the Clovis type site—when he was looking for early sites in the area. Blackwater Draw is located between the towns of Clovis and Portales in northeastern New Mexico (Cotter 1937; Howard 1935a, 1935b). The Clovis site was investigated for 30 years following its discovery (Holliday 2005; Sellards 1952; Warnica 1966). The investigations at this locality represent the first multidisciplinary research of Paleoindian archaeology, and made it possible to establish a geological framework for the archaeological record of the first Americans (Antevs 1935, 1948; Clarke 1938; Patrick 1938; Stock and Bode 1936).

At Blackwater Draw Locality 1 (the Clovis site), the remains of Clovis occupations were located at the margins of a spring-fed paleo-lake that measured 300 m by 300 m. The site was exposed on the surface by gravel mining. The archaeological remains are represented by eight mammoths and several bison bone beds (Sellards and Evans 1960). One of the bison beds, two campsites, and two bison with associated artifacts were dated at 10,800 cy B.P. (Holliday 2005; Meltzer 1983). Warnica (1966) reported that approximately 500 artifacts were collected from different localities at the site. At least 12 Clovis points were collected, together with end scrapers, blades, lateral scrapers, and debitage from the bone beds and the encampments.

Another important Clovis site of New Mexico is the Mockingbird Gap Site, located 40 km southeast of Socorro. One of the largest Clovis sites in western North America, the site consists of a Clovis lithic scatter in an area 800 m by 80 to 150 m on a northeast-southwest trending ridge composed of sand and gravel, with a cap of strongly developed gypsite or calcrete. The site borders the floor of Chupadera Wash. Projectile point bases, fluted point preforms, end scrapers, gravers, and other flake tools represent the principal artifacts. No bones were present at Mockingbird Gap, which appears to be a campsite located close to the surface. The site has not been dated (Holliday and others 2009).

Texas

Clovis points have been found throughout the state of Texas. The Llano Estacado has the highest density of Clovis artifacts, but they are also present in the panhandle, Denton County, the Edwards Plateau, and the Lubbock area. Here we discuss three sites: Aubrey, Gault, and Pavo Real. Other important Clovis sites have been found in Texas, including the Kincaid and Montell rock shelters.

The Aubrey Clovis site is located on a lag of a late Pleistocene channel at 7.9 to 9 m below the modern floodplain of the Elm Fork of the Trinity River. This drainage began aggrading during the Clovis period. The site is located in north-central Texas between the rolling Plains and the Gulf Coastal Plain (Ferring 2001; G. Haynes 2002). This site represents the oldest Pleistocene Clovis site on record in North America dated to ~11,550 B.P. (Ferring 2001). Approximately 170 1-m by 1-m units have been excavated. The Aubrey Clovis site is composed of seven localities with a wide range of lithic artifacts, numerous hearths, a bison kill site, and at least 12,000 fragments of bones (Ferring 2001; Haynes 2002). One bison kill locus with a blade and debitage from re-sharpening flakes was excavated. Two distinct camp areas are present at the site, with over 6,000 lithic artifacts that include Clovis points, blades, end scrapers, and bifaces (Ferring 2001). Two knapping activity areas appear to be present; one specialized in bifacial reduction and the other in unifacial reduction (Ferring 2001). Apparently, the Clovis occupations of the site were short (Ferring 2001; Witt 2005).

The Gault Site located midway between Georgetown and Ft. Hood, Texas, in a constricted head of a small valley. The site extends over an 800-m by 200-m area. It is a stratified site with a Clovis occupation, although the early and late Holocene occupations of the site are also well represented. Clovis people were attracted to the Gault site by several springs and a quarry of fine chert for tool knapping. The artifacts occur in primary contexts within pond clays and in overlying floodplain deposits. Localities at the site are composed of Clovis knapping stations, often in association with Pleistocene animal remains. A total of 600,000 lithic artifacts have been excavated at the site. Clovis artifacts include fluted projectile points, bifaces in all stages of reduction, blade cores, blades, core tablets, end scrapers, drills, knives, and debitage (Collins 1999a, 2002). At the Lindsay Pit locality, excavated by the Center for the Study of the First Americans, Texas A&M University, a knapping station was found for manufacturing blades and Clovis bifaces (Waters and others 2011; Dickens 2007). Blades and by-products of the Clovis blade technology were used to manufacture Clovis preforms, suggesting that blade technology and fluting were Clovis innovations (Dickens 2007). From the point of view of those who study lithic technology, Gault is one the most important sites in North America.

The Pavo Real site is located on the east side of the Leon Creek Valley, North of San Antonio, Texas. The site was quickly excavated in 1979 as part of a TxDOT highway project (Hester 2003). The geochronology, analysis, and interpretation were not completed until 2000 (Collins and Hudler 2003). The site measures 150 m × 100 m, and consists of lithic artifact scatters and fire-cracked rock distributed in five areas. It is a multi-component site with Clovis, Folsom, and Early and Late Archaic occupations. The fire-cracked rock features dated to 3600 to 2000 cy B.P. Areas 3 and 4 in the central section of the site have overlapping Clovis, Folsom, and Archaic occupations that appear to indicate that deposition at the site was slow during early Holocene times, with very little soil formation. There was no bone present at the site (Collins 2003). The Clovis artifact assemblage from the site indicates that many knapping activities took place there; the manufacture of blades appears to have been an important activity, along with bifaces and Clovis points. Area 5 contained 14 conical cores, together with core tables, and flakes from the rejuvenation of core platforms (Collins 2003).

The lithic complex at Pavo Real includes at least 5,000 pieces of lithic debitage, Clovis bifaces, Clovis point preforms, Clovis points, Folsom bifaces, Folsom point preforms, Folsom points, channel flakes for both Clovis and Folsom points, conical and wedge-shaped cores, blades, end scrapers, gravers, and a variety of unifacial tools (Collins 2003). The Pavo Real site appears to represent a lithic quarry, lithic manufacture, and encampment located near the river.

Summary of the Clovis Record in Arizona, New Mexico, and Texas

The early Paleoindian archaeological record in the Southwest and Texas is somewhat patchy and dispersed. It is apparent that south-central Texas was an important territory for Paleoindian groups. The southern High Plains was another territory that was well known and exploited by late Pleistocene inhabitants. In Arizona, the number of Clovis sites diminishes greatly, and only in the San Pedro River valley in the southeastern corner of the state is there is an archaeological record with excellent preservation. The major difference between the regions is the small number of conical blades cores and blades in Arizona, compared to the central region of Texas. From the archaeological record it is fair to say that good lithics, water, and megafauna were important commodities of the Paleoindian life style.

CONCLUSION

Sonora provides a remarkable context for studying the late Pleistocene occupation of North America and Mexico. When information about Late Pleistocene archaeological sites in Sonora is added to data from Paleoindian sites in Arizona, New Mexico, and Texas, important insights emerge about the peopling of the Americas.

If Paleoindian groups moved down the west coast of North America and reached the end of the Baja California peninsula, they either had to use watercraft to cross 100 km of open water to the mainland of Mexico or backtrack to the north where they would have encountered the Colorado River. Some groups may have chosen to follow the Colorado River northward into the interior of the continent, while other groups may have continued down the western coast of mainland Mexico, eventually reaching Central and South America.

Archaeological data in Sonora support the "staging-area" model of Clovis land use. The Clovis points found in Sonora were made using local raw material sources of varied quality. Knowing where to find the best local sources of stone for use in lithic tools indicates that Clovis people had a detailed knowledge of their environment. From this, I infer that Clovis groups stayed at sites for long periods of times, or that they visited the same sites recurrently as a part of a long-term strategy of land use.

The essential resources found in Sonora made this region an attractive place for place for pioneering human groups.

The Clovis groups that migrated to the Sonora Desert encountered fauna and flora that they had not previously seen elsewhere in North America. The climatic conditions in Sonora during the Late Pleistocene entailed warm and wet winters and cool and wet summers. This created a relatively rich environment with a diversity of animals and plants that could be hunted and gathered to enable long-term occupation of territories. The Paleoindian sites in Sonora provide evidence that multiple regional Clovis adaptations emerged with specific responses to plants, animals, and other resources.

Extensive Clovis campsites, hunting areas, stone procurement areas, and wild resources indicate that territories were used repeatedly. Clovis economic strategies were organized to exploit a large and pristine environment that contained a variety of animals and plants. Our investigations indicate that Clovis people used a variety of raw materials for tool making, including different sources of chert, quartzite, quartz crystal, rhyolite, obsidian, and basalt. The homogeneity of Clovis points, the sharing of artifacts between groups, and the sharing of raw materials suggest that Clovis groups maintained strong ties with extended populations at a regional level.

The 12 Clovis sites documented in Sonora indicate extensive use of the region by Paleoindian hunters and gatherers. El Bajío, in particular, was an important locality situated at the edge of the Llanos de Hermosillo and the Rio San Miguel valley. These landforms provided a natural north-south corridor for travel. The quarry at Cerro de la Vuelta was the most important and extensively used source of lithic material in the Sonoran Desert. At El Bajío, family groups congregated to make tools. The extensive camp areas and localities at the site that contain only one type of artifact indicate that other specific activities were also carried out, including the manufacture of clothing and shoes. Annual residential mobility probably was planned to take into account the El Bajío lithic source. Although there is no spring at El Bajío, in the past the San Miguel River and Zanjón River probably had more flow than today, and these would have provided a water source comparable to the permanent water at other Paleoindian sites in Sonora.

Radiocarbon dates from Fin del Mundo indicate Clovis people were hunting gomphotheres and other game animals at 11,550 B.P. (13,390 cal years) (Sánchez and others 2014). The gomphotheres found at Fin del Mundo are significant because this is the only place they have been found in a Paleoindian kill site in North America.

We have much more to learn about the Paleoindian occupation of Sonora. The rich archaeological record of Clovis in Sonora promises to yield significant new information as archaeologists work in the region in the future. This information will be important in understanding how the Paleoindian people used different environments to support themselves as they spread through the North and South America.

References Cited

Acosta, José de
1954 [1590] *Historia natural y moral de las Indias.*
Estudio preliminar y edición del P. Francisco
Mateos, Atlas, Madrid. Electronic document, Biblioteca Virtual Miguel de Cervantes,
http://www.cervantesvirtual.com/obra-visor/
historia-natural-y-moral-de-las-indias--0/html/
fee5c626-82b1-11df-acc7-002185ce6064_7
.html#I_23, accessed July 9, 2014.

Acosta Ochoa, Guillermo
2008a Poblamiento temprano y variabilidad cultural en
el sureste de Mexico. Paper presented at the 73rd
Annual Meeting of the Society for American
Archaeology, Vancouver.
2008b La cueva de Santa Marta y los cazadores-
recolectores del Pleistoceno final—Holoceno
temprano en las regiones tropicales de México.
Unpublished doctoral thesis. Universidad
Nacional Autónoma de México, México. D.F.

Agenbroad, Larry D.
1967 The Distribution of Fluted Points in Arizona.
The Kiva 32(4):113–120.

Aliphat Fernandez, Mario
1988 La Cuenca Zacoalco-Sayula: Ocupación humana
durante el Pleistoceno final en el Occidente
de México. In *Orígenes del hombre Americano,*
edited by Alba Gonzalez Jácome, pp. 145–177.
Secretaria de Educación Pública, México, D.F.
2008 The Zacoalco-Sayula Basin: The Early Human
Occupation in Western Mexico. Paper presented
at the 73rd Annual Meeting of the Society for
American Archaeology, Vancouver.

Alvarez, Ana María, and Gianfranco Cassiano
2013 Proyecto poblamiento Clovis en la región de
Metztitlán, Hidalgo, Mexico. Revista técnico del

Consejo de Arqueología 2012–2013. Archivo
Técnico Coordinacion de Arqueología, Instituto
Nacional de Antropología e Historia, México, D.F.

Amick, Daniel S.
1996 Regional Patterns of Folsom Mobility and Land
Use in the American Southwest. *World Archaeology* 27:411–426.

Anderson, David G.
1990 The Paleoindian Colonization of Eastern North
America: A View from the Southeastern United
States. In *Early Paleoindian Economies of Eastern
North America*, edited by Kenneth B. Tankersley
and Barry L. Isaac, pp. 163–216. Research in
Economic Anthropology, Supplement 5. JAI
Press, Greenwich, Connecticut.
1991 Examining Prehistoric Settlement Distribution in Eastern North America. *Archaeology of
Eastern North America* 19:1–22.
1996 Models of Paleoindian and Early Archaic Settlement in the Lower Southeast. In *The Paleoindian
and Early Archaic Southeast*, edited by David G.
Anderson and Kenneth Sassaman, pp. 29–57.
University of Alabama Press, Tuscaloosa.
2005 Pleistocene Human Occupation of the Southeastern United States: Research Directions
for the Early 21st Century. In *Paleoamerican
Origins: Beyond Clovis*, edited by Robson Bonnichsen, Bradley T. Lepper, Dennis Stanford,
and Michael R. Waters, pp. 29–43. Texas A&M
University Press, College Station.
2010 Human Settlement in the New World: Multidisciplinary Approaches, the "Beringian" Standstill,
and the Shape of Things to Come. In *Human
Variation in the Americas: The Integration of
Archaeology and Biological Anthropology*, edited

Anderson, David G. (*continued*)
    by Benjamin M. Auerbach, pp. 311–346. Center
    for Archaeological Investigations, Occasional
    Paper No. 38. Southern Illinois University,
    Carbondale.
2013   Paleoindian Archaeology in Eastern North
        America: Current Approaches and Future Direc-
        tions. In *In the Eastern Fluted Point Tradition*,
        edited by Joseph A. M. Gingerich, pp. 371–403.
        University of Utah Press, Salt Lake City.
Anderson, David G., and J. Christopher Gillam
2000   Paleoindian Colonization of the Americas:
        Implications from an Examination of Physiog-
        raphy, Demography, and Artifact Distribution.
        American Antiquity 65(1):43-66.
Anderson, David G., D. Shane Miller, Stephen J. Yerka,
J. Christopher Gillam, Erik N. Johanson, Derek T.
Anderson, Albert C. Goodyear, and Ashley M. Smallwood
2010   PIDBA (Paleoindian Database of the Americas)
        2010: Current Status and Findings. *Archaeology
        of Eastern North America* 38:1–28.
Andrefsky, William, Jr.
2009   The Analysis of Stone Tool Procurement, Pro-
        duction, and Maintenance. *Journal of Archaeo-
        logical Research* 17(1):65–103.
Antevs, Ernst
1931   *Late-Glacial Correlations and Ice Recession in
        Manitoba*. Memoir 168, Geological Survey of
        Canada, Ottawa.
1934   Climaxes of the Last Glaciation in North Amer-
        ica. *American Journal of Science* 28:304–311.
1935   The Spread of Aboriginal Man to North Amer-
        ica. *Geographical Review* 25(2):302–309.
1948   The Great Basin, with Emphasis on Glacial and
        Postglacial Times. *University of Utah Bulletin*
        38(20):168–191.
1955   Geologic Climatic Dating in the West. *American
        Antiquity* 20(4):317–355.
Arellano, Alberto R.
1946a   Datos geológicos sobre la antigüedad del
        hombre en la Cuenca de México. *Memoria del
        Segundo Congreso Mexicano de Ciencias Sociales*
        (5):213–219.
1946b   El elefante fossil de Tepexpan y el hombre primi-
        tivo. *Revista de Estudios Antropologicos* 8(1):89–94.
1951   The Becerra Formation (Late Pleistocene) of
        Central México. In *Proceedings of the 18th Inter-
        national Geological Congress*, Part 11, Section K:
        Correlation of Continental Vertebrate-bearing
        Rocks, pp. 55–62. International Geological
        Congress, London.

Armenta Camacho, Juan
1957   *Hallazgos prehistoricos en el Valle de Puebla.*
        Report 2. Centro de Estudios Históricos de
        Puebla, Puebla.
1959   *Hallazgo de un artefacto asociado con mamut,
        en el Valle de Puebla.* Report 7. Instituto Nacio-
        nal de Antropología e Historia-Departamento
        de Prehistoria, México, D.F. Arroyo-Cabrales,
        Joaquin, Eileen Johnson, and Luis Morett
2001   Mammoth Bone Technology at Tocuila in the
        Basin of Mexico. *The World of Elephants—Inter-
        national Congress*, pp. 419–423. Rome, Italy.
Arroyo-Cabrales, Joaquin, Oscar J. Polaco, and
Eileen Johnson
2006   A Preliminary View of the Coexistence of Mam-
        moth and Early Peoples of Mexico. *Quaternary
        International* 142–143:79–86.
Arroyo-Cabrales, Joaquin, Oscar J. Polaco, Eileen Johnson,
and A. Fabiola Guzman
2003   The Distribution of the Genus *Mammuthus* in
        Mexico. *Advances in Mammoth Research, Pro-
        ceedings of the Second International Mammoth
        Conference*, edited by Jelle W. F. Reumer, John de
        Vos and Dick Mol, pp. 27–39. DENSEA 9. Annal
        of the Natural History Museum, Rotterdam,
        Netherlands.
Arroyo-Cabrales, Joaquin, Oscar J. Polaco, C. Laurito, Eileen
Johnson, María Teresa Alberdi, and Lucía Valerio Zamora
2007   The Proboscideans (Mammalia) from Mesoamer-
        ica. *Quaternary International* 169–170:17–23.
Aschmann, Homer
1952   A Fluted Point from Central Baja California.
        American Antiquity 17(3):262–263.
Aveleyra Arroyo de Anda, Luis
1950   *Historia de México: Revisión de prehistoria Mexi-
        cana: El hombre de Tepexpan y sus problemas.*
        Ediciones Mexicanas, S.A., México, D.F.
1955   *El segundo mamut fósil de Santa Isabel Iztapan,
        México, y artefactos asociados.* Departamento
        de Prehistoria 1. Instituto Nacional de Antrop-
        ología e Historia, México, D.F.
1961   El primer hallazgo Folsom en el Territorio
        Mexicano y su relacion con el complejo puntas
        acanaladas de Norte América. In *Homenaje a
        Pablo Martinez del Rio, XXV aniversario de la
        edicion de los orígenes Americanos*, pp. 31–48.
        Instituto Nacional de Antropología e Historia,
        México, D.F.
1962   *Antigüedad del hombre en México y Centro-
        américa; Catalogo razonado de localidades y
        bibliografía selecta (1867–1961)*. Cuadernos del

Instituto de Historia Serie Antropológica 14. Universidad Nacional Autónoma de México, México, D.F.

1964 The Primitive Hunters. In *Natural Environment of Early Cultures,* edited by Robert West, pp. 384–413. Handbook of Middle American Indians, Vol. 1, general editor, Robert Wauchope. University of Texas Press, Austin.

1965 The Pleistocene Carved Bone from Tequixquiac, Mexico: A Reappraisal. *American Antiquity,* 30(3):261–277.

1967 *Los cazadores primitivos en Mesoamerica.* Instituto de Investigaciones Historicas Serie Antropología 21, Universidad Nacional Autónoma de México, México, D.F.

Aveleyra Arroyo de Anda, Luis, and
Manuel Maldonado-Koerdell

1953 Association of Artifacts with Mammoth in the Valley of Mexico. *American Antiquity* 18(4):332–340.

Bailey, Robert G.

2002 Ecoregions. In *The Physical Geography of North America,* edited by Antony R. Orme, pp. 235–245. Oxford University Press, New York.

Bamforth, Douglas B.

2009 Projectile Points, People, and Plains Paleoindian Perambulations. *Journal of Anthropological Archaeology* 28:142–157.

Ballenger, Jesse A. M., Vance T. Holliday, Andrew L. Kowler, William T. Reitze, Mary M. Prasciunas, D. Shane Miller, and Jason D. Windingstad

2011 Evidence for Younger Dryas Global Climate Oscillation and Human Response in the American Southwest. *Quaternary International* 242 (2011) 502–519.

Bárcena, Mariano

1882 Descripción de un hueso labrado, de llama Fosil, encontrado en los terrenos posterciarios de Tequixquiac, Estado de México. *Anales del Museo Nacional de Mexico,* Primera Época, Vol. 2, pp. 439-444. Museo Nacional de México, México, D.F.

Bárcena, Mariano, and Antonio Del Castillo

1885 Noticia acerca del hallazgo de restos humanos prehistóricos en el Valle de México. *La Naturaleza* (first series) 7:257–264.

Batt, C. M., and A. Mark Pollard

1996 Radiocarbon Calibration and the Peopling of North America. In *Archaeological Chemistry,* edited by A. Mark Pollard and Carl Heron, pp. 415–433. Royal Society of Chemistry, Cambridge, United Kingdom.

Benz, Bruce

2002 Origins of Mesoamerican Agriculture: Reconnaissance and Testing in the Sayula-Zacoalco Lake Basin. Electronic document, Foundation for the Advancement of Mesamerican Studies (FAMSI) http://www.famsi.org/reports/99074/, accessed March 30, 2015.

2005 Los orígenes de la agricultura Mesoamericana: Reconocimiento y estudios In la cuenca de los Lagos Sayula-Zacoalco. Electronic document, Foundation for the Advancement of Mesamerican Studies (FAMSI) http://www.famsi.org/reports/99074es/99074esBenz01.pdf, accessed March 30, 2015

Berry, Claudia F., and Michael S. Berry

1986 Chronological and Conceptual Models of the Southwestern Archaic. In *Anthropology of the Desert West: Essays in Honor of Jesse D. Jennings,* edited by Carol J. Condie and Don D. Fowler, pp. 253–327. Anthropological Papers 110. University of Utah Press, Salt Lake City.

Betancourt, Julio L.

1990 Late Quaternary Biogeography of the Colorado Plateau. In *Packrat Middens: The Last 40,000 Years of Biotic Change,* edited by Julio L. Betancourt, Thomas R. Van Devender, and Paul S. Martin, pp. 259–292. University of Arizona Press, Tucson.

Bettinger, Robert L

1991 Native Land Use: Archaeology and Anthropology. In *Natural History of the White-Inyo Range, Eastern California,* edited by Clarence. A. Hall, pp. 463–486. University of California Press, Berkeley.

Bever, Michael R., and David J. Meltzer

2007 Exploring Variation in Paleoindian Life Ways: The Third Revised Edition of the Texas Clovis Fluted Point Survey. *Bulletin of the Texas Archeological Society* 78:65–99.

Binford, Lewis R.

1980 Willow Smoke and Dogs' Tails: Hunter-Gather Settlement Systems and Archaeological Site Formation. *American Antiquity* 45(1):4–20.

1990 Mobility, Housing, and Environment: A Comparative Study. *Journal of Anthropological Research* 46(2):119–152.

Black, Glenn A.

1949 Tepexpan Man: A Critique of Method. *American Antiquity* 14(4):344–346.

Blick, John

1938 Chinobampo Skull. Manuscript in possession of the author.

Bleed, Peter
 1986 The Optimal Design of Hunting Weapons: Maintainability or Reliability. *American Antiquity* 51(4):737–747.

Bopp, Monica
 1961 El análisis de polen, con referencia especial a dos perfiles polínicos de la Cuenca de México. In *Homenaje a Pablo Martinez del Río en el vigésimoquinto aniversario de la edición de Los Orígenes Americanos*, pp. 49–56. Instituto Nacional de Antropología e Historia, México, D.F.

Bordes, François
 1967 *The Old Stone Age*. McGraw-Hill, New York.

Bradbury, Andrew P., and Jay D. Franklin
 2000 Raw Material Variability, Package Size, and Mass Analysis. *Lithic Technology* 25(1):42–58.

Bradley, Bruce A.
 1991 Flaked Stone Technology in the Northern High Plains. In *Prehistoric Hunters of the High Plains*, 2nd ed., edited by George C. Frison, pp. 369–395. Academic Press, New York.
 1993 Paleoindian Flaked Stone Technology in the North American High Plains. In *From Kostenki to Clovis: Upper Paleolithic-Paleoindian Adaptations*, edited by Olga Soffer and Nikolai Dmitrievich Praslov, pp. 251–262. Plenum Press, New York.

Bradley, Bruce A., Michael B. Collins, and Andrew Hemmings
 2010 *Clovis Technology*. Archaeological Series 17. International Monographs in Prehistory, Ann Arbor.

Brown, David E.
 1994 Sonora Savanna Grassland. In *Biotic Communities: Southwestern United States and Northwest México*, edited by David E. Brown, pp. 136–142. University of Utah Press, Salt Lake City.

Brown, David E, Charles H. Lowe, and Charles P. Pase
 1994 Appendix 1. In *Biotic Communities: Southwestern United States and Northwest México*, edited by David E. Brown, pp. 302–315. University of Utah Press, Salt Lake City.

Brown, Kenneth
 1980 A Brief Report on Paleoindian-Archaic Occupation in the Quiché Basin, Guatemala. *American Antiquity* 45(2):313–324.

Buchanan, Briggs, and Mark Collard
 2007 Investigating the Peopling of North America through Cladistic Analyses of Early Paleoindian Projectile Points. *Journal of Anthropological Archaeology* 26:366–393.

Bousman, C. Britt, Michael B. Collins, Paul Goldberg, Thomas Stafford, Jan Guy, Barry W. Baker, D. Gentry Steele, Marvin Kay, Glen Fredlund, Phil Dering, Susan Dial, Vance Holliday, Diane Wilson, Paul Takac, Robin Balinsky, Marilyn Masson, and Joseph F. Powell
 2002 The Paleoindian-Archaic Transition: New Evidence from Texas. *Antiquity* 76:980–990.

Bryan, Kirk
 1946 Datos geológicos sobre la antigüedad del hombre en La Cuenca de México. *Memorias del Segundo Congreso Mexicano de Ciencias Sociales* (5):220–225. Organizado por la Sociedad Mexicana de Geografía y Estadística, que se reunió en octubre de 1945. México, D.F.
 1948 Los suelos complejos y fósiles de la altiplanicie de México, en relación a sus cambios climáticos. *Boletín de la Sociedad Geológica Mexicana* 13(1):1–20.

Callahan, Errett
 1979 The Basis of Biface Knapping in the Eastern Fluted Point Tradition: A Manual for Flintknappers and Lithic Analysts. *Archaeology of Eastern North America* 7(1):1–180.

Cannon Michael D., and David J. Meltzer
 2008 Explaining Variability in Early Paleoindian Foraging. *Quaternary International* 191(1):5–17.

Carballal Stadtler, Margarita
 1997 Formación y características de la Cuenca de Mexico. Secuencias explicativas, génesis y naturaleza de los depósitos lacustres. In *A Propósito del Cuaternario; Homenaje a Francisco Gonzalez Rul*, edited by Margarita Carballal, pp. 25–38. Dirección de Salvamento Arqueológico, Instituto Nacional de Antropología e Historia, México, D.F.

Carballal Stadtler, Margarita (editor)
 1997 *A propósito del Cuaternario; Homenaje a Francisco Gonzalez Rul*. Dirección de Salvamento Arqueológico, Instituto Nacional de Antropología e Historia, México, D.F.

Carpenter, John
 2009 La Playa, Sonora. *Arqueología Mexicana* 17(97):50–53.

Carpenter, John, and Guadalupe Sánchez
 2013 El Holoceno Medio (Altitermal) y los inicios del Holoceno Tardío: La diversificación del Yuto-Aztecano y la difusión del maíz. *Diálogo Andina* 41:199–210.

Carpenter, John, Guadalupe Sánchez, and Elisa Villalpando
 1996 *Rescate Arqueológico La Playa (SON F:10:3), Municipio de Trincheras, Sonora, México.*

Preliminary report available at the Instituto Nacional de Antropología e Historia, México, D.F.

1997   *Rescate Arqueológico La Playa (SON F:10:3), Municipio de Trincheras, Sonora, México.* Preliminary report available at the Instituto Nacional de Antropología e Historia, México, D.F.

2003   Sonora precerámica: Del Arcaico y del surgimiento de aldeas agrícolas. *Arqueología* 29:5–29.

Carpenter, John, Guadalupe Sánchez, Elisa Villalpando, Natalia Martínez, Coral Montero, Juan Jorge Morales, and Cesar Villalobos

2001   Proyecto Arqueológico La Playa. Draft report available at the Instituto Nacional de Antropología e Historia, México, D.F.

2002   Of Maize and Migration: Mode and Tempo in the Diffusion of *Zea mays* in Northwest Mexico and the American Southwest. In *Traditions, Transitions, and Technologies: Themes in Southwestern Archaeology*, edited by Sarah Schlanger, pp. 245–258. University of Colorado Press, Boulder.

2005   The Late Archaic/Early Agricultural Period in Sonora, Mexico. In *New Perspectives on the Late Archaic Across the Borderlands*, edited by Bradley J. Vierra, pp. 3–40. University of Texas Press, Austin.

Carpenter, John, Elisa Villalpando, and Guadalupe Sánchez

2008   Environmental and Cultural Dynamics on the Southern Papaguería Periphery. In *Fragile Patterns, The Archaeology of the Western Papaguería*, edited by Jeffrey H. Altschul and Adrianne G. Rankin, pp. 287–307. SRI Press, Tucson.

2009   La Playa: An Early Agricultural Landscape. *Archaeology Southwest*, 23(1):14.

Cassiano, Gianfranco

1998   Evidencias del poblamiento prehistórico en el area de Mezquititlán, Hidalgo. *Revista de Arqueología* (second series) 19:25–44.

2008   Ocupaciones de fines del Pleistoceno y comienzos del Holoceno en el noreste de Hidalgo, México. Paper presented at the 73rd Annual Meeting of the Society for American Archaeology, Vancouver.

Cassiano, Gianfranco, and Alberto Vásquez

1990   Oyapa: Evidencias de poblamiento temprano. *Revista de Arqueología* (second series) 4:25–40.

Chavero, Alfredo

1881   Historia antigua y de la conquista. In *México a través de los siglos*, vol. 1. Ballescá y Comp., México, D.F.

Clarke, William T., Jr.

1938   Pleistocene Mollusks from the Clovis Gravel Pit and Vicinity. In The Occurrence of Flints and Extinct Animals in Pluvial Deposits Near Clovis New Mexico, part VII. *Proceedings of the Philadelphia Academy of Natural Science* 90: 119–121.

Collins, Michael B.

1999a   *Clovis Blade Technology: A Comparative Study of the Keven Davis Cache, Texas.* University of Texas Press, Austin.

1999b   The Gault Site, Kincaid Rockshelter, and Keven Davis Cache. Poster presented at the Clovis and Beyond Conference, Santa Fe.

2002   The Gault Site, Texas, and Clovis Research. *Athena Review* 3(2):31–42.

2003   Paleoindian Pavo Real. In *Pavo Real (41BX52): A Paleoindian and Archaic Camp and Workshop on the Balcones Escarpment, South Central Texas*, edited by Michael B. Collins, Dale B. Hudler, and Stephen L. Black, pp. 83-190. Studies in Archaeology 41. Texas Archaeological Research Laboratory, University of Texas, Austin.

Collins, Michael B., and Dale B. Hudler

2003   Site Setting, Environment, and Descriptions. In *Pavo Real (41BX52): A Paleoindian and Archaic Camp and Workshop on the Balcones Escarpment, South Central Texas*, edited by Michael B. Collins, Dale B. Hudler, and Stephen L. Black, pp. 23–38. Studies in Archaeology 41. Texas Archaeological Research Laboratory, University of Texas, Austin.

Collins Michael B., and John C. Lohse

2004   The Nature of Clovis Blades and Blade Cores. In *Entering America: Northeast Asia and Beringia Before the Last Glacial Maximum*, edited by David B. Madsen, pp. 159–183. University of Utah Press, Salt Lake City.

Collins, Michael B., Dale B. Hudler, and Stephen L. Black (editors)

2003   *Pavo Real (41BX52): A Paleoindian* and Archaic Camp and Workshop on the Balcones Escarpment, South Central Texas. Studies in Archaeology 41. Texas Archaeological Research Laboratory, University of Texas, Austin.

Cook, H. J.

1927   New Geological and Paleontological Evidence Bearing on the Antiquity of Mankind in America. *Natural History* 27:240–247.

1928   Glacial Age Man in New Mexico. *Scientific American* 139:38–40.

Copeland, Audrey, Jay Quade , James T. Watson,
Brett T. Mclaurin, and Elisa Villalpando
  2012   Stratigraphy and Geochronology of La Playa
         Archaeological Site, Sonora, Mexico. *Journal of
         Archaeological Science* 39 (2012):2934–2944.

Cordell, Linda
  1997   *The Archaeology of the Southwest*, second edi-
         tion. Academic Press, New York.

Cotter, John Lambert
  1937   The Occurrence of Flints and Extinct Animals in
         Pluvial Deposits near Clovis, New Mexico, Part
         IV. *Proceedings of the Philadelphia Academy of
         Natural Science* 90:113–117.

Crabtree, Don E.
  1966   A Stoneworker's Approach to Analyzing and
         Replicating the Lindenmeier Folsom. *Tebiwa*
         9(1):3–39.
  1972   *An Introduction to Flintworking*. Occasional
         Papers 28. Idaho University Museum, Pocatello.

Cruz Antillon, Rafael
  2012   Evidencias arqueológicas de los primeros
         pobladores de Chihuahua. Paper presented at
         the 16th Piña Chan Symposium: México-Brasil
         Arqueología en Desarrollo, México, D.F.

Cserna, Zoltan de
  1975   Mexico. In *The Encyclopedia of World Regional
         Geology*, Part 1: Western Hemisphere, edited by
         R. Fairbridge, pp. 348–360. Dowden, Huntchin-
         son and Ross, Stroudsburg, Pennsylvania.

Davis, Owen K., and R. Scott Anderson
  1987   Pollen in Packrat (*Neotoma*) Middens: Pollen
         Transport and the Relationship of Pollen to
         Vegetation. *Palynology* 11:185–198.

Davis, Owen K., and David S. Shafer
  1992   A Holocene Climatic Record from the Sonoran
         Desert from Pollen Analysis from the Mont-
         ezuma Well, Arizona. *Paleogeography, Paleo-
         climatology, Paaleoecology* 92:107–119.

Des Lauriers, Matthew R.
  2008   A Paleoindian Fluted Point from Isla Cedros,
         Baja California. *Journal of Island & Coastal
         Archaeology* 3:271–276.
  2011   Of Clams and Clovis: Isla Cedros Baja California,
         Mexico. In *Trekking the Shore: Changing Coast-
         lines and the Antiquity of Coastal Settlement*,
         edited by Nuno F. Bicho, Jonathan A. Haws, and
         Loren G. Davis, pp. 161–178. Springer, New York.

De Terra, Helmut
  1947a Preliminary Note on the Discovery of Fos-
         sil Man at Tepexpan in the Valley of Mexico.
         American Antiquity 13(1):40–44.

  1947b Teoria de una cronología geológica para el
         Valle de México. *Revista Mexicana de Estudios
         Antropológicos* 9 (1, 2 and 3):11–26.
  1957   *Man and Mammoth in Mexico*. Hutchinson,
         London.

De Terra Helmut, Javier Romero, and T. D. Stewart
  1949   *Tepexpan Man*. Publications in Anthropol-
         ogy 11. Viking Fund, New York.

Díaz del Castillo, Bernal
  1939[1632] *Historia verdadera de la conquista de la Nueva
              España*. Editorial Pedro Robledo, México, D.F.

Dickens, Williams A.
  2007   Clovis Biface Reduction at the Gault Site, Texas.
         Poster presented at the 72nd Annual Meeting of
         the Society for American Archaeology, Austin.

Dillehay, Tom D.
  1989   *Monte Verde: A Late Pleistocene Settlement in
         Chile: Paleoenvironment and Site Context*, Vol.1.
         Smithsonian Institution Press, Washington, D.C.
  1997   *Monte Verde: A Late Pleistocene Settlement in
         Chile: The Archaeological Context*, Vol. 2. Smith-
         sonian Institution Press, Washington, D.C.
  2009   Probing Deeper into First American Studies.
         Proceedings of the National Academy of Sciences
         106(4):971–978.

Dillehay, Tom D., C. Ramírez, M. Pino, M. B. Collins,
J. Rossen, and J. D. Pino-Navarro
  2008   Monte Verde: Seaweed, Food, Medicine, and the
         Peopling of South America. *Science* (new series)
         320:784–786.

Di Peso, Charles
  1965   The Clovis Fluted Point from the Timmy Site,
         Northwest Chihuahua. *The Kiva* 31(2):83–87.

Dunnell, Robert C.
  1990   The Role of the Southeast in American Archae-
         ology. *Southeastern Archaeology* 9(1):11–22.

Ekholm, Gordon
  1937   Fieldnotes. Manuscript on file at the American
         Museum of Natural History, New York.
  1938   Fieldnotes, Archaeological Survey of Sonora and
         Sinaloa (1938). Manuscript in possession of the
         author.
  1940   The Archaeology of Northern and Western
         Mexico. In *The Mayas and Their Neighbors*,
         edited by Clarence L. Hay, Ralph Linton, Sam-
         uel K. Lothrap, Harry L. Shapiro, and George C.
         Vaillant, pp. 307–320. Appleton-Century,
         New York.

Epstein, Jeremiah F.
  1961   The San Isidro and Puntita Negra Sites: Evidence
         of Early Man Horizon in Nuevo Leon, Mexico.

In *Homenaje a Pablo Martinez del Rio en el XXV aniversario de la edicion de los orígens Americanos*, pp. 71–74. Instituto Nacional de Antropología e Historia, México, D.F.

Ezell, Paul
  1954   An Archaeological Survey of Northwestern Papagueria. *The Kiva* 19(2–4):1–26.

Faugere, Brigitte
  1996   *Entre Zacapu y Río Lerma: Culturas en una zona fronteriza*. Centre Francais d´Etudes Mexicaines et Centroamericaines. México, D.F.
  2006   *Cueva de los Portales: Un Sitio Arcaico del Norte de Michoacan, Mexico*. Instituto Nacional de Antropología e Historia, CEMCA, México, D.F.

Faught, Michael K.
  1996   *Clovis Origins and Underwater Prehistoric Archaeology in Northwestern Florida*. Doctoral dissertation, Department of Anthropology, University of Arizona, Tucson. University Microfilms, Ann Arbor.

Faught, Michael K., and Andrea K. Freeman
  1998   Paleoindian Complexes of the Terminal Wisconsin and Early Holocene. In *Paleoindian and Archaic Sites in Arizona*, edited by Jonathan Mabry, pp. 33–54. Technical Report 97-7. Center for Desert Archaeology, Tucson.

Fay, George E.
  1955   Prepottery Lithic Complex from Sonora, Mexico. *Science* 121 (3152):777–778.
  1967   *An Archaeological Study of the Peralta Complex*. Occasional Publications in Anthropology, Archaeology Series, 1. Archaeology Series 1. Occasional Publications in Anthropology, University of Northern Colorado, Greeley.

Ferring, C. Reid
  1994   The Role of Geoarchaeology in Paleoindian Research. In *Method and Theory for Investigating the Peopling of the Americas*, edited by Robson Bonnichsen and D. Gentry Steele, pp. 57–72. Center for the Study of the First Americans, Corvallis, Oregon.
  2001   *Archaeology and Paleoecology of the Aubrey Clovis Site (41DN479) Denton County, Texas*. U.S. Army Corps of Engineers. Fort Worth District, Fort Worth.

Fiedel, Stuart J.
  1999   Older Than We Thought: Implications of Corrected Dates for Paleoindians. *American Antiquity* 64(11):96–116.
  2004   Rapid Migrations by Arctic Hunting Peoples: Clovis and Thule. In *The Settlement of the American Continent*, edited by C. Michael Barton, Geoffrey A. Clark, David R. Yesner, and Georges A. Pearson, pp. 79–84. University of Arizona Press, Tucson.

Figgins, Jesse D.
  1927   The Antiquity of Man in America. *Natural History* 27:229–239.
  1933   A Further Contribution to the Antiquity of Man in America. *Proceedings of the Colorado Museum of Natural History* 12(2):4–10.

Fish, Suzanne K., and Stephen A. Kowaleski.
  1990   *The Archaeology of Regions: The Case for Full Coverage Survey*. Smithsonian Institution Press, Washington, D.C.

Flannery, Kent V.
  1986   Guilá Naquitz in Spatial, Temporal, and Cultural Context. In *Guilá Naquitz: Archaic Foranging and Early Agriculture in Oaxaca*, edited by Kent V. Flannery, pp. 31–63. Academic Press, New York.

Flemming, N., G. Bailey, V. Courtillot, G. King, K. Lambeck, F. Ryerson, and C. Vita-Finzi.
  2003   Coastal and Marine Palaeo-environments and Human Dispersal Points Across the Africa-Eurasia Boundary. In *The Maritime and Underwater Heritage*, edited by C. A. Brebbia, and T. Gambin, pp. 61–74. WIT Press, Southampton, United Kingdom.

Foradas, James G.
  2003   Chemical Sourcing of Hopewell Bladelets: Implication for Building a Chert Database for Ohio. In *Written in Stone: The Multiple Dimensions of Lithic Analysis*, edited by P. Nick Kardulias and Richard W. Yerkes, pp. 87–112. Lexington Books, Rowman & Littlefield, Lanham, Maryland.

Frison, George C.
  1991   *Hunters of the High Plains*. Academic Press, New York.
  2000   Progress and Challenges: Intriguing Questions Linger after 75 Years of Answers. *Scientific American Discovering Archaeology* (January/February):40–42.

Fujita, Harumi
  2002   Evidencia de presencia humana en el continente Americano hace 40,000 años en el Espíritu Santo, B.C.S. In *Revista de Arqueología Mexicana*, Mayo Junio 2002, pp. 14–15. Instituto Nacional de Antropología e Historia, México, D.F.
  2007   En torno a la antigüedad de la primera ocupación de la Covacha Babisuri de la Isla del Espíritu Santo. In *Memoria del seminario de arqueologia del norte de México*, edited by

Fujita, Harumi (*continued*)
>Cristina García and Elisa Villalpando, pp. 15–24 (digital edition). Centro Instituto Nacional de Antropología e Historia, Sonora, Hermosillo.

>2008 Cuarto informe del proyecto El Poblamiento de América visto desde la Isla del Espíritu Santo, Baja California Sur. Manuscript in the Consejo de Arqueología, el archivo de la Coordinación de Arqueología, México, D.F.

Gaines, Edmund P.
>2006 Paleoindian Geoarchaeology of the Upper San Pedro River Valley, Sonora, Mexico. Unpublished master's thesis, Department of Anthropology, University of Arizona, Tucson.

Gaines, Edmund P., Guadalupe Sánchez, and Vance Holliday
>2009a Geoarchaeolgy of El Gramal, a Multi-component Site in Central Sonora, México. Poster presented at the 74th Annual Meeting of the Society for American Archaeology, Atlanta.

>2009b Paleoindian Archaeology of Northern Sonora, Mexico: A Review and Update. *Kiva* 74(3):305–336.

García Bárcena, Joaquin
>1975 Estudios sobre fechamientos por hidratación de la obsidiana. *Boletin INAH* (second series) 12:27–38.

>1979 *Una punta acanalada de la Cueva de los Grifos, Ocozocoautla, Chiapas.* Cuaderno de Trabajo del Departamento de Prehistoria 17. Instituto Nacional de Antropología e Historia, México, D.F.

>1989 El hombre y los proboscideos de América. In *Homenaje a Jose Luis Lorenzo*, edited by Lorena Mirambell, pp. 41–79. Serie Prehistoria, Instituto Nacional de Antropología e Historia. México, D. F.

García-Bárcena, Joaquín, and Diana Santamaría
>1982 *La Cueva de Santa Marta Ocozocoautla, Chiapas. Estratigrafía, cronología y cerámica*, Colección Científica 111. Instituto Nacional de Antropología e Historia, México D.F.

Garcia Cook, Angel
>1973 Una punta acanalada en el estado de Tlaxcala, México. *Comunicaciones* 9:39–42.

García Moreno, Cristina
>2008 *El complejo San Dieguito en el noroeste de México*, Instituto Nacional de Antropología e Historia, Colección Premios Instituto Nacional de Antropología e Historia, México, D.F.

Gingerich, Joseph A.M.
>2007 *Shawnee-Minisink Revisited: Re-evaluating the Paleoindian Occupation.* Unpublished master's thesis, Department of Anthropology, University of Wyoming, Laramie.

>2011 Down to Seeds and Stones: A New Look at the Subsistence Remains from Shawnee-Minisink. *American Antiquity* 76(1):127–144.

Gio Argaez, Rauel, and Yunuen Rodriguez Arevalo
>2003 Panorama general de la paleontología en México. *Ciencia ergo sum* (Revista Científica de la Universidad Autónoma del Estado de Mexico) 10(1):85–95. Toluca.

Goebel, Ted, Michael R. Waters, and Dennis H. O'Rourke
>2008 The Late Pleistocene Dispersal of Modern Humans in the Americas. *Science* 319:1497–1502.

Gonzalez, Silvia, and David Huddart
>2007 The Late Pleistocene Human Occupation of Mexico. Manuscript in possession of the author. Conference Proceedings: Section on Pleistocene Archaeology at www.ljmu.ac.uk/ECL/83451.htm.

Gonzalez, Silvia, David Huddart, and Matthew Bennett
>2006 Valsequillo Pleistocene Archaeology and Dating: Ongoing Controversy in Central México. *World Archaeology* 38(4):611–627.

Gonzalez, Silvia, David Huddart, Matthew Bennett, and Alberto Gonzalez-Huesca
>2006 Human Footprints in Central Mexico Older than 40,000 Years. *Quaternary Science Review* 25:201–222.

Gonzalez, Silvia, David Huddart, Luis Morett-Alatorre, Joaquin Arroyo-Cabrales, and Oscar J. Polaco
>2001 Mammoths, Volcanism and Early Humans in the Basin of Mexico during the Late Pleistocene/Early Holocene. In *The World of Elephants—International Congress,* pp. 704–706. Rome.

Gonzalez, Silvia, José Concepción Jiménez, Robert Hedges, David Huddart, James C. Ohman, Alan Turner, and José Antonio Pompa
>2003 Earliest Humans in the Americas: New Evidence from Mexico. *Journal of Human Evolution* 44:379–387.

>2006 Early Humans in Mexico: New Chronological Data. In *El hombre temprano en América y sus implicaciones en el poblamiento de la Cuenca de México*, edited by José Concepción Jiménez, Silvia González, José Antonio Pompa and Francisco Ortiz, pp. 67–76. Colección Científica,

Instituto Nacional de Antropología e Historia, México, D.F.

Gonzalez, Silvia, Luis Morett, David Huddart, and Joaquin Arroyo-Cabrales
2006 Mammoth from the Basin of Mexico: Stratigraphy and Radiocarbon. In *El Hombre Temprano en América y sus Implicaciones en el Poblamiento de la Cuenca de México*, edited by José Concepción Jiménez, Silvia González, José Antonio Pompa y Francisco Ortiz, pp. 263–274. Colección Científica, Instituto Nacional de Antropología e Historia, Mexico City.

González-González, Arturo, Carmen Rojas, Alejandro Terrazas, Martha Benavente, and Wolfgang Stinnesbeck
2006 Poblamiento temprano en la Península de Yucatán: Evidencias loalizadas en Cuevas Sumergidas de Quintana Roo, México. In *América*, edited by José Concepción Jiménez, Oscar Polaco, and Gloria Martínez, pp.73–90. Instituto Nacional de Antropología e Historia and Impretei, México, D.F.

Gonzalez Quintero, Lauro, and Fernando Sánchez
1980 Determinación polínica del ambiente en que vivieron los mamutes en la Cuenca de Mexico. In *Coloquiosobre paleobotanica y palinología*, edited by Fernando Sánchez, pp. 195–200. Colección Científica, Instituto Nacional de Antropología e Historia,, México, D.F.

Gramly, Richard M.
1990 *Guide to the Palaeo-indian Artifacts of North America*. Persimmon Press, New York.

Green, F. E.
1963 The Clovis Blades: An Important Addition to the Llano Complex. *American Antiquity* 29 (2):145–165.

Guevara Sánchez, Arturo
1989 Vestigios prehistóricos del Estado de Sinaloa, dos casos. *Arqueología* 1:9–29.

Guillermin-Tarayre, E.
1867 *Rapport sur lexploration minéralogique des régions Mexicaines*, Archives de la Comission Scientifique du Mexique, Vol. 3, pp. 173–470. Imprimerie Impériale, Paris.

Gutierrez, María de la Luz, and Justin R. Hyland
1994 La punta Clovis de El Batequi. *Arqueología Mexicana* 2(8):82–83.
1998 El yacimiento de obsidiana Valle de Azufre, Baja California Sur. *Revista Arqueología* (second series) 19:45–54.
2002 Arqueologia de la Sierra de San Francisco.

Colección Científica, Instituto Nacional de Antropología e Historia, México, D.F.

Hamilton, Marcus
2008 Quantifying Clovis Dynamics: Confronting Theory with Models and Data Across Scales. Unpublished doctoral dissertation, Department of Anthropology, University of New Mexico, Albuquerque.

Hamy, E. T.
1884 Mission scientifique au Mexique et dans l'Amérique centrale. Recherches zoologiques, Part I: *Anthropologie du Mexique*. Imprimerie Nationale, Paris.

Hardaker, Christopher
2007 *The First American: The Suppressed Story of the People Who Discovered the New World*. Career Press, Franklin Lakes, New Jersey.

Haury, Emil W., Ernst Antevs, and J. F. Lance
1953 Artifacts with Mammoth Remains, Naco, Arizona. *American Antiquity* 19(1):1–14.

Haury, Emil W., E. B. Sayles, and William W. Wasley
1959 The Lehner Mammoth Site, Southeastern Arizona. *American Antiquity* 25(1):2–30.

Hayden, Julian D.
1956 Notes of the Archaeology of the Central Coast of Sonora, Mexico. *The Kiva* 21(3-4):9–23.
1965 Fragile-Pattern Areas. *American Antiquity* 31 (2):272–276.
1967 A Summary Prehistory and History of the Sierra Pinacate, Sonora, Mexico. *American Antiquity* 32(3):335–344.
1969 Gyratory Crushers of the Sierra Pinacate, Sonora. *American Antiquity* 34(2):154–161.
1976 Pre-Altitermal Archaeology in the Sierra de Pinacate, Sonora, Mexico. *American Antiquity* 41(3):274–289.
1987 Early Man in the Far Southwestern United States and Adjacent Sonora, Mexico. Paper presented at the 11th Congress of the International Union for Pre- and Proto-Historic Sciences, Commission for the Peopling of the Americas, Mainz, West Germany.
1998 *The Sierra Pinacate*. University of Arizona Press, Tucson.

Haynes, C. Vance. Jr.
1964 Fluted Projectile Points: Their Age and Dispersion. *Science* 145:1408–1413.
1966 Elephant-Hunting in North America. *Scientific American* 214:104–112.
1967 Muestras de carbon-14 de Tlapacoya, Estado de

Haynes, C. Vance. Jr. (*continued*)

 Mexico. *Boletin* 29:49–52, Instituto Nacional de Antropología e Historia, México, D.F.

1968 Geochronology of a Late Quaternary Alluvium. In *Means of Correlation of Late Quaternary Successions*, edited by Roger B. Morrison and Henry E. Wright, pp. 591–631. University of Utah Press, Salt Lake City.

1969 The Earliest Americans. *Science* 166:709–715.

1975 Pleistocene and Recent stratigraphy: In *Late Pleistocene Environments of the Southern High Plains*, edited by Fred Wendorf and James J. Hester, pp. 57–96. Publication 9. Fort Burgwin Research Center, Taos.

1976 Archaeological Investigations at the Clovis Site at Murray Springs, Arizona, 1968. *National Geographic Society Research Reports*, 1968:165–171.

1980 The Clovis Culture. *Canadian Journal of Anthropology* 1(1):115–121.

1982 Archaeological Investigations at the Lehner Site, Arizona, 1974–1975. *National Geographic Society Research Reports* 14:325–334.

1987 Curry Draw, Cochise County Arizona: A Late Quaternary Stratigraphic Record of Pleistocene Extinction and Paleo-Indian Activities. In *Cordilleran Section of the Geological Society of America*, edited by M. L. Hill, pp. 23–28. Centennial Field Guide, Vol. 1. Geological Society of America, Boulder.

1991 Geoarchaeological and Paleohydrological Evidence for a Clovis-age Drought in North America and its Bearing on Extinction. *Quaternary Research* 35(3):438–450.

1993 Clovis-Folsom Geochronology and Climatic Change. In *From Kostenki to Clovis: Upper Paleolithic-Paleo-Indian Adaptations*, edited by Olga Soffer and N. D. Praslov, pp. 219–236. Plenum Press, New York.

1995 Geochronology of Paleoenvironmental Change, Clovis Type Site, Blackwater Draw, New Mexico: *Geoarchaeology* 10:317–388.

2000a New World Climate. *Scientific American Discovering Archaeology*, January/February 2000:37–39.

2000b Stratigraphic Evidence of Climate Changes during Paleoindian Times. *Archaeology Southwest*, 14(2):3.

2007 Quaternary Geology of the Murray Springs Clovis Site. In *Murray Springs: A Clovis Site with Multiple Activities Areas in the San Pedro Valley, Arizona*, edited by C. Vance Haynes and Bruce B. Huckell, pp. 16–54. Anthropological Papers 71. University of Arizona Press, Tucson.

Haynes, C. Vance, and Bruce B. Huckell (editors)

2007 *Murray Springs: A Clovis Site with Multiple Activities Areas in the San Pedro Valley, Arizona*. Anthropological Papers 71. University of Arizona Press, Tucson.

Haynes, Gary

2002 *The Early Settlement of North America, The Clovis Era*. Cambridge University Press, New York.

Haynes, Gary, David G. Anderson, C. Reid Ferring, Stuart J. Fiedel, Donald K. Grayson, C. Vance Haynes Jr., Vance T. Holliday, Bruce B. Huckell, Marcel Kornfeld, David J. Meltzer, Julie Morrow, Todd Surovell, Nicole M. Waguespack, Peter Wigand, and Robert M. Yohe II

2007 Comment on "Redefining the Age of Clovis: Implications for the Peopling of the Americas." *Science* 317:320.

Hemmings, E. Thomas

1970 Early Man in the San Pedro Valley, Arizona. Unpublished doctoral dissertation, Department of Anthropology, University of Arizona, Tucson.

Hemmings, E. Thomas, and C. Vance Haynes, Jr.

1969 The Escapule Mammoth and Associated Projectile Points, San Pedro Valley , Arizona. *Journal of the Arizona Academy of Science* 5:184-188.

Hesse, India S., Willam J. Parry, and Francis E. Smiley

1998 Badger Springs: A Late Paleoindian Site in Northeastern Arizona. *Current Research in the Pleistocene* 16:27–29.

2000 Badger Springs. *Archaeology Southwest* 14(2):6.

Hester, Thomas R.

1977 The Current Status of Paleoindian Studies in Southern Texas and Northeast New Mexico. In *Paleoindian Lifeways*, edited by Elieen Johnson, pp. 169–186. West Texas Museum Journal 17. Texas Tech University, Lubbock.

2003 Introduction. In *Pavo Real (41BX52): A Paleoindian and Archaic Camp and Workshop on the Balcones Escarpment, South Central Texas*, edited by Michael B. Collins, Dale B. Hudler, and Stephen L. Black, pp. 3–6. Studies in Archaeology 41. Texas Archaeological Research Laboratory, University of Texas, Austin.

Hill, Matthew Glenn

2001 Paleoindian Diet and Subsistence Behavior on the Northwestern Great Plains of North America. Unpublished doctoral dissertation, University of Wisconsin, Madison.

Hinton, Thomas
　1955　A Survey of Archaeological Sites in the Altar Valley, Sonora, In *The Kiva* 21 (1-2):1–12.
Hofman, Jack L., and Russell W. Graham
　1998　The Paleoindian Cultures of the Great Plains. In *Archaeology on the Great Plains*, edited by W. Raymond Wood, pp. 87–139. University Press of Kansas, Lawrence.
Hole, Frank
　1986　Chipped Stone Tools. In *Guilá Naquitz: Archaic Foraging and Early Agriculture in Oaxaca*, edited by Kent V. Flannery, pp. 97–140. Academic Press, New York.
Holliday, Vance T.
　1985　Archaeological Geology of the Lubbock Lake Site, Southern High Plains of Texas. *Geological Society of America Bulletin* 96(12):1483–1492.
　1997　*Paleoindian Geochronology of the Southern High Plains.* University of Texas Press, Austin.
　2005　Ice-Age People of New Mexico. In *New Mexico's Ice Ages*, edited by Spencer G. Lucas, Gary S. Morgan and Kate E. Zeigler, pp. 263–276. Bulletin 28. New Mexico Museum of Natural History and Science, Albuquerque.
Holliday, Vance, B. Huckell, R. Weber, M. Hamilton, W. Reitze, and J. Mayer
　2009　Geoarchaeology of the Mockingbird Gap (Clovis) Site, Jornada del Muerto, New Mexico. *Geoarchaeology* 24(3):248–370.
Holmgren, Camille A., Jodi Norris, and Julio L Betancourt
　2007　Inferences about Winter Temperatures and Summer Rains from the Late Quaternary Record of C4 Perennial Grasses and C3 Desert Shrubs in the Northern Chihuahuan Desert. *Journal of Quaternary Science* 22(2):141–161.
Holzkamper, Franz M.
　1956　Artifacts from Estero Tastiota, Sonora, Mexico. In *The Kiva* 2(3-4):12–19.
Howard, Edgar B.
　1933　Association of Artifacts with Mammoth and Bison in Eastern New Mexico. *Science* 78:524.
　1935a　Evidence of Early Man in North America, *The Museum Journal* (University of Pennsylvannia Museum) 24:61–175.
　1935b　The Occurrence of Flints and Extinct Animals in Fluvial Deposits near Clovis, New Mexico, Part 1, Introduction. *Proceedings of the Academy of Natural Sciences of Philadelphia* 87:299–303.
Huddart, David, and Silvia Gonzalez
　2006　A Review of the Environmental Change in the Basin of Mexico, Implications for Early Humans.

In *El hombre temprano en América y sus implicaciones en el poblamiento de la Cuenca de México*, edited by José Concepción Jiménez, Silvia González, José Antonio Pompa, and Francisco Ortiz, pp. 77–106. Colección Científica, Instituto Nacional de Antropología e Historia, México, D.F.
Huckell, Bruce B.
　1978　*The Oxbow Hill-Payson Project.* Contributions to Highway Salvage Archaeology 48. Arizona State Museum, University of Arizona, Tucson.
　1981　The Navarrete Site: A Third Clovis Locality on Greenbush Draw, Arizona. Manuscript on file, Arizona State Museum Archives, University of Arizona, Tucson, AZ.
　1982　*The Distribution of Fluted Points in Arizona; A Review and Update.* Archaeological Series 145. Arizona State Museum, University of Arizona, Tucson.
　1996　The Archaic Prehistory of the North American Southwest. *Journal of World Prehistory* 10:305–373.
　2004　Clovis in the Southwest. In *New Perspectives of the First Americans*, edited by Bradely T. Lepper and Robson Bonnichsen, pp. 93–99. Center for the Study of the First Americans, College Station, Texas.
　2007　Clovis Lithic Technology a View from the Upper San Pedro Valley. In *Murray Springs: A Clovis Site with Multiple Activities Areas in the San Pedro Valley, Arizona*, edited by C. Vance Haynes and Bruce B. Huckell, pp. 170–213. Anthropological Papers 71. University of Arizona Press, Tucson.
Huckell, Bruce B., and C. Vance Haynes, Jr
　2003　The Ventana Complex: New Dates and New Ideas on Its Place in Early Holocene Western Prehistory. *American Antiquity* 68(2):353–371.
Irwin-Williams, Cynthia
　1967　Association of Early Man with Horse, Camel, and Mastodon at Hueyatlaco, Valsequillo, Puebla, Mexico. In *Pleistocene Extinctions: The Search for a Cause*, edited by Paul S. Martin and H. E. Wright. Jr., pp. 337–347. Yale University Press, New Haven.
　1981　Commentary of Geologic Evidence for Age of Deposits at Hueyatlaco Archaeological Site, Valsequillo, Mexico. *Quaternary Research* 16(2):258.
Irwin-Williams, Cynthia, and C. Vance Haynes
　1970　Climatic Change and Early Population Dynamics in the Southwestern United States. *Quaternary Research* 1(1):59–71.

Ives, Ronald
  1963   The Problem of the Sonoran Littoral Cultures.
          The Kiva 28(3-4):28–32.
Jelinek, Arthur J.
  1971   Early Man in the New World: A Technological
          Perspective. *Arctic Anthropology* 8:15–21.
Johnson, Albert
  1963   The Trincheras Culture of Northern Sonora.
          American Antiquity 29(2):174–186.
Johnson, Eileen, J. Arroyo, and Oscar Polaco
  2006   Climate, Environment and Game Animal
          Resources of the Late Pleistocene Mexican
          Grassland. In *El hombre temprano en America y
          sus implicaciones en el poblamiento de la Cuenca
          de México*, edited by José Concepción Jimenez,
          Silvia Gonzalez, José Antonio Pompa, pp.
          231–247. Colección Cientifica, Instituto Nacio-
          nal de Antropología e Historia. México, D.F.
Judge, W. James
  1973   *Paleoindian Occupation of the Central Rio
          Grande Valley in New Mexico.* University of New
          Mexico Press, Albuquerque.
Justice, Noel D.
  2002a   *Stone Age Spear and Arrow Points of California
          and the Great Basin.* Indiana University Press,
          Bloomington.
  2002b   *Stone Age Spear and Arrow Points of the South-
          western United States.* Indiana University Press,
          Bloomington.
Kelly, Robert L.
  1992   Mobilty/Sedentism: Concepts, Archaeological
          Measures, and Effects. *Annual Review of Anthro-
          pology* 21:43–66.
  1995   *The Foraging Spectrum.* Smithsonian Institution
          Press, Washington, D.C.
  1996   Ethnographic Analogy and Migration to the
          Western Hemisphere. In *Prehistoric Mongoloid
          Dispersals,* edited by Takeru Akazawa and
          Emöke J. E. Szathmary, pp. 228–240. Oxford
          University Press, New York.
  1999   Hunter-Gatherer Foraging and Colonization
          of the Western Hemisphere. *Anthropologie*
          37(1):143–153.
  2003   Maybe We Do Know when People First Came to
          North America; and What does It Mean If We
          Do? *Quaternary International* 109-110:133–145.
Kelly, Robert L., and Larry C. Todd
  1988   Coming into the Country: Early Paleoindian
          Mobility and Hunting. *American Antiquity*
          53:231–244.

Kilby, J. David
  2008   An Investigation of Clovis Caches: Content,
          Function, and Technological Organization.
          Unpublished doctoral dissertation, Department
          of Anthropology, University of New Mexico,
          Albuquerque.
Krieger, Alex D.
  1950a   Notes and News: Early Man. *American Antiquity*
          16:181–182.
  1950b   Review Work: The Tepexpan Man, by Helmut de
          Terra, Javier Romero and T. D. Stuart. *American
          Antiquity* 15(4):343–347.
Kuhn, Steven L.
  1991   New Problems, Old Glasses: Methodologi-
          cal Implications of an Evolutionary Paradigm
          for the Study of Paleolithic Technologies. In
          *Perspectives on the Past: Theoretical Biases in
          Mediterranean Hunter-Gatherer Research*, edited
          by Geoffrey A. Clark, pp. 243–257. University of
          Pennsylvania Press, Philadelphia.
Lavín, M. F., and S. G. Marinone
  2003   An Overview of the Physical Oceanography of
          the Gulf of California. In *Nonlinear Processes
          in Geophysical Fluid Dynamics*, edited by O. U.
          Velasco Fuentes, J. Sheinbaum, and J. Ochoa, pp.
          173–204. Kluwer Academic, New York.
Lehmer, Donald J.
  1949a   Archaeological Survey of Sonora Mexico.
          Chicago Natural Museum Bulletin (December
          1949):4–5.
  1949b   Fieldnotes, Archaeological Survey of Sonora.
          Manuscript in possession of the author.
Lepper, Bradley, and Robson Bonnichsen (editors)
  2004   *New Perspectives on the First Americans.* Center
          for the First Americans, College Station, Texas.
Lohman, Richard C.
  1969   *Marine Magnetic and Bathymetric Profiles in the
          Gulf of California, 1967.* Naval Oceanographic
          Office, Washington, D.C.
Long, Austin
  1966   Late Pleistocene and Recent Chronologies
          of Playa Lakes in Arizona and New Mexico.
          Unpublished doctoral dissertation, University of
          Arizona, Tucson.
Lorentzen, L. H.
  1998   Appendix: Common Paleoindian and Archaic
          Projectile Points in Arizona. In *Paleoindian and
          Archaic Sites of Arizona*, edited by Jonathan B.
          Mabry, pp. 138–151. Technical Report 97-7.
          Center for Desert Archaeology, Tucson.

Lorenzo, José Luis

1953   A Fluted Point from Durango, Mexico. *American Antiquity* 4:394–395.

1958   *Los glaciares de México.* Instituto de Geofísica Monografía 1. Universidad Nacional Autónoma de México, México, D.F.

1967   *La etapa lítica in México.* Departamento de Prehistoria 20. Insituto Nacional de Antropología e Historia, México, D.F.

1969   *Condiciones periglaciares de las Altas Montañas de México.* Departamento de Prehistoria, Instituto Nacional de Antropología e Historia, México, D.F.

1978   Early Man Research in the American Hemisphere: Appraisal and Perspectives. In *Early Man in America, from a Circumpacific Perspective,* edited by Alan Lyle Brian, pp. 35–77. Occasional Papers 1. Department of Anthropology, University of Alberta, Edmonton.

1988   Historia de la prehistoria en México. In *Orígenes del hombre Americano,* edited by Alba González Jácome, pp. 21–38. Secretaría de Educación Pública, México, D.F.

1991   Fechamiento de la mujer de Tepexpan. *Boletín del Instituto Nacional de Antropología e Historia,* Suplemento 28:1–35. Instituto Nacional de Antropología e Historia, México, D.F.

Lorenzo, José Luis, and Lorena Mirambell

1985   Preliminary Report on Archaeological and Paleoenvironmental Studies in the Area of El Cedral, San Luis Potosi, Mexico, 1977–1980. In *New Evidence for the Pleistocene Peopling of the Americas,* edited by Alan Lyle Bryan, pp. 107–114. Peopling of the Americas Symposia Series, Center for the Study of Early Man, Orono, Maine.

1986a   *Mamutes excavados en la Cuenca de Mexico (1952–1980).* Departamento de Prehistoria, Instituto Nacional de Antropología e Historia, México, D.F.

1986b   *Tlapacoya 35,000 años de historia del Lago de Chalco.* Serie Prehistoria, Insituto Nacional de Antropología e Historia,México, D.F.

1999   The Inhabitants of Mexico during the Upper Pleistocene. In *Ice Age People of North America,* edited by Robson Bonnichsen and Karen L. Turnmire, pp. 482–496. Center for the Study of the First Americans, Corvallis, Oregon.

Lozano Garcia, Socorro, Beatriz Ortega Guerrero, Margarita Caballero-Miranda, and Jaime Urrutia-Fucugauchi

1993   Late Pleistocen/Early Holocene Paleoenviroments of Chalco Lake, Central Mexico. *Quaternary Research* 40:332–342.

Mabry, Jonathan B.

1998a   Frameworks for Arizona's Early Prehistory. In *Paleoindian and Archaic Sites in Arizona,* edited by Jonathan B. Mabry, pp. 1–18. Technical Report 97-7. Center for Desert Archaeology, Tucson.

1998b   Introduction. In *Archaeological Investigations of Early Village Sites in the Middle Santa Cruz Valley: Analysis and Synthesis,* edited by Jonathan B. Mabry, pp. 1–29. Anthropological Papers 19. Center for Desert Archaeology, Tucson.

Mabry, Jonathan, John Carpenter, and Guadalupe Sánchez

2008   Archaeological Models of Early Uto-Aztecan Prehistory in the Arizona-Sonora Borderlands. In *Archaeology Without Borders: Contact, Commerce, and Change in the U. S. Southwest and Northwestern Mexico,* edited by Laurie Webster and Maxine McBrinn, pp. 259–311. University Press of Colorado, Boulder.

Mabry, Jonathan B., and Michael K. Faught

1998   Archaic Complexes of the Early Holocene. In *Paleoindian and Archaic Sites in Arizona,* edited by Jonathan B. Mabry, pp. 53–64. Technical Report 97-7. Center for Desert Archaeology, Tucson.

MacNeish, Richard S.

1950   A Synopsis of the Archaeological Sequence in the Sierra de Tamaulipas. *Revista Mexicana de Estudios Antropologicos* 11:79–96.

MacNeish, Richard S., and Frederick A. Peterson

1962   The Santa Marta Rock Shelter, Ocozocoautla, Chiapas *Papers of the New World Archaeological Foundation* 14 (1962):1–46.

MacWilliams, Arthur C., John R. Roney, Karen R. Adams, and William L. Merrill

2006   Investigaciones de los sitios de cultivo de maíz temprano en Chihuahua. Manuscript available at the Consejo de Arqueología, Instituto Nacional de Antropología e Historia, México, D.F.

Malde, Harold, Virgina Steen-McIntyre, Charles W. Naeser, and Sam L. Van Landingham

2007   The Stratigraphic Debate at Huayatlaco, Valsequillo, Mexico. Manuscript in the possession of the author.

Martin, Paul S.

1963   *The Last 10,000 Years: A Fossil Pollen Record of the American Southwest.* University of Arizona Press, Tucson.

1967   Prehistoric Overkill. In *Pleistocene Extinctions the Search for a Cause,* edited by Paul S. Martin and H. E. Wright, pp. 75–120. Yale University Press, New Haven.

1973   The Discovery of America. *Science* 179:969–974.

Martinez Tagueña, Natalia, Vance T. Holliday, Rafael Cruz, and Alberto Peña

2011   Paleoindian Sites and Artifacts from Northern Chihuahua, Mexico. Paper presented at the 69th Annual Plains Anthropological Conference, Tucson.

Martinez, Natalia, Guadalupe Sánchez, John Carpenter, and Michael Brack

2002   Localidad del complejo San Dieguito-Malpais: Análisis. In *Cuarto informe de la temporada 2001 del proyecto de salvamento arqueológico La Playa,* edited by John Carpenter, Guadalupe Sánchez, and Elisa Villalpando, pp. 140–148. Reporte al Consejo de Arqueologia del Instituto Nacional de Antropología e Historia, Mexico.

McDowell, Fred W., Jaime Roldan Quintana, and Ricardo Amaya Martinez

1997   Interrelationship of Sedimentary and Volcanic Deposits Associated with Tertiary Extensions in Sonora, México. *Geological Society of American Bulletin* 109:1349–1360.

McIntyre, Kenneth G., and Marian McIntyre

1976   Paleoindian Occupation of Northwestern Sonora: A Preliminary Report of Investigations Carried out in July and August 1974. Manuscript in possession of C. Vance Haynes Jr., School of Anthropology, University of Arizona, Tucson.

Mehringer, Peter J., and C. Vance Haynes, Jr.

1965   The Pollen Evidence for the Environment of Early Man and Extinct Mammals at the Lehner Mammoth Site, Southeastern Arizona. *American Antiquity* 31(1):17–23.

Meltzer, David J.

1983   The Antiquity of Man and the Development of American Archaeology. In *Advances in Archaeological Method and Theory,* vol. 6, edited by Michael B. Schiffer, pp. 1–51. Elsevier, Cambridge, Massachusetts.

1989   Why Don't We Know When the First People Came to North America? *American Antiquity* 54(3):471–490.

1993   Is There a Clovis Adaptation? In *From Kostenki to Clovis: Upper Paleolithic-Paleo-Indian Adaptions,* edited by Olga Soffer and Nikolai Dmitrievich. Praslov, pp. 293–310. Plenum Press, New York.

1995   Clocking the First Americans. *Annual Review of Anthropology* 24:21–45.

2002   What Do You Do When No One's Been There Before? Thoughts on the Exploration and Colonization of New Lands. In *The First Americans: The Pleistocene Colonization of the New World,* edited by Nina G. Jablonski, pp. 27–58. California Academy of Sciences, San Francisco.

2004   Modeling the Initial Colonization of the Americas: Issues of Scale, Demography, and Landscape Learning. In *The Settlement of the American Continent: A Multidisciplinary Approach to Human Biogeography,* edited by C. Michael Barton, Geoffrey A. Clark, David R. Yesner, and Georges A. Pearson, pp. 123–137. University of Arizona Press, Tucson.

2009   *First Peoples in a New World: Colonizing Ice Age America.* University of California Press, Los Angeles.

Miller, D. Shane, and Joseph A. M. Gingerich

2013   Paleoindian Chronology and the Eastern Fluted Point Tradition In *In the Eastern Fluted Point Tradition,* edited by Joseph A. M. Gingerich, pp. 9–22. University of Utah Press, Salt Lake City.

Mirambell, Lorena

1972   Una osamenta fosil en el exlago de Texcoco. *Bolletin* 2:9–16. Instituto Nacional de Antropología e Historia, México, D.F.

1994   Los primeros pobladores del actual territorio Mexicano. In *Historia antigua de México,* Vol. 1, edited by Linda Manzanilla and Leonardo Lopez Lujan, pp. 177–208. Instituo Nacional de Antropología e Historia-Universidad Nacional Autónoma de México-Editorial Porrua, México, D.F.

2012   *Rancho "La Amapola," cedral, un sitio arqueológico-paleontológico, Pleistocénico-Holocénico con restos de actividad humana.* Instituto Nacional de Antropología e Historia, México, D.F.

Molina-Freaner, Francisco E., Therese A. Markow, Edward J. Pfeiler, Octavio R. Rojas-Soto, Alejandro Varela-Romero, Adrián Quijada-Mascareñas, Martín Esqueda, and Gloria Yépiz-Plascencia

2010   Diversidad genética de la biota. In *Diversidad biológica de Sonora,* edited by Francisco E.

Molina-Freaner and Thomas R. Van Devender, pp. 97–127. Universidad Nacional Autónoma de México, México, D.F.

Montané, Julio C.

1968 Paleo-Indian Remains from Laguna de Tagua Tagua, Central Chile, *Science* 161:1137–1138.

1985 Desde los origenes hasta 3000 años antes del presente. In *Historia general de Sonora*, Vol. 1, *Periodo prehistórico y prehispanico*, pp. 171–221. Gobierno del Estado de Sonora, Hermosillo.

1988 El poblamiento temprano de Sonora. *In Orígenes del hombre Americano,* edited by Alba Gonzalez Jácome, pp. 83–116. Secretaria de Educación Pública, México, D.F.

Morett, Luis., Joaquín Arroyo-Cabrales, and Oscar Polaco

1998 Tocuila, a Remarkable Mammoth Site in the Basin of Mexico. *Current Research in the Pleistocene* 15:118–120.

Morett, Luis. A, Silvia González, Joaquín Arroyo-Cabrales, Oscar J. Polaco, Graham J. Sherwood, and Alan Turner

2003 The Late Pleistocene Paleoenvironment of the Basin of Mexico—Evidence from the Tocuila Mammoth Site. In *Advances in Mammoth Research, Proceedings of the Second International Mammoth Conference*, edited by Jelle W. F. Reumer, John de Vos and Dick Mol, pp. 267–272. DEINSEA, Annal of the Natural History Museum, Rotterdam.

Morrow, Juliet E.

1997 End Scraper Morphology and Use-Life: An Approach for Studying Paleoindian Lithic Technology and Mobility. *Lithic Technology* 22(1):32–45.

Muhs, Daniel R., Kathleen R. Simmons, George L. Kennedy, and Thomas K. Rockwell

2004 Quaternary Sea-Level History of the United States. In *The Quaternary Period in the United States*, edited by Alan R. Gillespie, Stephen C. Porter, and Brian F. Atwater, pp. 147–183. Elsevier, New York.

Nabhan, Gary P.

1985 *Gathering the Desert*. University of Arizona Press, Tucson.

1989 *Enduring Seeds: Native American Agriculture and Wild Plant Conservation*. North Point Press, San Francisco.

Nárez, Jésus

1990 *Materiales arqueológicos de Tlapacoya*. Colección Científica, Instituto Nacional de Antropología e Historia, México, D.F.

Newberry, John

1885 Discusiones acerca del hombre del Peñon. *La naturaleza* (first series) Vol. 7, pp. 284–285, México, D.F.

Noguera, E.

1958 *Reconocimiento arqueológico in Sonora*. Dirección de Monumentos Prehispánicos 10. Instituto Nacional de Antropología e Historia, México D.F.

Northon, Chris D., Michael S. Foster, John M. Lindly, and Douglas R. Mitchell

2005 A Newly Discovered Clovis Point from the Phoenix Basin and an Update on Arizona Clovis Point Attributes. *Kiva* 70(2):293–307.

Nuñez Elvis E., Bruce J. Macfadden, Jim I. Mead, and Arturo Baez

2010 Ancient Forests and Grasslands in the Desert: Diet and Habitat of Late Pleistocene Mammals from Northcentral Sonora, Mexico. *Paleogeology, Paleoclimatology and Paleoecology* 297(2010):391–400.

Ochoa-Castillo, Patricia, Mario Perez-Campa, Ana Lilian Martin del Pozo, and Joaquín Arroyo-Cabrales

2003 New Excavations at Valsequillo, Puebla, Mexico. *Current Research in the Pleistocene* 20:61–63.

Orozco y Berra, Manuel

1880 *Historia antigua y de la conquista de Mexico*, Vol. 2. Tipografía de Gonzalo A. Esteva, México D.F.

Owen, Rogers C.

1984 The Americas: The Case Against an Ice-Age Human Population. In *The Origins of Modern Humans: A World Survey of the Fossil Evidence*, edited by Fred H. Smith, and Frank Spencer, pp. 517–563. Alan R. Liss, New York.

Paleoindian Database of the Americas (PIDBA)

2014 Paleoindian Database of the Americas. Electronic database, http://pidba.utk.edu, accessed March 30, 2015.

Pastrana, Alejandro

1998 *La explotación Azteca de la obsidiana en la Sierra de las Navajas*. Colección Científica, Instituto Nacional de Antropología e Historia, México, D.F.

Patrick, R.

1938 The Occurrence of Flints and Extinct Animals in Pluvial Deposits near Clovis, New Mexico, Part V, Diatom Evidence from the Mammoth Pit. *Proceedings of the Philadelphia Academy of Natural Science* 90:15–24.

Pearson, Georges A.

2004 Pan-American Paleoindian Dispersals and the Origins of Fishtail projectile Points as Seen

Pearson, Georges A. (*continued*)
> through the Lithic Raw-material Reduction Strategies and Tool-manufacturing Techniques at the Guardiría Site, Costa Rica. In *The Settlement of the American Continent,* edited by Barton, Michael, Geoffrey Clark, David Yesner, and Georges Pearson, pp. 85–102. University of Arizona Press, Tucson.

Perez Rebollo Raul
> 1985   Geografía de Sonora. In *Historia general de Sonora,* Vol. 1, edited by Calderón Valdés, pp. 111–172. Gobierno del Estado de Sonora, Hermosillo.

Pitblado, Bonnie L.
> 2011   A Tale of Two Migrations: Reconciling Recent Biological and Archaeological Evidence for the Pleistocene Peopling of the Americas. *Journal of Archaeological Research* 19(4):327–375.

Prascuinas, Mary M.
> 2008   Clovis First? An Analysis of Space, Time, and Technology. Unpublished doctoral dissertation. Department of Anthropology, University of Wyoming, Laramie.
> 2011   Mapping Clovis: Projectile points, Behavior, and Bias, *American Antiquity* 76(1):107–126.

Punzo, José Luis, and Bridget Zavala
> 2007   Investigaciones recientes en el Valle de Guadiana. In *Memorias del seminario de arqueología del norte de México,* edited by Cristina Garcia and Elisa Villalpando, pp. 181–191. Centro-Instituto Nacional de Antropología e Historia-Sonora, Hermosillo. Electronic document, http://www.scribd.com/doc/241411516/Memorias-del-Seminario-de-Arqueologia-del-Norte-pdf, accessed March 2, 2015.

Renne, Paul, Joshua Feinberg, Michael Waters, Joaquin Arroyo Cabrales, Patrivia Ochoa Castillo, and Mario Perez Campa
> 2005   Age of Mexican Ash with Alleged "Footprints." *Nature* 438:E7–E8.

Riviale, Pascal
> 2001   Eugène Boban ou les aventures d'un antiquaire au pays des américanistes. *Journal de la Société des Américanistes* 87:351–362.

Robles Ortiz, Manuel
> 1974   Distribución de artefactos Clovis en Sonora. *Boletín* (second series) 9:25–32. Instituto Nacional de Antropología e Historia, México, D.F.

Robles Ortiz, Manuel, and Francisco Manzo Taylor
> 1972   Clovis Fluted Points from Sonora, Mexico. *The Kiva* 37(2):199–206.

Rodríguez, Francoise, and Nelly Silva
> 1987   *Ethnoarqueología de Quitovac, Sonora: Reporte de la temporada 1987.* Archivo Técnico del Instituto Nacional de Antropología e Historia Sonora, Hermosillo.

Rodríguez-Loubet, Francoise, Michel Antochiw, and Elizabeth Araux
> 1993   *Quitovac, Ethnopréhistoire du Désert de Sonora, Mexique.* Editions Recherches sur les Civilisations, Paris.

Rogers, Malcolm
> 1939   *Early Lithic Industries of the Lower Basin of the Colorado River and Adjacent Desert Areas.* Archaeological Papers 3. San Diego Museum of Man, San Diego.
> 1958   San Dieguito Implements from the Terraces on the Rincon, Pantano and Rillito Drainage System. *The Kiva* 24(1):1–23.

Rzedowski, Jerzy
> 1981   *Vegetación de México.* Limusa Editores, México, D.F.

Sánchez, Guadalupe M.
> 1998   Of Roasting Pits and Plant Remains: Preliminary Analyses of Archaeobotanical Remains from La Playa, Sonora, Mexico. Unpublished master's thesis, Department of Anthropology, University of Arizona, Tucson.
> 2001   A Synopsis of Paleo-Indian Archaeology in Mexico. *Kiva* 67(2):119–136.
> 2010   Los Primeros Mexicanos: Late Pleistocene/Early Holocene Archaeology of Sonora, México. Unpublished doctoral dissertation, Department of Anthropology, University of Arizona, Tucson.

Sánchez, Guadalupe, and John Carpenter
> 2009   La industria litica Clovis Sonorense: del Pleistoceno Terminal/Holoceno temprano: Una mirada desde el sitio de El Bajío. In *Investigaciones recientes sobre la lítica arqueológica en México,* edited by Lorena Mirambell and Leticia González, pp. 19–37. Colección Cientifica 561. Instituto Nacional de Antropología e Historia, México, D.F.
> 2012   Paleoindian and Archaic Traditions in Sonora, Mexico. In *From the Pleistocene to the Holocene Human Organization and Cultural Transformations in Prehistoric North America,* edited by C. Britt Bousman and Bradley J. Vierra, pp. 125–147. Texas A&M University Press, College Station.

Sánchez, Guadalupe M., and Natalia Martinez
> 2001   Analisis de la litica lasqueada. In *Tercer informe de las temporadas 1998–1999 and 2000 del*

Proyecto de Salvamento Arqueológico La Playa, edited by Elisa Villalpando and John P. Carpenter, pp. 170–193. Report submitted to Consejo de Arqueologia del Instituto Nacional de Antropología e Historia, México, D.F.

Sánchez, Guadalupe, Edmund Gaines, Vance T. Holliday, and Joaquin Arroyo-Cabrales
  2009 Fin del Mundo. *Archaeology Southwest* 23(3):6–7.

Sánchez, Guadalupe, Vance T. Holliday, Edmund P. Gaines, Joaquín Arroyo-Cabrales, Natalia Martínez-Tagüeña, Andrew Kowler, Todd Lange, Gregory W. L. Hodgins, Susan M. Mentzer, and Ismael Sánchez-Morales
  2014 Human (Clovis)–Gomphothere (*Cuvieronius* sp.) Association ~13,390 Calibrated yBP in Sonora, Mexico. *PNAS.* Electronic document, www.pnas.org/cgi/doi/10.1073/pnas.1404546111, accessed July 15, 2014.

Sánchez-Morales, Ismael
  2012 Las industrias líticas de puntas de proyectil y bifaciles en los sitios Arcaicos de Sonora. Licenciatura thesis, Escuela Nacional de Antropología e Historia, México, D.F.

Sanders, Thomas
  1990 *Adams: The Manufacturing of Flaked Stone Tools at a Paleoindian Site in Western Kentucky.* Persimmon Press Monographs in Archaeology, Buffalo.

Santamaría, Diana, and Joaquin García Barcena
  1984 *Raspadores verticales de la Cueva de los Grifos.* Cuadernos de Trabajo de Prehistoria 22. Instituto Nacional de Antropología e Historia, México, D.F.
  1989 *Puntas de proyectil, cuchillos y otras herramientas de la Cueva de los Grifos, Chiapas.* Cuaderno de Trabajo 40. Instituto Nacional de Antropología e Historia, México, D.F.

Saunders, Jeffrey J.
  1980 A Model for Man-Mammoth Relationships in Late Pleistocene North America. *Canadian Journal of Anthropology* 1(1):87–98.

Sayles, Edwin. B. and Ernst Antevs
  1941 *The Cochise Culture.* Medallion Papers 29. Gila Pueblo, Globe, Arizona.

Sedov, Sergey, Socorro Lozano-García, Elizabeth Solleiro-Rebolledo, Emily McClung de Tapia, Beatriz Ortega-Guerrero, and Susana Sosa-Nájera
  2010 Tepexpan Revisited: A Multiple Proxy of Local Environmental Changes in Relation to Human Occupation from a Lake Shore Section in Central Mexico. *Geomorphology* 122:309–322.

Sellards, Elias H.
  1952 *Early Man in America.* University of Texas Press, Austin.
  1955 Fossil Bison and Associated Artifacts from Milnesand, New Mexico. *American Antiquity* 20:336–344.

Sellards, Elias H., and Glen L. Evans
  1960 The Paleo-Indian Cultural Successoin in the Central High Plains of Texas and New Mexico. In *Men and Cultures,* edited by Anthony F. C. Wallace, pp. 639–649. University of Pennsylvania Press, Philadelphia.

Shott, Michael J.
  1986 Technological Organization and Settlemnt Mobility: An Ethnographic Examination. *Journal of Anthropological Research* 42:15-51.

Shreve, Forrest
  1937 The Vegetation of Sinaloa. *Bulletin of the Torrey Botanical Club* 64:605–613.

Siebe, Clauss, and J. Urrutia-Fucugauchi
  1999 Mammoth Bones Embeded in a Late Pleistocene Lahar from Popocatepetl Volcano, Near Tocuila, Central Mexico. *Geological Society of American Bulletin* 111(10):1550–1562.

Sliva, R. Jane
  1997 *Introduction to the Study and Analysis of Flaked Stone Artifacts and Lithic Technology.* Center for Desert Archaeology, Tucson.

Smallwood, Ashley M.
  2011 Clovis Technology and Settlement in the American Southeast. Unpublished doctoral dissertation. Department of Anthropology, Texas A&M University, College Station.

Smith, Bruce D.
  1997 The Initial Domestication of *Cucurbita pepo* in the Americas 10,000 years Ago. *Science* 276 (May):932–934.

Sollberger, J. B.
  1977 On Fluting Folsom: Notes on Recent Experiments. *Bulletin of the Texas Archeological Society* 48:47–52.

Stanford, Dennis
  1991 Clovis Origins and Adaptations: An Introductory Perspective. In *Clovis: Origins and Adaptations,* edited by R. Bonnichsen and K. L. Turnmire, pp. 1-14. Center for the Study of the First Americans, Corvallis, Oregon.

Steen-McIntyre, Virginia, Roald Fryxell, and Harold E. Malde
  1981 Geologic Evidence for Age of Deposits at Huayatlaco Archaeological Site, Valsequillo, Mexico. *Quaternary Research* 16(1):1–17.

Steponaitis, Vincus P.
1986   Prehistoric Archaeology of the Southeastern
        U.S. *Annual Review of Anthropology* 15:383–393.

Stock, Chester, and Bode, Francis D.
1936   The Occurrence of Flints and Extinct Animals in
        Pluvial Deposits near Clovis, New Mexico, Part
        III, Geology and Vertebrate Paleontology of the
        Quaternary near Clovis, New Mexico: *Proceed-
        ings of the Philadelphia Academy of Natural
        Sciences* 88:219–241.

Surovell, Todd A.
2000   Early Paleoindian Women, Children, Mobility,
        and Fertility. *American Antiquity* 65(3):493–508.

Taylor, R. E.
2009   Six Decades of Radiocarbon Dating in New
        World Archaeology. *Radiocarbon*, 51(1):173–212.

Taylor, R. E., C. Vance Haynes Jr., and M. Stuiver
1996   Clovis and Folsom Age Estimates: Stratigraphic
        Context and Radiocarbon Calibration. *Antiquity*
        70:505–525.

Tankersley, Kenneth B.
2004   The Concept of Clovis and the Peopling of the
        Peopling of North America. In *The Settlement
        of the American Continent,* edited by Barton,
        Michael, Geoffrey Clark, David Yesner, and
        Georges Pearson, pp. 49–63. University of
        Arizona Press, Tucson.

Turner, Raymond M., and David E. Brown
1994   Sonoran Desert Scrub. In *Biotic Communi-
        ties: Southwestern United States and Northwest
        México,* edited by David E. Brown, pp. 181–222.
        University of Utah Press, Salt Lake City.

Valadez Moreno, Moises
2006   La ocupación temprana de Nuevo Leon. Paper
        presented at the IX Conferencia Anual de
        Arqueología de la Zona Norte, Nuevo Casas
        Grandes.
2008   La tradición Arcaica del noreste. Manuscript in
        possession of the author.

Van Devender, Thomas R.
1990   Late Quaternary Vegetation and Climate of the
        Sonoran Desert, United States and México. In
        *Packrat Middens: The Last 40,000 Years of Biotic
        Change,* edited by Julio L. Betancourt, Thomas
        Van Devender, and Paul Martin, pp. 134–165.
        University of Arizona Press, Tucson.
2007   Ice Age in the Sonoran Desert: Pinyon, Pine,
        and Joshua Trees in the Dry Borders Region. In
        Dry Borders, edited by Richard Felger and Bill
        Broyles, pp. 58–70. University of Utah Press,
        Salt Lake City.

Van Devender, Thomas R., and W. Geoffrey Spaulding
1979   Development of Vegetation and Climate
        in the Southwestern United States. *Science*
        204:701–710.

Van Devender, Thomas R., Tony.L. Burgess,
Richard S. Felger, and Raymond M. Turner
1990   Holocene Vegetation of the Hornaday Moun-
        tains of Northwestern Sonora, México. *Proceed-
        ings of the San Diego Society of Natural His-
        tory* 2:1–19.

Van Devender, Thomas R., Tony L. Burgess, Jessie C. Piper,
and Raymond M. Turner
1994   Paleoclimatic Implications of Holocene Plant
        Remains from the Sierra Bacha, Sonora, Mexico.
        Quaternary Research 41:99–108.

Van Devender, Thomas R., R. S. Thompson, and
Julio L. Betancourt
1987   Vegetational History in the Southwest: The
        Nature and Timing of the Late Wisconsin-
        Holocene Transition. In *North America and
        Adjacent Oceans During the Last Deglaciation,*
        edited by William F. Ruddiman, and Henry E.
        Wright, pp. 323–352. Geology of North America,
        Vol. K-3, Geological Society of America, Boulder.

Vega Granillo, Eva Lourdes
1992   Estudio hidrogeológico de la Cuenca del Río
        Mátape, Sonora. *Boletin del Departamento de
        Geologia* 9(2):75–84. Universidad de Sonora,
        Hermosillo.

Villalobos Acosta, César
2007   *La diversidad emergente: Complejidad y metá-
        foras textuales en la investigación arqueológica
        de Sonora, México.* Estudios, Programa Edito-
        rial de Sonora, Instituto Sonorense de Cultura,
        Hermosillo.

Villalpando Canchola, Maria Elisa, John P. Carpenter,
James T. Watson, and Sahira Rincon Montero
2009   Proyecto arqueológico La Playa [SON F:10:3],
        Informe Temporada IV, Primavera 2008.
        Archivo Técnico, Centro Instituto Nacional de
        Antropología e Historia Sonora, Hermosillo.

Villalpando Canchola, Maria Elisa, James T. Watson, and
John P. Carpenter
2010   Proyecto arqueológico La Playa [SON F:10:3],
        Informe Temporada 2009. Archivo Técnico,
        Centro Instituto Nacional de Antropología e
        HistoriaSonora, Hermosillo.
2012   Proyecto arqueológico La Playa [SON F:10:3],
        Informe Temporada I, 2011–2012. Archivo Téc-
        nico, Centro Instituto Nacional de Antropología
        e Historia Sonora, Hermosillo.

Waguespack, Nicole M.
  2003 Clovis Hunting and the Organization of Subsistence Labor. Unpublished doctoral dissertation. Department of Anthropology, University of Arizona, Tucson.
  2007 Why We're Still Arguing About the Pleistocene Occupation of the Americas. *Evolutionary Anthropology* 16:63–74.
Warnica, James M
  1966 New Discoveries at the Clovis Site. *American Antiquity* 31(3):345–357.
Waters, Michael R.
  1985 Early Man in the New World: An Evaluation of the Radiocarbon Dated Pre-Clovis Sites in the Americas. *In Environments and Extinctions: Man in Late Glacial North America*, edited by Jim I. Mead and David J. Meltzer, pp. 125–144. Center for the Study of Early Man, Orono, Maine.
  1986 *The Geoarchaeology of Whitewater Draw, Arizona.* Anthropological Papers 45. University of Arizona Press,Tucson.
Waters, Michael R., and Thomas W. Stafford, Jr.
  2007 Redefining the Age of Clovis: Implications for the Peopling of the Americas. *Science* 315:1122–1126.
Waters, Michael R., Joaquin Arroyo-Cabrales, Patricia Ochoa-Castillo, and Paul Renne
  2008 Geoarchaeological Investigations of the Hueayatlaco Site, Valsequillo Reservoir, Mexico. Paper presented at the 73rd Annual Meeting of the Society of American Archaeology, Vancouver.
Waters, Michael R., Charlotte D. Pevny, and David L. Carlson
  2011 *Clovis Lithic Technology: Investigation of a Stratified Workshop at the Gault Site, Texas.* Texas A&M University Press, College Station.
Wheat, Amber D.
  2012 Survey of Professional Opinions Regarding the Peopling of the Americas. *The SAA Archaeological Record* 12(2):10–14.

White, Richard S., Jim I. Mead, Arturo Baez, and Sandra L. Swift
  2010 Localidades de vertebrados fósiles del Neógeno (Mioceno, Plioceno y Pleistoceno): Una evaluación preliminar de la biodiversidad del pasado. In *Diversidad Biológica de Sonora*, edited by Francisco E. Molina-Freaner and Thomas R. Van Devender, pp. 51–72. Universidad Nacionál Autónoma de México, México, D.F.
Whittaker, John C.
  1994 *Flintknapping: Making and Understanding Stone Tools.* University of Texas Press, Austin.
Willig, Judith A.
  1991 Clovis Technology and Adaptation in the Far Western North America: Regional Pattern and Environmental Context. In *Clovis: Origins and Adaptations*, edited by Robson Bonnichsen and Karen L. Turnmire, pp. 91–118. Center for the Study of the First Americans, Corvallis, Oregon.
Winter, Marcus, Cira Martínez López, and Robert Markens
  2008 Early Hunters and Gatherers of Oaxaca: Recent Discoveries. Paper presented at the 73rd Annual Meeting of the Society for American Archaeology, Vancouver.
Witt, A. Benjamin
  2005 Differential Use of Space: An Analysis of the Aubrey Clovis Site. Unpublished master's thesis, University of North Texas, Denton.
Wormington, H. Marie
  1957 *Ancient Man in North America.* Publication 4. Denver Museum of Natural History, Denver.
Xelhuantzi Lopez, María Susana
  2008 Informe del analisis de polen de dos perfiles estratigráficos enel sitio Clovis de El Aigame, Sonora. Report in the archives of the Subdireccion de Laboratorios y Apoyo Academico, Coordinación de Arqueologia, Instituto Nacional de Antropología e Historia, México, D.F.

Index

ABSTRACT

Mexico is a significant region for understanding the colonization of the continent because it is shaped like a funnel. When the first Americans moved inland from Beringia to South America, they crossed what is now the border between the United States and Mexico, a territory that it is more than 1,600 km long. These people then walked south to the Isthmus of Tehuantepec, a narrow strip of land 160 km wide between the Pacific Ocean and the Atlantic Ocean.

The archaeological record of the first people of Mexico is scarce, and the previously published information is confusing and unsystematic. During the last decade, however, investigations of Paleoindian sites have increased exponentially, even though only a handful of Mexican researchers focus their investigations on Pleistocene sites. Systematic investigations of Paleoindian sites in the state of Sonora, in particular, have increased enormously what is known about the Pleistocene landscape and the first people who inhabited this region.

This book reviews what is currently known about the Pleistocene archaeology of Mexico, with an emphasis on Sonora. It describes the landscape, paleoenvironment, and physiographic provinces of Sonora, and provides a regional cultural history. Data from 12 Paleoindian sites in that state are analyzed, including the Clovis lithic industry at the site of El Bajío. The patterns of land use, subsistence strategies, organization of labor, and chronology of the Clovis period are defined.

Archaeological data from Sonora support the "staging-area" model of Clovis land use. Extensive Clovis campsites, hunting areas, stone procurement areas, and the availability of wild resources indicate that people repeatedly used the region. The Clovis points found in Sonora were made using local materials of varied quality including chert, quartzite, quartz crystal, rhyolite, obsidian, and basalt. Knowing where to find the best local sources of stone for tool making indicates that Clovis people had a detailed knowledge of their environment. From this, it is inferred that Clovis groups stayed at sites for long periods of times, or that they visited the same sites recurrently as a part of a long-term strategy of land use. The homogeneity of Clovis points, the sharing of artifacts between groups, and the sharing of raw materials suggest that Clovis groups maintained strong ties with extended populations at a regional

RESUMEN

México es una región significativa para entender la colonización del continente porque tiene forma de embudo. Cuando los primeros americanos se transportaron por tierra de Beríngia hacia Sudamérica cruzaron lo que es ahora la frontera entre Estados Unidos y México, un territorio que tiene más de 1,600 km de longitud. Esta gente posteriormente caminó al sur por el Istmo de Tehuantepec, una franja delgada de 160 km de ancho entre el Océano Pacífico y el Océano Atlántico.

El registro arqueológico de la primera gente de México es escasa, y la información previamente publicada es confusa y poco sistemática. Sin embargo, en la última década, las investigaciones de sitios Paleoindios se ha incrementado exponencialmente, aunque solamente media docena de investigadores se especializan en sitios Paleoindios. Las exploraciones de los sitios Paleoindios en el estado de Sonora, en particular, han incrementado enormemente y ahora conocemos de los paisajes del Pleistoceno y los primeros pobladores que habitaron esta región.

Éste libro hace una revisión de lo que actualmente sabemos de la arqueología del Pleistoceno de México con énfasis en Sonora. Describe el paisaje, paleoambiente, y las provincias fisiográficas de Sonora, y presenta una historia regional cultural. Se analizan los datos de doce sitios Paleoindios en Sonora, incluyendo la industria lítica Clovis del sitio de El Bajío. Se definen los patrones del uso del suelo, estrategias de subsistencias, la organización laboral y cronología del periodo Clovis en Sonora.

Los datos arqueológicos de Sonora soportan el modelo "área de función" para explicar el uso del territorio Clovis. Las puntas Clovis encontradas en Sonora fueron elaborados usando materia prima local de diversa calidad. El conocimiento de dónde encontrar las mejores fuentes de piedra local para usar en las herramientas indica que la gente Clovis conocía en detalle su medioambiente. De esto, infiero que los grupos Clovis permanecieron en los sitios por largos periodos de tiempo, o visitas recurrentes a las mismas localidades como parte de las estrategias de largo tiempo del uso del territorio. Los recursos esenciales encontrados en Sonora hicieron esta región un lugar atractivo para los grupos pioneros.

La presencia de localidades con extensos campamentos, áreas de caza, áreas de extracción de rocas para hacer herramientas, y recursos silvestres indican que los

level. The essential resources found in this region made it an attractive place for pioneering human groups.

Clovis economic strategies were organized to exploit a large and pristine environment that contained a variety of animals and plants. Radiocarbon dates from Fin del Mundo indicate Clovis people were hunting gomphotheres and other game animals at 11,550 B.P. (13,390 cal B.P.) (Sánchez and others 2014). The gomphotheres found at Fin del Mundo are significant because this is the only place they have been found in association with humans in North America.

The rich Paleoindian archaeological record of Clovis in Sonora promises to yield significant new information as archaeologists continue to work in the region. This information will be important in understanding how Paleoindian people used different environments to support themselves as they spread through North and South America.

territorios fueron usados repetidamente. Las estrategias económicas Clovis fueron organizadas para explotar ambientes prístinos grandes que contenían una variedad de plantas y animales. Fechas de radiocarbono obtenidas del sitio Fin del Mundo indican que la gente Clovis estaba cazando gonfoterios y otros animales alrededor de 11,550 B.P. (13,3990 años calibrados) (Sánchez y otros 2014). Los gonfoterios encontrados en el Fin del Mundo son importantes ya que es en el único lugar donde se han sido hallados en Norte América.

Estas investigaciones indican que la gente Clovis usaba una variedad de materia prima para hacer herramientas, incluyendo diversas fuentes de sílex, cuarcita, cristal de cuarzo, riolita, obsidiana y basalto. La homogeneidad de las puntas Clovis, la coincidencia de artefactos y el intercambiar materias primas entre grupos, sugiere que los grupos Clovis mantenían fuertes lazos con poblaciones de la región.

El abundante registro arqueológico de Paleoindios Clovis en Sonora promete proporcionar nueva información si los arqueólogos continúan trabajando en la región en el futuro. Esta información será importante para entender como la gente Paleoindia uso diferentes ambientes cuando se esparcieron a lo largo del Norte y Sur América.

ANTHROPOLOGICAL PAPERS OF THE UNIVERSITY OF ARIZONA